A SPACE ON THE SIDE OF THE ROAD

CULTURAL POETICS IN AN "OTHER" AMERICA

Kathleen Stewart

PRINCETON UNIVERSITY PRESS   PRINCETON, NEW JERSEY

Portions of chapters 2, 6, and 8 first appeared as a chapter titled
"Back-talking the Wilderness: 'Appalachian' En-genderings," in
Uncertain Terms: Negotiating Gender in American Culture,
ed. Faye Ginsburg and Anna Lowenhaupt Tsing, pp. 43–56,
© 1990 by Faye Ginsburg and Anna Lowenhaupt Tsing.
Reprinted by permission of Beacon Press.
A portion of chapter 2 first appeared as "Nostalgia—A Polemic,"
Cultural Anthropology 3 (3): 227–41, © by *Cultural Anthropology*.
A portion of chapter 3 first appeared as "On the Politics of Cultural
Theory: A Case for 'Contaminated' Critique," *Social Research* 58 (2):
395–412, © 1991 by *Social Research*.

Library of Congress Cataloging-in-Publication Data
Stewart Kathleen, 1953–
A space on the side of the road : cultural poetics in an
"other" America / Kathleen Stewart.
p.   cm.
Includes bibliographical references and index.
ISBN 0-691-01104-4 (alk. paper). — ISBN 0-691-01103-6 (pbk. : alk. paper)
1. West Virginia—Rural conditions.   2. Coal miners—West Virginia.
3. Ethnology—West Virginia.   4. Folklore—West Virginia.
5. West Virginia—Social life and customs.   I. Title.
HN79.W4S74   1996
306'.09754—dc20   95-24365   CIP

For my mother, Claire Driscoll Stewart,
and my father, Frank Stewart

_____

Contents

Photographs ─────────────────────

Acknowledgments ⸻

THIS BOOK is pieced together out of moments of talk and friendship with many people in West Virginia. Although in most cases I have changed their names to protect their privacy, I am especially grateful to Riley and Sylvia Hess; Joanna Roberts; Patty, Jimmy, Shawn, and Vanessa Halsey; Joyce, Herb, Barbara, Crystal, and Lance Smith; Alfred and Kitty Guerrant; Julie Bowens; Lisa Harless; Sue and Lou Aries; Pinky and Kenny Rose; Betty Cadle; Jerry Graham; Riley Meadows; Miss Shutt; Mr. Henry; Creed Polk; Eva Mae; Johnny McBride; Bobby and Easter Johnson; Helen and James Mullins; Red and Alma Sheets; Dora Hancock; Amos Howerton; Carl, Rosa, and Hollie McKinney; Ollie McKinney; Jessie McVey; Miss Patterson; Tiny Rhinehart; Hershel and Naomi Shrewsbury; Nancy Taylor; David and Juanita Polk; Jethro and Lenna Walker; and Martha and Harvey Thaxton.

Funding for writing was assisted in the early stages by the Institute for Southern Culture and in the final stages by a Rockefeller Postdoctoral Fellowship at the Center for Cultural Studies, University of California, Santa Cruz (1992–1993) and by the University Research Institute, University of Texas. At Santa Cruz, James Clifford, Susan Harding, and David Schneider offered invaluable friendship and support and joined Anna Tsing, Donna Haraway, Shelly Errington, and Lisa Rofel in providing a wonderful context for discussion and critique. At Texas I am grateful to all of my colleagues and I would especially like to thank Steven Feld, Greg Urban, Joel Sherzer, Ward Keeler, Robert Fernea, Liza Shapiro, Samuel Wilson, Henry Selby, and Pauline Strong. Students in seminars at the University of Texas from whom I have learned a great deal include, especially, Susan Lepselter, Aaron Fox, Margaret Lott, Randall Tillery, Benjamin Feinberg, and Glen Perice.

I am also grateful for invitations to participate in seminars and symposia where chapters or sections of the book were first drafted and critiqued including, especially, an NEH Advanced Seminar on Lament in 1988 at the University of Texas organized by Steven Feld, the Society for Cultural Anthropology meetings in Santa Monica in 1989, an Advanced Seminar on Senses of Place at the School of American Research in 1992 organized by Keith Basso and Steven Feld, a symposium on Ethnographic Surrealism at Columbia University in 1993 organized by Michael Taussig, and talks at the University of Washington, the University of Chicago, the University of California, San Diego, Rice University, and at the division of Critical Studies, California Institute of the Arts. Participation in an ongoing seminar on Public Culture and Counter-Publics at the Center for Psychosocial Studies in Chicago organized by Ben Lee also provided a new and challenging context for thinking through the book. In addition to those already mentioned in these contexts I would especially like to thank Lauren Berlant, Dick Hebdige, Marilyn Ivy, George Marcus, John Pemberton, Vincent Raphael, Roger Rouse, Julie Taylor, and Steven Tyler.

I owe the greatest intellectual debt in the development of my own thinking to Ross Chambers, James Clifford, Steven Feld, Susan Harding, Susan Stewart, Michael Taussig, and Elizabeth Taylor, as well as to the works of James Agee, Roland Barthes, Mikhail Bakhtin, and Walter Benjamin. I would also like to thank Richard Bauman, Steven Caton, Ruth Finnegan, Mike Yarrow, John Hartigan, and Marilyn Strathern for their influence on my thinking whether in brief encounters or through long association.

Mary Murrell has been an astonishingly wonderful editor who has made it a pleasure to publish with Princeton University Press; I thank her for her care and efficiency in moving the manuscript through its stages, for her knowledge of and sensitivity to my particular theoretical and aesthetic concerns for the shape of the book, and even for the very title of the book itself. Nicholas Dirks, James Peacock, and Mary Steedly offered powerful and engaged critiques of the manuscript and excellent suggestions for revision. Lauren Lepow was a brilliant manuscript editor and was both painstaking and considerate. Susan Lepselter's index demonstrates her own deep knowledge of the theoretical and ethnographic problematics I have tried to address. Em Herzstein, Harriette Hartigan, and John Hartigan came with me in return visits to the field to shoot photographs, and I thank them for their stunning contributions to the book; much more than "illustrations," these photographs have been long-standing companions to the writing and objects of rumination in themselves. John Allison, Liza Shapiro, Emily Socolov, and Danny Webb offered valuable aesthetic advice on the cover, and Emily has been a willing computer consultant and friend at all hours of the day and night. I thank Danny Webb for his unfailing support and loyalty over the years, his local knowledge of rural southern discourses and ways of life, and his own daily flood of crazy stories and haunting images that provided constant distraction from the insular world of a book-in-progress and kept its "point" very firmly in mind. Finally, I thank my parents, Claire Driscoll Stewart and Frank Stewart, to whom this book is dedicated, for everything.

A SPACE ON THE SIDE OF THE ROAD

Prologue

THIS IS A STORY about the fabulation of a narrative "space on the side of the road" that enacts the density, texture, and force of a lived cultural poetics somewhere in the real and imagined hinterlands of "America." It takes place in the hard-core Appalachian coal-mining region of south-western West Virginia—a region that constitutes an "Other America" not because it is somehow "outside" or marginal to "America's" cultural landscape but because it has, through a long history of exploitation and occupation by an industry and an incessant narrativization of a cultural real, come to imagine its place within its spaces of desire.

This makes it "other" than the story of "America" that arises in the abbreviated shorthand account of nationalist myth—a second-order semiological system that empties cultural signifiers of their history and sociality by appropriating them to an abstract rhetorical project of its own (Barthes 1957). Here we are told over and over again, in a chant of certainty, that the story of America is a story of the West versus the rest, of capitalism and modernization, of individualism, materialism, education, reason, democracy. An exegetical list of traits comes to us as if from a news brief from Washington or from the memory of a fourth-grade textbook on American Civilization. Here, the cultural productions that constitute an "America" of sorts are frozen into essentialized "objects" with fixed identities; a prefab landscape of abstract "values" puts an end to the story of "America" before it begins.

The narrative space that I am calling here a "space on the side of the road" is the site of an opening or reopening into the story of America. In West Virginia, and in other like "occupied," exploited, and minoritized spaces, it stands as a kind of back talk to "America's" mythic claims to realism, progress, and order. But more fundamentally, and more criti-cally, it opens a gap in the order of myth itself—the order of grand sum-marizing traits that claim to capture the "gist" of "things." The "space on the side of the road" is both a moment in everyday stories in West Vir-ginia and an allegory for the possibilities of narrative itself to fashion a gap in the order of things—a gap in which there is "room for maneuver" (Chambers 1991).

Like so many other encompassed and de-centered places in the United States and around the world, the coal-mining region of West Virginia is a place that insists on the necessity of gaps in the meaning of signs and creates a place for story—for narrativizing a local cultural real. Here a prolific narrative space interrupts the search for the gist of things and the

quick conclusion with a poetics of deferral and displacement, a ruminative reentrenchment in the particularity of local forms and epistemologies, a dwelling in and on a cultural poetics contingent on a place and a
time and in-filled with palpable desire.

In the daily practices of textualizing "thangs that happen," a local cultural real emerges in a precise mimetic tracking of events and grows dense
with cultural tensions and desires. Local voices are launched from within
a space of contingency, and the "truth" of things is lodged in the concrete
yet shifting life of signs—a network of tellings and retellings, displacements and re-memberings. Here, unlike in the "America" of listed traits
and abstract values, it is not only possible but compelling to imagine the
life of signs as a "first-order" semiological system where precise interpretive practices flesh out the story of an "Other America" in-filled with
texture and the force of imagination and desire. This is a space of story,
then, that both back talks "America" and becomes the site of its intensification in performance.

The "space on the side of the road" begins and ends in the eruption of
the local and particular; it emerges in imagination when "things happen"
to interrupt the expected and naturalized, and people find themselves surrounded by a place and caught in a haunting doubled epistemology of
being in the midst of things and impacted by them and yet making something of things. This is the space of the gap in which signs grow luminous
in the search for their elusive yet palpable meanings and it becomes
hauntingly clear that, as they say in the hills, "thangs are not what they
seem." It is a space that marks the power of stories to re-member things
and give them form. In it, the West Virginia coal-mining camps and
hollers become a place that is at once diffused and intensely localized,
incorporated into a national imaginary and left out, intensely tactile and
as ephemeral as the ghostly traces of forgotten things. These hills—at
once occupied, encompassed, exploited, betrayed, and deserted—become
a place where the effects of capitalism and modernization pile up on the
landscape as the detritus of history, and where the story of "America"
grows dense and unforgettable in re-membered ruins and pieced-together
fragments.

The problem of this book is how to imagine this "space on the side of
the road" without freezing its moves in a grand totalizing scheme of "objects" and "gists." As an "object" "Appalachia" already has its place in
an American mythic imaginary. There is the list of traits that has been
assigned to it as a "poverty region" and "backwater" or as a "folksy"
place. There is its heroic status in the master narrative of American labor
history. There is the easy assumption that "it" is essentially "other,"
"outside," and "resistant." There is the place it holds in the romantic,
antimodernist dream of escape from "America's" list of traits that make

it seem not one thing ("modern," "materialist," "fast-paced," "alien-ated," etc., etc.) but another ("simple," "essential," "authentic," "time-less," "lived," etc., etc.). The very distance that holds the mythic story's cultural "objects" at bay and captures their "gist" turns on itself to wax nostalgic for the cut details, the sensate memories, the remainders and excesses excluded from its own abbreviated account.

Across the distance of all such totalizing schemas, culture itself appears elusive and mysterious and gathers into signs of life grown luminous across a lyrical divide like picturesque scenes at the far end of a cultural landscape. There is a dream that somewhere out there—in the space of marginalia and ex-centricity—there are "places" still caught in the on-going density of sociality and desire. Places to which "we" might return—in mind, if not in body—in search of redemption and renewal. The place of the hills of West Virginia snaps into place in the "black" and "white" order of "center" and "margin," "self" and "other," "dominant" and "resistant" culture. Seen against the backdrop of the empty list that is "America," "difference" itself marks the space of culture and is at once confined in a bounded space on the margins and given license to "be itself."

With things so "black" and "white" it is not surprising that African-American culture has become the talisman of "cultural difference" or culture-that-makes-a-difference in America. Within this frame, the poli-tics of "othering" and the marking of difference remain subject to the old enclosures and to perverse appropriations. The problem remains, then, how to imagine and re-present cultural differences that make a difference in a way that might itself begin to make a difference.

In order to re-present the "space on the side of the road," then, we need more than assertions that the local has its own epistemology or that everything is culturally constructed. We need to approach the clash of epistemologies—ours and theirs—and to use that clash to repeatedly re-open a gap in the theory of culture itself so that we can imagine culture as a process constituted in use and therefore likely to be tense, contradictory, dialectical, dialogic, texted, textured, both practical and imaginary, and in-filled with desire. That is, the theory of culture itself must be brought into the space of the gap between signifier and meaning—the "space on the side of the road"—so that we can begin to imagine it as a "thing" that is not self-identical with itself but given to digression, deflection, displace-ment, deferral, and difference. Culture in this "model," if we can call it that, resides in states of latency, immanence, and excess and is literally "hard to grasp." This, I think, is the implication of the work of theorists like Barthes, Bakhtin, and Benjamin who each in his own way pointed to this "hard-to-grasp" quality and the sense of a "something more" in cul-ture: for Barthes, there is the textedness of things, the indeterminacy of "meaning" in the text, the importance of concepts of the void or the gap, and the "something more" of pleasure; for Bakhtin there is the radical dialogics of cultural production, the genealogical "meaning" of signs and forms discoverable only in their social and historical usage, and the ungraspable "something more" of genre and especially voice; Benjamin is the most explicit in his claim for a "something more" in a redemptive critique and in the divided, dialectical "meaning" of images and objects. The point is not that culture is a "complex" "thing" but rather that it cannot be gotten "right," that it is, as they say in the hills, "nothin' but just talk is all," or the tense rhythm of action and "just settin'," or a hunting for "signs" in the face of the inexplicable. It is not an end, or a blueprint for thinking and acting, but a constant beginning again— a search, an argument, an unfinished longing. The very effort to imagine it, then, is itself a continuous effort to reopen stories, and spaces of cultural critique, that are just as continuously being slammed shut with every new "solution" to the problem of culture and theory.

This book, then, does not propose a solution to the problem of representing cultural difference. If anything, it is an argument against the search for the perfect text and the quick textual solution in which the author attempts to cover all the bases with formal representations of self-reflexivity, self-positioning, and dialogic exchange. These are all important interpretive moves in the process of writing culture, but the question is how to fashion them into a productive gap in the theory of culture itself—a space that gives pause to consider the density and force of cultural politics.

To tell the story of "America" and the fabulation of "Other" spaces is to tweak the anxieties and desires that motivate the master narratives of center and margin, self and other, and naturalize an order of things "in here" and a space of culture "out there." It is to imagine an imaginative life that stands as a remainder both to the list of traits that put an end to the story of "America" and to the dread and romance of a cultural real "somewhere else."

This is a story, then, that cannot be told from the safe distance of a relativist chant or gathered into a collection of discrete and bounded "cultures" organized like rocks on a world map. It cannot simply claim to debunk stereotypes, or to counter romance with realism, or to "disprove" the myths of an "American" ideology. It depends instead on the more painful, dangerous, and perpetually unfinished task of unforgetting (Heidegger 1971) the complicity of cultural critique-as-usual in the story of "America" in order to begin again with a story that catches itself up in something of the force, tension, and density of cultural imaginations in practice and use.

This book, then, is not a smooth story that follows the lines of its own progress from beginning to end as a master narrative would but a collection of fits and starts in the moves of master narrative itself. It is made up of moments of encounter, shock, recognition, retreat. It grows nervous, and whatever "system" it is able to glimpse is itself a nervous system (Taussig 1992). It is a story in which there is always something more to be said. It is an attempt not to set the story of "America" straight but to open a gap in it so that we might at least begin to imagine "America" and the "spaces" within it. It tells its story through interruptions, amassed densities of description, evocations of voices and the conditions of their possibility, and lyrical, ruminative aporias that give pause. It tries to dwell in and on the formed particularity of things and the spaces of desire (and dread) they incite in the imagination. It fashions itself as a tension between interpretation and evocation, mimicking the tension in culture between the disciplinary and the imaginary (Cantwell 1993). It attempts to perform the problematics of the American imaginary—the problematics of subject and object, power and powerlessness, distance and closeness, certainty and doubt, stereotype and cultural form, forgetting and re-membering—so that these become constitutive elements of the story itself.

It is a nervous, overstuffed, insistent story about a nervous, over-stuffed, insistent place on the margins, and in the interstices, and at the center of "America." It mimics and attempts to perform the diacritical cultural poetics of an "Other" (story of) America—the "space on the side of the road" with its incessant compulsion to story things that happen to interrupt the progress of events, its endless process of re-membering, re-telling, and imagining things, its tactile mimesis of decomposing objects and luminous signs that speak to people and point to the possibility of the "something more" in culture.

The project has itself been a process of re-membering and retelling, and the resultant account stands as an allegory of the cultural processes it is trying to re-present. It began with two years of fieldwork from August 1980 to September 1982 and continued through a dozen return visits in the years that followed and through the twists and turns of field notes, tape recordings, memories, photographs, phone calls, postcards, letters, telegrams, and professional papers. Over time, it has become a process of long dwelling on things re-membered and retold, forgotten and imagined.

The fieldwork began and ended with hanging out with people and stopping to talk to people on the street. I used a tape recorder when I could, but, as they say in the hills, "thangs happen" and more often than not I was forced to rely on memory. I would run off to scribble notes in shorthand and then fill them in in as much detail as I could in long hours

dwelling on every phrase and word and scanning for signs of "culture."
Gaps would appear in the notes where I could not remember a strange
phrase or follow all the endless digressions in a flood of stories. Those
missing phrases and strange moves in a story then stood out as signs when
I heard them again, and they became objects of fascination for me and the
site of a further rumination on things ephemeral yet tactile, empirical and
imaginary. Missing pieces and unknown meanings taught me to listen not
just more intently, but differently—a listening in order to retell. Over
time, as I came to recognize patterns in modes of telling, it was easier to
follow along with stories and to remember them verbatim. And of course
over time it became necessary to tell stories in a local *way with words* so
that people would still visit me and stop to talk.

I spent the first year in Egeria—a place named after a biblical story of
an idyllic oasis—in a remote mountain cabin with views on all sides of
dispersed settlements where people still kept chickens and cows and pigs
and had fields of hay and huge gardens. It was imagined, locally, as well
as in my own "American" imaginary, as an *old timey* place indexing a
nostalgia for a time and place apart from the cities and the postindustrial
present of life in the hills. Yet people here, like those living in the fragments of the old coal camps in the hollers below, worked in the mines
when they could or in the new supermarkets in town or were enabled to
"return" to this place to "retire" only through devastating disabilities
incurred in long decades of backbreaking work in the mines and in the
northern cities.

Not through isolation alone, but also, and at the same time, through
long, close participation in "America," local *ways of talkin'* and *ways of
doin' people* have become metacultural markers of a local way of life in
deliberate distinction from the demonized ways of the cities. The seemingly "natural" or "immediate" way of life in Egeria is itself a production
of the scripts of stories and a constant scanning for signs. An elaborate
taxonomy of ways with words indexes precise forms of representation
and ways of reading them: the term *lying* refers to highly stylized, performative competitions, usually between older men, as each one claims to be
able to *do* the other *one better*; an appreciation for poetic performance is
indexed in the recognition that so-and-so has a *nice turn of phrase* or is
good to talk to; people who cannot *turn a phrase* are considered *backward* and *no account*, yet there can also be accusations made that someone is *just talkin'* or *runnin' their mouth*; the accusation that someone
may be *braggin'* or *preachin' at people* warns of the social consequences
of socially irresponsible speech, and there are subtle distinctions made
between how one speaks to a neighbor or a relative (distant or near), an
older person or a younger person, a Christian or a sinner; talk of *ideals*

and *signs* points to a mysterious sensibility that there is something more to things than what meets the eye. Claims that people are *squirrelly, holed up, down with the nerves,* or *runnin' the roads* index states of depression and restless anxiety. Claims that there are *confusions* in families and churches or that people are *carryin' on* up the hollers or that *thangs have got down* index intense states of social conflict and the political-economic malaise of a subjected region.

My own effort to re-member and retell, too, grew dense in the thickets of a storied sociality. Things happened and were retold in ways that drew people together or pushed them apart. There were people and places I knew to avoid from the stories some told about them. Talking to some neighbors, I found myself prohibited from talking to others; attending a church, I found myself isolated from the "sinners" and their ways and unable to keep beer in the house or to play country music. When the church went into the *confusion* of a violent schism, I became associated with one faction and cut off from the other half of the congregation. Eventually I moved, joined by my colleague, Elizabeth Taylor, to Amigo—a coal camp in a dark holler with one of the worst reputations in the area for people "carrying on" and living all piled up in the remnants of an industrial landscape. Here there was endless talk, not only about the hills versus the city, but about the character of one camp versus another or one section of Amigo versus another or those wild places way up the holler away from the hard road. And here I not only heard and learned to retell the stories that people told me but listened, as well, to the stories that Betsy heard and retold. I can no longer always remember who originally heard what since by now we have both retold the "same" stories, though differently, in notes and talks and papers. In my own experience with constant re-memberings and retellings, then, I can imagine something of the epistemological effects of a thoroughly narrativized cultural real.

The final writing of this book, then, began with an effort to make a space for these stories in an "American" academic discourse and to insert the storied sensibility of culture as a "truth" that is performed and imagined in precise practices of retelling. Culture in this account is a space of imagination, critique, and desire produced in and through mediating forms. It is not something that can be set "straight" but it has to be tracked through its moves and versions, its sites of encounter and engagement, its pride and regrets, its permeabilities and vulnerabilities, its nervous shifts from one thing to another, its moments of self-possession and dispersal. Nor is culture in this sense easy to re-present. I have used every trick I could imagine to catch the reader up in the dialogic provisionality of its "truths" including dense descriptions with amassed details, direct polemics, reproduced stories, realist assessments and romantic interludes, evocations and exegeses, seductions and confessions, and direct appeals to the reader to "picture" this and "imagine" that.

In the retelling of the stories themselves I have used ethnopoetic notations in an effort to evoke something of the intensely elaborated cultural poetics of this speech (see Hymes 1975, 1981, 1985; D. Tedlock 1972, 1983; Derrida 1978) and to mimic the effects of poetics in performance (see Bauman 1977, 1986; Bauman and Briggs 1990). I use bold lettering to indicate emphasis, line breaks to indicate pauses or gaps, and occasional representations of spoken pronunciations to evoke the differences between Appalachian dialect and "Standard English." This, of course, is a process of translation both of the oral to the written and of a local (and stigmatized) language to a particular audience for desired effects. It is by no means an effort to represent a purely objective linguistic reality but an ideological strategy informed by Bakhtin's translinguistics (1981, Volosinov 1986), which traces forms in their social and political use. It is an effort to evoke some of the density and texture of expressive forms that voice a cultural poetic embedded in a way of life and the politics of its constant subversion and reproduction in the face of national and transnational forces and precise encounters with the story of "America."

To the same end, I use italics throughout the text to indicate culturally marked local terms or terms that have some marked cultural relevance in their social use. Many of these terms are italicized only the first time they are used or only at moments when it seems necessary to mark off their local usage in a particular context or in the structure of a particular sentence. These are terms like *camps, hollers, the old timey, the anymore, thugs, scrip, holed up, ramps, smothering, the nerves, the dizzy, confusion, aggravation, studyin' on thangs, makin' somethin' of thangs, just settin', the stand, what nots, big meanings, foolin' with thangs, takin' to thangs, ornery, mean, no account, backward, showin' hisself, ignorance, cuttin' up, tearin' up, roamin', tradin', visitin',* getting *squirrelly* or getting *tickled, crazy, white trash, runnin' the roads, runnin' your mouth, lyin', braggin',* and things that *just happen* or *just come* to people. A few terms are marked as specifically local throughout the text, and so remain in italics, because of their central place in the local imaginary. These include the terms *places, remember, ideals, signs,* and often *talk* or *just talk*.

The chapters of the book move through some of the particular issues in othering and storying in America and some of the twists and turns, determinants and effects of stories in an "Other" America, including the shape of their social imaginary and the "space on the side of the road" from which they arise. Each chapter condenses and performs a set of particular associations of place, home, memory, history, exile, excess, spectacle, social performance, encounter, contingency, agency, social hierarchy, the body, the mythic, talk, ideals, and imagination.

Chapter 1, "The Space of Culture," evokes a home place emptying out and the fashioning of the "space on the side of the road" for narrative re-membering. It posits an immanent critique capable of tracking the sensibilities of mimesis in narrative and the densities of a textured and re-membered landscape. Finally, it introduces the sociality of narrative performance and the doubled epistemology of narrative that both places people in the midst of unfolding events and elicits a metadiscursive attention to modes of telling.

Chapter 2, "Mimetic Excess in an Occupied Place," explores the social imaginary of a place at once subject to the booms and busts of an industry and locally occupied in its own right. It describes its restlessness and rumination, its poetics of encounter, sheer action, and intensity, its abjection, its states of exile and dreams of return, its spectacles of impact, and its experimental activities of foolin' with things. It traces the negative, reversible logic of hope or faith arising out of the signs of a world got down.

Chapter 3, "Unforgetting: The Anecdotal and the Accidental," argues that the disciplinary apparatus of the bourgeois social order forgets and interrupts cultural particularity and texture through a rigid distinction of "subjects" and "objects" and a hierarchy of reason, idea, and truth claim over the anecdotal, the accidental, the contingent, and the fragmentary. It then traces the practices of unforgetting in the watchful narrative attention to things that happen and forms that relate moments of surprise.

Chapter 4, "Chronotopes," explores the dialectics of a historical perspective based on roaming the ruins of life in postindustrial America and an allegorical poetics of melancholic intensification that imagines a utopic potential still clinging to fragments. At moments when organized conventional symbols and signs meet a signification that is receptive, uncertain, undetermined, and inconclusive, a ruined landscape becomes a dense signification of social memory and meaning. Encountered places and scenes become social texts in themselves that enact the traces of a political unconscious.

Chapter 5, "Encounters," explores the diacritics of encounter between the story of "America" and its storied "Othered" places. Against the smooth surfaces of finished codes and projected concepts, the "Other" insists on the logic of encounter itself and heightens its differences from "the center" in performances of semiotic action. Signs of place and agency are enacted and made tactile in plastic performances of the body as a subjected subject and concretized metaphors of situation and locale.

Chapter 6, "The Space of the Sign," explores the poetic gap in signification that displaces the purely nominative and referential functions of language into a cultural real and shakes the conviction of a naturalized Real World with the intimation of unseen forces and unrealized agencies. Naming itself becomes an act caught up in the densities of mediating social and aesthetic forms of seeing, acting, and talking. Signification grows inflected with the weight of social responsibility and care. Accusations of shamelessness and meanness embed abstract hierarchical identities of class, race, and gender in a space of social performance that marks the possibility of dramatic eruptions of heroic agency, mysterious forces, and loudmouthed back talk.

Chapter 7, "The Accident," demonstrates moments of fate or the sudden, forceful revelation of the inescapable relatedness of things. In the face of unspeakable events, narrative plot fragments into overwhelming lyric images that stand as revealed signs of an immanent sensibility uncaptured by the order of things. Narrative, in other words, is not just the recounting of events but the thread of a thought that traces the precise turn of events in which the possible becomes probable, the mythic reveals itself within the ordinary, and the immanent or emergent is instantiated in the actual.

Chapter 8, "The Place of Ideals," pits the accusation that everything is *just talk* and people are just *runnin' their mouths* against an order of ideas—pronounced, significantly, as *ideals*—which betray a sense of something more emergent in the inescapably mediated space of a narrated world. The very gap between word and world becomes an object of fascination signaling unforeseen possibilities. The world speaks itself as a story filled with narrative coherence, and yet claims to ideals, like everything else, remain a form of *talk* in social use and are filled with the density and texture of sociality, history, and cultural politics.

The final chapter recalls the place of the nervous and ruminative, contingent and intensely imagined "space on the side of the road" in the "American" cultural landscape. It is a space often crowded into the margins, and yet it haunts the center and reminds it of something it cannot quite grasp.

1

The Space of Culture

PICTURE HILLS so dense, so tightly packed in an overwhelming wildness of green that they are cut only by these cramped, intimate *hollers* tucked into the steep hillsides like the hollow of a cheek and these winding, dizzying roads that seem somehow tentative, as if always threatening to break off on the edges or collapse and fall to ruins among the weeds and the boulders as so many others before them have done. Picture hills so tucked away that the sun shines down on them for only a few hours a day before passing over the next ridge. Picture hills slashed round and round with the deep gashes of strip mining like a roughly peeled apple and hilltops literally lopped off by machines the size of ten-story buildings. And these creeks—this ever-audible soundscape to the everyday—that in the spring swell and rage at the bridges and overhanging shacks and leave behind a wake of mud and trash that extends high into the trees. Picture mountainous slag heaps of mining refuse that catch fire from internal combustion under all the thousands of tons of their own weight and burn for months or years at a time, letting off a black stench of oily smoke. Picture how the hills burst into red and orange flames at all hours of the night and how the flames are likened to the pits of hell. Picture sagging creek banks shored up with tires, rusted trucks, and refrigerators and treacherous slag "dams" holding back lakes of black oily water from the mines. Picture how, when it rains, the men go on watch through the night, climbing the steep hills to peer into the blackness and wonder if the dam will hold through the night.

Picture the tattered remnants of the old coal-mining *camps* crowded into the hollers, how people's *places* perch precariously on the sides of the hills or line the roads with the hills pressed hard against their backs. Some stand freshly painted in yards filled with kitsch figurines and plastic swimming pools. Others bear the faded pastel blues, greens, and yellows they have worn for many years, the paint worn through in places to weathered boards, their porches starkly swept and lined with chairs. Others still are deeply decayed, with broken porches, partially caved-in roofs, broken water pipes gushing out the underside, and relatives' trailers packed tight into their yards for lack of land to rent or buy.[1]

Picture the *places* way up the hollers in a wilder, more dangerous zone away from the hardtop and neighbors. Here whole compounds may be

1. Tommy Creek, Amigo. Photograph © Em Herzstein.

2. A place up the holler, Tommy Creek holler, Odd. Photograph © Harriette Hartigan, Artemis.

pieced together with the remains of the *old places* now long fallen into ruin. A main house may be surrounded by tiny shacks made out of scrap metal and no bigger than a bed, where grown sons or crazy relations stay. There may be an outhouse, a cold cellar, a pump house, chicken coops, a pigsty, and several small gardens. Or there may be only a grassless yard heaped with metals and woods, bits of toys, and dismembered machines. There will be chairs stuck out in the middle of it all—the *place* where Fred or Jake or Sissy sits—and further out, encircling the compound, a ring of rusted, disemboweled trucks and cars, a pen filled with baying hounds, and, beyond that, only the hills themselves where you will come across the graveyards, the orchards, the ruins, the named *places*, the strip mines, the trucks belly-up, the damp, decayed mattresses, some scattered items of clothing, some campfire sites, some piles of beer cans, some bags of trash . . .

Imagine life in a place that was encompassed by the weight of an industry and subject to a century of boom and bust, repeated mass migrations and returns, cultural destabilizations and displacements, and then the final collapse of mining and the slow, inexorable emigration of the young. Imagine a history remembered not as the straight line of progress but as a flash of unforgettable images. Remember the *old timey* cabins in the hills, the fires, the women dead in childbirth, the slick company representatives who dropped by unsuspecting farmers' cabins, stayed for dinner, and casually produced a bag of coins in exchange for parcels of "unused ridgeland" (Eller 1982:54), the company camps that sprang up around mines like someone else's mirage complete with company *scrip*, company stores, company doctors, company *thugs*, company railroads, company schools, company churches, and company baseball teams. Company thugs carried sawed-off shotguns, **policing** who came and went on the trains. They say the thugs stood sentry in the hills over a camp in the night. You could see their lanterns and that's how you knew they were there. Then the lights would go out and you didn't know. Imagine all the arresting images of strikes, lockouts, house evictions, people put out in the alleys with their stuff all around them and the snow coming down.

> They was a settin' in chairs
> like they was in their own **livin' room**.
> And that's the **truth**.
> They had nowhere to go and the snow comin' down right on top of 'm.
> People lived in tents and the babies lay upon the quilts on the ground.

Armed miners *holed up* on a mountain and the federal government was called in to drop bombs on them from airplanes.

There were the dizzying swings of boom and bust, the mechanization of the mines, the mass migrations of the fifties and sixties, the final boom during the oil crisis, the final mine closings in the eighties, the collapse of the place, the painful hanging on, the unthinkable leavings. Imagine how the place became a migrational space that caught people in the repetition of drifting back and forth from the hills to the cities looking for work (Ardery 1983; Coles 1971; Cunningham 1987; Gitlin and Hollander 1970). How country songs of heartache and displacement became their theme songs. How ecstatic fundamentalism boomed in a performative excess of *signs* of the spirit and dreams of another world beyond. How the place itself drew them back to dig themselves in—"so far in I ain't never comin' out." How the place grew palpable to the remembered senses: the smell of snakes in the air, the sound of slow voices chatting in the yard, the breeze striking the tin pie plates in a garden, the taste of *ramps* and dandelion greens.

Imagine a place grown intensely local in the face of loss, displacement, exile, and a perpetually deferred desire to return to what was always already lost or still ahead, just beyond reach. Picture how a home place long threatening to dissolve into the sheer shiftiness of history might grow in-filled with an intense synesthesia of person, sociality, and landscape, how a haunted cultural landscape becomes a dizzying, overcrowded presence. Imagine how people say they *smother* and are hit by waves of *the dizzy* and *the nerves*, how they say they wouldn't never want to leave. Imagine how they find themselves "caught between a rock and a hard place," *re-membering* a home place that is always emptying out and backing away from the cold impossibility of the foreign land of the cities "beyond" that remains their only option.

Imagine, in short, how culture in an occupied, betrayed, fragmented, and finally deserted place might become not a corpus of abstract ideas or grounded traditions but a shifting and nervous space of desire immanent in lost and *re-membered* and imagined things. Picture the effort to track a cultural "system" that is "located," if anywhere, in the nervous, shifting, hard-to-follow trajectories of desire and in-filled with all the *confusion* and *aggravation* of desire itself. Imagine a world that dwells in the space of the gap, in a logic of negation, surprise, contingency, roadblock, and perpetual incompletion. Picture how it oscillates wildly between its dreams of order and its prolific excesses, how it drifts in the flux of desire and condenses under its weight and force. Picture how it gives itself over to "a thousand plateaus of intensification" (Deleuze and Guattari 1991) and becomes a kind of anticipation, a mode of questioning the world, an incessant search (E. Taylor 1992a).

Picture how the space of desire in such a place could grow at once tactile and imaginary, at once pressingly real and as insubstantial as ghostly traces. Imagine the need to *re-member* through the constant repetition of images fixed, condensed, *studied on*, and made visceral, the need to watch, to chronicle, to *make something of thangs*, the attachment to things that matter, the fascination with objects on which the mind can stare itself out.[2] Remember all the named *places* in the hills that mark the space of accidents and tragedies. Imagine how people *just set* and talk at the old gas stations and *stands*[3]—the beat-up old stores on the side of the road that sell daily necessities with long shelf lives like cigarettes, soda pop, candy, cakes, and the canned milk for the endless pots of coffee. Picture how people watch for things that happen and scan for *signs*. Imagine them sitting on porches at the end of the day as the hills come in to darken the sky. Picture the endless proliferation of stories throughout the day and over the years and on these darkening porches.

Picture the proliferation of signs of a local life written tentatively yet persistently onto the landscape. The tiny wooden or cinder-block post offices that bear the names Amigo, Red Jacket, Ruin, Helen, Black Eagle, Viper, Iroquois, Hard Shell, Winding Gulf, Odd, East Gulf, Coal City, Cook Town, Persistence, Lillybrook. The tiny particleboard entrepreneurial shacks with signs that read "BEeR CiGArETs PoP" in huge irregular lettering. The trucks perched on the side of the road selling watermelons or made-in-Mexico velveteen wall hangings of the Last Supper,

3. The stand, Amigo. Photograph © Harriette Hartigan, Artemis.

the Sacred Heart, the rebel flag. Hand-painted road signs—"Please Don't Throw Your Trash Here," "Anteeks," "Eggs For Sale," "WATCH IT! Road Washed Out Up Ahead Aways." Church signs advertising a welcome and a warning: "Sinners Welcome," "Sinners Apply Within," "Repent, For The Day Is Near." The massive coal trucks rushing around steep curves, their names mounted in bold letters on the grille— "Heaven's Highway," "Good Time Buddy," "Let the Good Times Roll." At one curve, two hand-painted billboards crammed with biblical quotations face each other in a heated debate over how literally to interpret the *signs* of the End Times. At another, a hand-painted road sign perched at the top of a treacherous hill offers only the starkly haunting warning: "ETERNITY AHEAD."

Picture the porches piled high with couches, chairs, plastic water jugs. The yards filled with broken toys, washing machines, scrap metal and salvaged wood, cars and trucks on blocks or belly-up being dismembered piece by piece. All the living room walls crowded with signs of absent presence: the pictures of kin who have left and the dead in their coffins, the paintings of the bleeding Sacred Heart of Jesus with the beautiful longing eyes. All the mantels and tabletops covered with *what nots* and shrines. The newspaper clippings of deaths and strikes. The children's drawings and trophies. The heart-shaped Valentine's Day chocolates boxes saved every year for twenty years and mounted on bedroom

4. Church sign, Rhodell. Photograph © Harriette Hartigan, Artemis.

5. Sylvia Hess's phone table with photographs of Riley taken by Em Herzstein. Photograph © Harriette Hartigan, Artemis.

walls. All the velveteen tapestries of J. L. Lewis,[4] John F. Kennedy,[5] and Elvis.

Imagine how an encompassed and contested way of life can grow immanent, how it might be scripted right into the matter of things, how objects and bodies could become images that twist and turn in the strands of desire and rise like moons on the horizon. Imagine how "meaning" can coalesce in the tactility of a cryptic object. How representation might not represent its "objects" with the closure of information gleaned, code decoded, or explanation dis-covered but might become instead a literal, graphic mimesis that re-presents in order to *re-member* and provoke. Imagine how people search for an otherness lurking in appearances. How they find excesses that encode not "a meaning" per se but the very surplus of meaningfulness vibrating in a remembered cultural landscape filled with contingency and accident, dread and depression, trauma and loss, and all these dreams of escape and return. Imagine the desire to amass such a place around you, to dig yourself into it, to occupy it . . .

A Space of Critique

If, following Marcus and Fischer (1986), I take anthropology to be—at least potentially—a form of cultural critique, the question is what kind of critique and where to begin? What is the "object" of such a critique? I have begun to describe this place—these hills—as a nervous system (Taussig 1992) in which "culture" is a wild, politicized oscillation between one thing and another and the very image of "system" itself slips out of the grasp of all those quick assumptions that associate it with things like order, unity, (ancient, timeless) tradition, coherence, and singularity. This is a "system" that is not either/or but both/and: both global and local, both tactile and imaginary, both set and fleeting, both one thing and another. It is a system in which moments of cultural naturalization and denaturalization are fundamentally interlocked (Culler 1975), a place where centripetal and centrifugal forces (Bakhtin 1981) form a unity of opposed forces (Gates 1988). It depends at once on a radical condensation or intensification of meaning in text and performance and on the persistence of gaps in code and concept that elicit a continuous search for meaning.

The first question for cultural critique is how to picture a place like this—a place like so many others that find themselves in a like position—where there is both a constant proliferation of expressive signs in all their density, texture, and force and a constant naturalization of "the world as it is" as signs are written into the very nature of things. A place where it is the quality and feeling of forms—their intensity, their density, texture, and force—that constitute the local "culture" as a feeling-full mediation. Deleuze and Guattari (1983, 1991) describe it as a schizophrenic tension that produces force and proliferates forms. It is a radically dialogic structure emergent in practice (Bakhtin 1981) and yet a thoroughly texted form in which meanings reverberate through intertextual reference (Kristeva 1976, 1980). Barthes (1957, 1974, 1975, 1982) tracked the infinite particularity of its interpretive moves, while Benjamin (1969, 1977), perhaps more than any other theorist, realized the dramatic complexity of its cultural politics.

The question, then, is how to dwell in such a "system" long enough to track its moves and cultural politics. How to picture its constitutive "structures of feeling" (Williams 1973, 1977), its "force" (R. Rosaldo 1984, 1989), its texted politics of desire (Chambers 1984, 1991; White 1981). How can we take it as an object except through the mediating forms it itself produces—in this case, mimesis, narrative, allegory, the insistence on particularity, ruin, and remembrance, the process of being caught up in discourses and signs and carried into states of the nerves and the dizzy and studyin' on thangs.

How is it possible to imagine such a "system" except by first arresting that all too well-known form of transcendent critique that holds tension, density, and texture at bay in favor of the generalization, the exegesis, the finalizable system that makes sense of things in a recognizable frame of types and causes and elements? Holding all that at bay, what, then, would be the "object" of cultural critique and who would be its "subject," agent, author? What, then, might happen to (and in) the space of critique itself? Or at least what might we be able to imagine?

"Subjects" and "Objects" in the Space of an Immanent Critique

Take the life of objects themselves. If I had fifty thousand words to describe the life of watched and *remembered* things in these hills, I would use them, as James Agee did in *Let Us Now Praise Famous Men* (1941), to heap detail upon detail so that we might at least imagine an escape from the "you are there" realism of ethnographic description into a surreal space of intensification. Like Agee, I could describe the rooms and rafters, the cracks in the walls, the damp underneath of the houses where dogs and fleas and other creatures lie, the furniture, the contents of drawers, the smell of coal soot ground into the floors over years and covering the walls with a thin greasy layer, a second-story bedroom ceiling open to the sky where the roof has fallen in, the way gauzy curtains are drawn across the windows so that everything outside can be seen without knowing it is being watched, a poor family of six huddled together on mattresses on the living room floor because that is the only room that gives shelter in the winter.

For Agee, every "thing" he encountered became a sign communicating exploitation, injustice, disappointment, and desire. Writing during the Depression, he railed against existing forms of documentary in an effort "to open up a passionately ambiguous new space" (Reed 1988:160) beyond any claims to be able to represent such "things" as tenant farmers (or hillbillies). He turned his book into a political allegory about relations between Us who represent them and Them represented in an effort to destabilize not just a particular representation of "them" but the very claim to know the "meaning" of such "things" at all. The subject of the book had to be twofold, constantly shifting back and forth between Them represented and Us with the power to represent. The inevitable failure of representation to capture an absolute "real" meant only a further commitment to the political act of poesis—the continuous effort to imagine what might be called a "cultural real." Escape, he said, is impossible: ruin is our only hope—a complete abandonment to the currents of existence.

In the effort to clear a space to imagine the cultural poesis of an "Other America," his writing grew nervous and experimental, shifting from one object to another and finding itself caught first in one mode of representation and then in another. Caught in the gap between "subject" and "object," it fastened onto the traces of remembered things, tracking along in their wake. It grew hypergraphic, pushing minutely described things into a space of "mimetic excess" (Taussig 1993) in which things are at once naturalized as the real and marked in their very textualization as a cultural construction.

For Agee, writing with a kind of mimetic excess himself, reality and writing seemed to transpose themselves in cultural objects (Reed 1988: 161); a cultural poesis seemed to have somehow scripted itself right into the matter of things. The texture of wood on a country church wall appeared "as if it were an earnest description" (Agee 1941:38). "A chain of truths did actually weave itself and run through: it is their texture that I want to represent, not betray or pretty up into art" (240). He wished he could put bits of wood, fabric, and excrement on the page rather than words. He wished the book could be printed on newsprint so that it would fade and fall apart with use, mimicking the ephemerality of everyday life and cultural meaning.

The interweaving of aesthetic and political impulses became, for Agee, both a utopian critique of politics and an aesthetic critique of the imaginative poverty of quick explanations and facile codes. Fastening onto the traces of a lived cultural poesis, he aimed his words like a sniper's gun at

6. Old diner and stand on the side of the road. Photograph © Em Herzstein.

the dreamy documentary bubble that would contain an "Other," sub-jected life world in the prefabricated good intentions of the order of things.

> This is a book about "sharecroppers" and is written for all those who have a soft place in their hearts for the laughter and tears inherent in poverty viewed at a distance, and especially for those who can afford the retail price; in the hope that the reader will be edified, and may feel kindly disposed toward any well-thought-out liberal efforts to rectify the unpleasant situation down south ... and in the hope, too, that he will recommend this little book to really sympathetic friends, in order that our publishers may at least cover their invest-ments and that (just the merest perhaps) some kindly thought may be turned our way, and a little of your money fall on us. (1941:14–15)

Adopting a poetics of implication and entanglement against a poetics of purity and transcendence, Agee proposed an ethnographic account to be read not for its truth value and congruence with fact but for its tense, halting evocation of difference and desire at the very heart of a doubly constructed "real." It is an account that, far from proposing to "solve" the problems of documentary or ethnographic representation in a perfect text, tries to wrest cultural representation free of the very claim to prob-lem-solving absolute knowledge. His text became an interpretive space in-filled with the failures of representing otherness. It may be that the "new ethnography," too, could make a space for such inevitable failures rather than rush to contain them in a discipline of correctives and asides that dreams, once again, the old dream of the perfect text in new textual solutions such as author positionings, formally dialogic presentations, ironic distance, and self-reflection. Without such a space for imagining the inevitable failures of representation, new claims of textual solutions to the political problems of subject and object, meaning, difference, and cause take on the gray tint of a new positivism.

Agee, in his own impassioned and imperfect effort to imagine something of the density and texture of tenant farm life, roamed indiscriminately and promiscuously between modes of writing from the romantic to the skeptical, from the confessional to the encyclopedic, from the biographical to the sociological without fixing on any one mode or building an edifice to enclose them all together. Nothing worked and yet an almost palpable "view" of sorts emerged from the effort of writing and imagination—a view that lay firmly caught in the writing and drew force as a contingent effect of that writing. This is something like what we might imagine as the performance of a nervous cultural "system" itself, and it leads to the same partial and engaged attachment to re-membered things.

You could say that it is a kind of applied grammatology (Ulmer 1985) that plumbs poesis for its politics and ends not in an abstract free play of signifiers but in a treatment of signs as graphic performances. Like Benjamin (1977), Agee dreamed of an immanent critique that could follow along in the wake of an "Other" cultural poesis mimicking its forms until the writing reached a point of subtle disorientation where critical text and cultural poesis draw together (Nägele 1988:20). This would be a cultural critique that is not so much a decoding as an engagement, not so much a hermeneutical interpretation as a crafted mimesis or re-presentation (Auerbach 1953; Barthes 1986b; Tyler 1986; Ulmer 1985) in the same way that an "interpretation" of a piece of music or a play is not an exegesis but a performance. It is a reading akin to what Barthes called the blissful reading of a text: "you cannot speak 'on' such a text, you can only speak 'in' it, in its fashion, enter into a desperate plagiarism, hysterically affirm [it]" (Barthes 1975:22).

Like montage or collage, it operates through a poetics of and by citation that can only "grasp" its "object" by following its interpretive moves into their tense and varied effects. In it, the power to comment becomes fragmentary with a built-in incompletion and abruptness of statement. It operates like a series of captions (Benjamin 1977), drawing attention to culturally texted "objects." Its effort is to hold attention on them in all their texture and particularity long enough to delay the rush to quick explanation and harmonizing synthesis that scans past them on a track of its own. Critique becomes a search through the traces of a cultural real for

Agee's utopic dream of a "chain of truths [that] did actually weave itself and run through" (1941:240).

If there is a cultural politics to style, the style of immanent critique in anthropology might stand as a provocation to a "decontaminated" modernist critique (K. Stewart 1991) that demanded a self-conscious, self-controlled distance between observer and observed. Modernist critique, built on a relativist apparatus in which all frames and concepts could be seen as "culture bound" and dependent on "context" and "perspective," fixed "culture" as an object of analysis that was whole, bounded, and discrete. While it enjoined the anthropologist to specify, and guard against, his or her own ethnocentrism, it also charged him or her with the task of illuminating a total field of data under observation (Strathern 1987b). The anthropologist, empowered to move between cultures and translate their differences, had only to document contextual gaps in meaning, manipulating familiar concepts to convey alien ones; what "we" mean by exchange is not what "they" mean, what is bizarre to Us is to Them—in an "Other" context—familiar and ordinary (Strathern 1987b:258–59). The constant, ritual decontamination of the anthropologist's own ethnocentrism through self-conscious relativism and systematic data collection legitimated the anthropologist's critical role as model builder (and model world citizen). This is a utopic dream of another kind in keeping with the ideology of a bourgeois subject capable of self-discipline and distanced, discriminating judgment (Lowe 1982; Bourdieu 1984; Stallybrass and White 1986; Frykman and Löfgren 1987).

Now, of course, critiques abound of the essentializing moves of modernist theory to fix a culture in place and time, to "picture" it in an overview, to name it "in a word," or to reduce it to an allegory of anthropological theories. Correctives include a renewed search for context and history, the recognition of transnational cultural production and precise cultural practices, and theories of culture that highlight internal contestation and intercultural hybridity, cultural invention and imagined community, and an ironic self-consciousness embedded even in the processes of "following traditions."[6] Feminist critiques of theories of discrete "subjects" and "objects" have been extended into critiques of the nature of culture, and experiments in feminist ethnography have become perhaps the most exciting and productive strand of the "new ethnography."[7] Subaltern, postcolonial, and minority studies have pushed cultural theory beyond relativism to track how actual cultural constructions are produced in difference.[8] Discourse-centered approaches to culture have extended theories of symbolic meaning into questions of the meaning of form, the public life of signs, and the pragmatics of signs in social use.[9] Performance theory has documented the rhetorical and emergent nature of culture.[10] And dialogic, reflexive, and deconstructive approaches to writing culture have demonstrated the inevitable link between poetics and politics.[11]

Yet in the wake of myriad critiques, there is always the temptation to seek the perfect ethnographic text, to fix the problem of cultural politics in a presumed textual solution. Part of the task of a "new ethnography" as I see it is to give pause and to call for something of the intense cultural-politics of any space of critique. It means throwing up a roadblock to the very daydreams of progress that would seek facile explanation and final solutions to the problem of alterity and cultural translation. It means using cultural critique to open up something like Agee's passionately ambiguous space to fashion emergent insights that culture is dialogic, hybrid, contested, situated, and imagined into techniques of imagining and re-presenting the complex interpretive moves that constitute a cultural real. It means fashioning something like Benjamin's dialectical image—an image that arrests the progress of ideology with a defamiliarizing shock of disjuncture and leaves us in a space of tense confabulation (Buck-Morss 1989).

The "new ethnography" that I try to imagine here would take a cue from the tactile, imaginary, nervous, and contested modes of critique of the subjects we study not in order to decide what these interpretive modes "mean" in the end but to begin to deploy them in a cultural politics. Its effort would be to displace not just the signs or products of essentialism (generalizations, reifications) but the very desires that motivate academic essentialism itself—the desire for decontaminated "meaning," the need to require that visual and verbal constructs yield meaning down to their last detail, the effort to get the gist, to gather objects of analysis into an order of things. It would mean an effort to dwell in the uncertain space of error or gap not just to police the errors and crimes of representation but to imagine the ontology and epistemology of precise cultural practices including our own modes of exegesis and explanation. It would mean displacing the rigid discipline of "subject" and "object" that sets Us apart and leaves Them inert and without agency. It would mean displacing the premature urge to classify, code, contextualize, and name long enough to imagine something of the texture and density of spaces of desire that proliferate in Othered places.

The Space of Story

Picture "culture" in the coal camps, then, not as a finished text to be read or as a transparent "object" that can be abstracted into a fixed representation but as a texted interpretive space in itself—a space produced in the slippage, or gap, between sign and referent, event and meaning, and gath-

ered into performed forms and tactile reminders. Picture the wild proliferations of a cultural space in all the restless coming and going, all the
dismembering and *re-membering* of things, people's eccentricities
amassed over the years, the automatic scanning for *signs*, the continuous
imagining of the "real" through the mediation of stories of things that
happen.

Then picture me, the ethnographer, trying to re-present the shifting
memories and desires of a haunting absent presence, to capture a "system" that has the fragmentary, contested qualities of the discursive process itself, to track "culture" through the tense confabulation of social
and discursive practices in use (Scott 1988).

Picture me, in the length of an afternoon, grilling Sylvie Hess for an
accurate outline of her kinship lines as she grew steadily more confused,
reeling off names and connections that didn't mesh and spinning off wild
digressions of stories until she arrived at the repeated roadblocks of double and triple relations ("Well, I believe he was her uncle, and her cousin
and then he was her stepdaddy . . ."). Picture how the effort to reckon kin
ends in the aggravated disclaimer—"Oh, I don't have no *ideal*, Katie, hit's
a mess is all, everbody 'round here's related to everbody else is all."

Picture me in the length of another afternoon grilling Riley Hess for an
accurate outline of his work history in the mines so that I could help him
document his eligibility for black lung benefits. Sifting through a suitcase
full of old pay stubs and papers, I tried to reconstruct the requisite twenty
years of mining out of his fragmented documentation of a work history of
fits and starts and migrations back and forth from one camp to another
and from the hills to Detroit and Arizona and back. Riley, sitting with me,
grew nervous and digressed from my futile attempts at chronology into
stories of dramatic encounters, hilarious failures, and bitterly hard times.
I remember the baffled look on his face. And I remember that his stories
grew progressively more graphic and imaginary until they had wrenched
us (or at least him) into a narrative space that is at once more situated and
contingent and yet opens an interpretive, expressive space—a space, in
short, in which there is more room to maneuver (Chambers 1991). Picture how, in story, world is mediated by word, fact moves into the realm
of interpretation to be plumbed for significance, how act moves to action
and agency, how the landscape becomes a space in-filled with paths of
action and imagination, danger and vulnerability.

> I bet you didn't know there's hills underground, same as above,
> a hill's got a inside same way its got a outside. They're **two sided.**
> And this **one** time, buddy, I started out and I was pullin' two hundred and ten
> cars and ever' one of 'm loaded up over the **top.**
> I always checked my brakes but I reckon they were **wet** because they weren't no
> good a' **tall** and I didn't know a thang **about** it.

And at the bottom of one a them hills there's a right smart **twist** where the track takes a **turn**.

And it's a low ceilin' and no room on the sides but just for the **train** to git through.

You have to **feel** your way through.

You kin lose your **head** if you stick it out like that Reed boy got **kilt**.

You gotta keep your head and feel your way through.

Well we started down and we was goin' perty good, y' know.

And I tried the brakes and honey they weren't nothin' **there**.

Well I told the brakeman, **buddy**, we're a **runnin'** away.

I said, find yourself a **place** and **jump off** if you can because I knowed we was gonna come **off**.

Well the **brakeman**, he was on t'other side and he found hisself a **place** and he **jumped**. There wasn't no place on **my** side and **I knowed** it.

Well I called the **dispatcher** and I **told** him, I said, **buddy** I'm a **runnin'** away and I got down inside the engine and let it **go**.

We hit that **ceilin'**,

and **buddy**,

there's **coal** and **steel** a **flyin'**.

We went right **into** that hill and they said twenty-eight cars come in after us and they hadda **time** of it.

They hadda take that thang out a there a piece at a time

where they said it done melted together.

They hadda tear that engine **apart** to git me outta that **thang**.

Well, they wanted me to go to the **hospital** and they had the **ambulance** a waitin' at the mouth and the lights a flashin' but I said **huh uh, NO-OOO**,

now I've had **enough**,

and I got up and went home.

But I never did work no more **motor**man job no more after that.

Picture the simultaneous frustrations and seductions for me, the American ethnographer, faced with the incessant narrative aporias of an out-of-the-way place. Imagine yourself standing not on the cleared ground of realist ethnographic description but in an intensely occupied and imagined space, fashioning an "object" of analysis out of filled spaces with the power to deflect and transform desire, to dramatize and fabulate, to situate and surround. Imagine yourself caught in the middle of things, tracking movements already in motion and the traces of *re-membered* impacts, searching for a culture that acts like a force field pushing you forward and lies ahead, drawing you on.

Imagine yourself caught in the space of story that opens when plans are interrupted by the accidental and the progress of time gives way to a graphic rumination through spaces of danger and desire, trial and transformation, self-extension and return. Imagine the constant effort to seize the fundamental as text, the daily struggle to lift up the "ground" of meaning in narrative poesis (E. Taylor 1992a). Imagine culture itself as an act of poesis—a creation that works through an act of mediation (Genette 1979; Todorov 1981). Then imagine how, in a place like this—a place, we might say, that literally "finds itself" and dwells in something like a space on the side of the road—the poetic mediation of meaning in forms could become an end in itself, how an "Other" world could emerge in the form of local *ways of talkin'* and *ways of doin' people*.

Narrative can be seen as the ordering of events in a particular spatio-temporal orientation or worldview (Bakhtin 1981; Ricoeur 1981, 1984). It can be seen as an act of emplotment—a grasping together, language that is "woven" (Ricoeur 1984)—or as the structure of a quest composed of functions and modes of resolution (Propp 1968) or as the search for moral and ideological closure in the face of a tension between desire and the law of things (White 1981). It can be taken as a speech form in performance that fashions "meaning" into the complex social and political act of a narrator relating events to an audience (Bauman 1977, 1986; Maclean 1988) or as a lexicon of speech genres that order social life (Bakhtin 1986) or as a series of linguistic transformations that add tone, mood, and voice to simple expository speech and so place action in a landscape of consciousness (Todorov 1981). It can be taken as a mode of ideological foreclosure—the space of a master narrative (Jameson 1981)—or as an expressive form with a built-in evaluative, metanarrative register (Babcock 1977). It can be seen as a forceful claim to the "truth" and the "original" (E. Bruner and Gorfain 1984; Said 1986) or as a tense, polyphonic fabulation of positions, voices, and registers (Barthes 1974; Bakhtin 1981, 1984) or as an intertextual structure of meaning launched in prior tellings and possible retellings (Kristeva 1980; Smith 1981). It can be taken as a relation of authority and desire between narrator and audience (Tompkins 1980; Jauss 1982; Chambers 1984, 1991) and the reported speech of characters in the story (Hurston 1935; Gates 1988) or as a form of mimesis that places speakers and actors in the middle of things as events unfold and fashions the world into a surround of traces and tactile impacts (LeGuin 1981; Taussig 1991). It can be read as a poetics of contingency, uncertainty, and partiality elevated to the level of epistemological principle (E. Bruner 1985; J. Bruner 1986; R. Rosaldo 1989; B. Tedlock 1992). It can be read as the imprint of the desire to leave a trace, to bear witness (LeGuin 1981), or as a space of desire in itself that produces both the "real" and interpretive "spaces" for the deflection and conversion of desire (Chambers 1984, 1991; S. Stewart 1984).

But whatever its presumed motives or traceable effects, and whether it takes a relatively authoritative, monologic form or a more open, dialogic form, narrative is first and foremost a mediating form through which "meaning" must pass. Stories, in other words, are productive. They catch up cultural conventions, relations of authority, and fundamental spatio-temporal orientations in the dense sociality of words and images in use and produce a constant mediation of the "real" in a proliferation of signs. They mark the space of a searching or scanning, the space of the sheer creativity of "making something of thangs," the sense of a surplus of meaning, the space of a positioned subject. The question of narrative in culture, then, is not so much the question of the meaning of any particular story or narrative structure but the question of the meaning of narrative itself—of narrativizing the world (Chambers 1984, 1991).

Picture me waiting over the length of another afternoon for Riley Hess to come to visit so that I could record his stories. When he finally arrived three hours late, the question "How are you?" opened immediately into a story of the **time** he had of it gettin' up that ol' **road**.

> Honey I **started up.**
> **Come on** past Creed **Walker's,** past Sonny **Lilly's**
> come on,
> and I come to the place down by **Fred's** where the creek branches out Barker's **ridge,**
> and **buddy,** that old Chevy truck, **hit** tuk to **smokin'** and great big ole **flames** like a **demon** grabbed a holt of it, I'm a tellin' **you.**
> **Buddy** I jumped out a that **thang** and I hated to **look.**
> Like ta **skeered** me to **death.**
> And it **did** too.
> Well, I threw open the **hood,**
> **Oh Lord!**
> And I looked at that **thang,** and I looked **agin',** honey it weren't nothin' but the **radiator** hose done blowed.
> Course I knowed it was **bad.**
> And I went down **Beckley,** b'lieve it was last **week.**
> Yessir, b'lieve it was last **Wednesday** I went in there and I got me a piece a **hose** at Priddy's and put it back a th' seat.
> **Hah.**
> Well, I went to git that **radiator** hose out from back the seat and sure 'nough there it **was.**
> **All right.**
> An' I said, said, **well** I'll have to git me some **water** and I didn't have nothin' to **hold** it, **you** know.
> So I said well I'll just go down the **creek** and git me some **water** while this here **cools** hitself.
> Cause, now, **hit** was **hot.**

Although there were houses nearby—Sonny Lilly's mommy's place is right there, side the road—he went down to the creek and roamed the banks scanning through trashed objects until he found himself lost in

reverie of his childhood on the creek and caught in an imaginary landscape. The chewed remains of a Styrofoam cup set off an imagined reverie
of an old alcoholic who must have lived at that place on the creek for
years and no one had ever seen him. He must have chewed at the cup out
of loneliness and "where he didn't have no food." Then Riley took the
little piece of cup and walked back and forth between the creek and the
truck over and over again—"must a been a hundred times"—until he had
the radiator full to the brim again. Then he came on to my place, armed
with his story: "And how are **you** today?"

It was only much later that I came to recognize such stories of people
finding themselves caught on the literal and metaphorical "side of the
road" as a conventional opening to what they called *just talk*—talk that
rises to the surface to overwhelm the merely referential with a rush of
poetic forms and the living phantasms of a sociality embedded in remembered drama. Imagine such a space on the side of the road.

Imagine being so caught up in the space of story that action follows
fabulation, as when Riley took up the Styrofoam cup, already laden with
an imagined history of use, and trekked back and forth, back and forth
between the creek and the radiator enacting a tactical digression from the
failed progress of a trip up the road. Imagine how the insertion of fabulation into action and the mythic into the real is not just an isolated experience but an already-texted relation told and retold in the myriad stories
of the *places* in these here hills. Like the story, for instance, about the two
old men, both practiced *liars*, who had argued back and forth for years
over whether a copperhead bite could kill a man. Finally one day one of
them was bitten while out roaming the hills. As his leg swelled to grotesque proportions, he trekked a long path over the hills to his friend's
house rather than get someone to take him to the hospital in town because he wanted to see the look on his friend's face. No one telling this
story ever mentions whether the old man lived or died because that is not
the point. The point, rather, is to dwell on the pull of storied claims on
people and the power of fabulation itself to draw them into eccentricity so
there's no telling **what** they might do.

Imagine that the space of narrativity—the constant practice of narrativizing the real—has itself become both the locus and the object of a local
epistemology. Note, for instance, how the moments of the plot of Riley's
story enact the moments of narrativity itself: the fastening on to the mys-
tery of the accidental (being stopped in his tracks), the intense dramatiza-
tion and personification of things and events (the demonic fire), the call
to dramatic action from a space in the midst of things (flinging open
the hood as the truck is about to explode), the demonstration of how in
the face of events a realist frame can be overwhelmed by the fabulous (the
routine preparation of buying a new hose becomes an omen), the dwelling in the wild "space on the side of the road" where anything can hap-

pen, the scanning for *signs* and the revelation of things that *just come* (the childhood memories set off by *places* on the creek, the fabulation of the meaning of the cup), the ruminative drifting from story to story, the piling up of stories on the landscape.

Note, too, how dialogic performance and dialogic exchanges within the story stretch the meaning of narrated events into the complex sociality of narrativity itself: Riley the narrator talks to Riley the hero, Riley the hero finds himself listening to found objects that speak, Riley the child speaks to Riley the old man, the past speaks to the present, Riley relates the story to me by way of introduction to our *talk* about stories. He constructs his story, even at the very moment of his experience of its events, for a range of implied audiences: the ethnographer and friend who has been waiting, and wondering, throughout the duration of events, his wife Sylvie who has lived through many mishaps with him and who would be worried if she knew he had not yet made it to my place, his old *lying* buddy Ralph who, as Riley knows from the past, will listen to the story only to respond with a story that aims to "do" Riley "one better."

Picture a world, then, in which events are always mediated by story and in which the story of finding oneself on the side of the road is a conventional opening that posits, among other things, that things happen, that *places* mark the space of lingering impacts and unseen forces, that the world speaks to people who find themselves caught in it. Picture how in the expansive scan of narrative space connections between things are always partial (Strathern 1991); there is always something more to say, always an uncaptured excess that provokes further questions, new associations that just come, and fresh gaps in understanding. Rather than complete or "exemplify" a thought, narratives produce a further searching. Imagine how, in a cultural space that finds itself in a space on the side of the road, stories run rampant and become the cultural center, how they have the power to fashion an "Other" world in contradistinction to the "realist" world of routines, plans, and progress, how they become the storehouse for local ways of talkin' and ways of doin' people in sharp, polemical distinction from the feared and despised ways of the cities.

The Space on the Side of the Road

Picture the space on the side of the road. How the space of story situates meaning and event in a dense discursive landscape of encounter as the narrator encounters the accidental event and finds herself roaming in a graphic scene in which objects speak to her and meaning, memory, and motive seem to adhere to storied things to become a force encountered. Picture how the authority to narrate comes of having been somehow

7. Josephine. Photograph © Harriette Hartigan, Artemis.

marked by events, in mind if not in body, and how the listeners, too, place themselves in the scene of story and follow along in its track so that they too can be somehow marked with its impression. Picture the dense sociality of mutual impact. Picture narrative's tense dialectic of mimetically re-presented impressions and discursively fashioned verbal art, how, as they say in the hills, stories "just come" and yet they are "nothin' but just talk is all."

Imagine how narrator and audience find themselves in the space of a doubled, haunting epistemology that comes of speaking from within the object spoken of. How they find themselves both subject and object of story, both inside and outside storied events, simultaneously seduced and watchful, firmly placed in the immanence of remembered scenes and unfolding events yet always cognizant of the culturally marked skill of "makin' somethin' of thangs." Picture the dialectic at a standstill, frozen in the time and space of a traveler stopped dead in his tracks and caught in a rumination that displaces the image of the progress of a truck traveling down the road.

Picture the space on the side of the road as a scenic re-presentation of the force of a lyric image with the power to give pause to the straight line of a narrative ordering of events from beginning to end and to place people in a fecund ground of wide-ranging associations and *re-memberings*. Imagine how an interpretive space, a cultural epistemology, can be culled into a lyric image that gives pause, how it is these lyric images—this imaginary space—that seem to matter most, how this low point in action could become the high point of cultural practice: the place from which *big meanings* emerge. Imagine how finding oneself on the side of the road could become an epistemological stance.

Picture Clownie Meadows arriving at the stand in Odd one day when several of us were standing around talking. At a pause in the talk Madie Plumly asked him how he was "gettin' along." I was, as usual, taken aback by the quick assumption of a story line without even the briefest abstract characterization of the self (as in "I'm fine" or "They've got us working seven days a week" or "I've been down with the flu").

Well, I started down the road,
oh must a been last Thursday I'd say it was.
Well it was the day we had all that rain and the rain comin' down, buddy, I'm a tellin' you.

There were several comments from the others about "that rain that day."

An hit was right there out yonder at that big ole red barn down past Miss Walker's and there's a stand a pine right there.
And that old Ford truck a mine, hit tuk to shakin' and a carryin' on, buddy.

Then the audience set off a series of digressions from the story line as if to participate in the construction of a scene on the side of the road. Jethro Graham wanted to know if he meant the place by the Harmons', and Clownie said no it was down past that "to where them Birdsong boys was a **drankin'** and a carryin' on that time." Madie, who had heard the story about the **drankin'** and carryin' on wanted to know just exactly where that was because poor old Miss Graham, living all alone out there, "like to died" of fright and "hit ain't right." Someone else guessed it "must a been up close to that old broke down shack a Harley's grandaddy, wan't it?" and Clownie said no, he didn't b'lieve it **was**. Bud Mc-Kinney told the man, "**You** know where he's a **talkin'** 'bout. Hit's where them **little girls** went out and died in the **woods** and couldn't nobody **find** 'm," and Clownie said well it might be, but now he couldn't say for sure because he never saw them girls.

From there the story went on. When Clownie pulled off the road, and the rain still comin' down, here comes Sonny Smith leading his cow back up the road.

Said, "**Sonny** whyn't you fix your **fence?**"
Said,"**that way** that cow cain't **git out** and **you** ain't runnin' up and down the road like some old **fool**."
"**Well**," he said, "I just might **do**."
He said, "**Well**, Clownie," said, "looks like you got you some **trouble**."
Said, "I got me some **tools** up the house," said, "le' me take this **cow** up there and I'll be **back**."
"**Well**," I said, "all right, Sonny, if you **want** to and I'll just wait **here**."
I don't reckon I was a goin' nowhere, do **you?**

Again, the audience gave pause. Someone from the back of the store said, "No sir, I don't reckon you was a goin' nowhere," and I heard an echo from somewhere in the back: "He ain't **goin'** nowhere, **is** he." Then, as Clownie took up his story line again, Sonny came back with his tools and again there was a series of digressions into joking comments about how Sonny thinks he has the biggest "toolbox" in the county and maybe even in the world.

So Sonny says, "**Buddy**, I b'lieve it might be the **carburetor**."
Now **understand** me, the man ain't **yet** looked under the **hood**.
   BUD: Ain't looked under the **hood**.
   CLOWNIE: No **sir**, buddy, he ain't looked under the hood and I ain't looked under the hood.
And we just went to work, and us **in the downpourin' of the rain,**
And we tuk apart ever' **piece** a that old **truck**, put it on the road,

tuk it out, **put it down,**
tuk it out, **put it down.**
And we **did too.**

He described the dismantling operation step by step in an almost singsong preaching style, the only other sound in the store now the rain falling on the roof and the occasional "yeah boy" or "ah hah."

Well, we got that ole truck tuk apart perty **good.**
And we's just about down to the **tires,** buddy, and here come that little ole **Graham** girl in from **school,**
said, "Well, **Clownie,**" said, "looks like Sonny sold **you** a bad **tire** don't it."
[Sonny runs a tire salvage and sales business out of his house.]
And I **looked** at that thang and I looked agin and I'm a tellin' **you** that **tire,** hit was as flat as my **foot**
an' just a **settin'** under that pore old **truck** like a pancake on the wrong side th' **pan.**
Tire trouble all the time and do you know we didn't never **once't** look at that tire?
I said, "**Lord** have **mercy,** let me git on **home** 'fore somethin' **happens.**"
And **I mean** I went **home.**
Sure did, buddy.
I left that thang in the mud and went home.
I ain't **stud'**in' it.
And this is the first I been out.
Buddy, I'm a tellin' **you.**

There was a series of straight-faced "well"s as the audience gave pause. Then Madie took up the conjured space on the side of the road in a story of a childhood experience "at that same place." She had been walking to the school bus pickup and got about a mile from her house when she felt a ghostly presence and could not pass. The sky darkened, the breeze disappeared, all ordinary sound and movement stopped. She stood for a very long time in a state of *remembrance.* Then she heard her grandfather's voice coming from out of a stand of hickory, and as she watched he slowly materialized. He was crying. He spoke to her of how he missed his grandchildren, how his wife had not kissed him good-bye when he died. Madie told him she missed him too, and then, as he was fading, she thought she heard her mother calling to her from some place way off and she, like Clownie, turned and went home.

Madie recalled her story by a free association with "that same place," although the descriptive details are different; Clownie's place is right down past Miss Walker's at a place where there is a big ol' red barn and a stand of pine, while Madie's place is an isolated spot with a stand of hickory. That is, her association is with the scene of a person caught in a space on the side of the road—a "place" that comes into view when something happens to interrupt the ordinary flow of events and leaves the narrator surrounded by a scene that palpitates with vulnerability. Uncertainty and challenge, painful memory and self-parody, eccentric characters and unearthly voices all point to a world in which there is more to things than what meets the eye and people are marked by events and drawn out of themselves. These are stories that dwell on what Benjamin (1969b) called the self-forgetfulness of the storyteller. They are opening stories that place the speaker in relation to others and the world and demonstrate an authority to speak as one who has "been there" and been impacted or changed.

When Clownie walked into the stand to find the rest of us standing around watching for news and amusement, he found his footing with a self-parodying, universalizing story about human blindness or *foolishness* and the lengths to which people will carry things once something happens to set them off. The audience participated in the intensification of a narrative space through the repetition of phrases for emphasis, the spinning digressions into multiple, diverging associations of *places*, the shared parody of Sonny and his "toolbox," and the general attitude that this was all *just talk*—a "story" infiltrating "experience" to the core.

Madie's story then followed the lines of performance and fabrication into a mystical condensation of the space of story itself—the image of the scene on the side of the road where meanings or messages lie immanent in things and the narrator/protagonist finds herself in an "Other" world. Here a cultural epistemology is not only implicit in the content of narrated events but is also given in the ideology of form itself (Jameson 1981).

These are stories about how "things happen" in life, and the action of the story itself moves forward only through, and by means of, an interruption (Kristeva 1982; de Lauretis 1984) and condenses in the lyrical image of the scene on the side of the road—a narrative space opened against the naturalized flow of the everyday. The lyric aporia points to an "Other" world caught up in the sheer creativity of narrative and grown overstuffed with semiotic significance so that the world seems to speak itself and speak itself as story (White 1981; E. Taylor 1992a). The story grows all-encompassing, linking people, places, and things together metonymically as its parts. The sky darkens, the breeze disappears, all ordinary sound and movement stop, the rain falls unrelentingly. Objects grow animated and speak: the truck "tuk to **shakin'** and a carryin' **on**," smashed beer bottles *remember* the Birdsongs' drunken spree and Miss Graham's fright, truck parts lie scattered in the mud as signs of disarray and contingency, a stand of hickories gives off a ghostly presence. *Places* on the side of the road stand as icons of things that happen and the people they happen to—the place where the little girls got lost in the woods and died, the big old red barn, the old broke down shack that had been Harley's grandaddy's, the hickory stand where the ghost of Madie's grandfather slowly materializes around his voice.

It seems to me that it is this moment of slippage and condensation more than anything else that is the "point" of stories here. Somewhere in the course of any visit talk will slow and slip into a place from which the world seems, at once, to have fallen away and to have grown more pressing. You could say that this is the "low point" in which people find themselves at home in a place *got down*. You could say that it is a point of poetic condensation or decomposition in which a naturalized cultural order can be dis-membered and re-membered in the space of desire. You could say that it places narrator and audience inside a narrative tradition in such a way that when they move outside again they are no longer who they were. I am sure, at any rate, that it is a moment that motivates a further proliferation of stories and that in this fecund indeterminacy of a narrativized life the world grows at once more tactile and more fabulous.

The "space on the side of the road" stands as a graphic model to think with. It narrativizes social and moral orders and makes a text not just an object of knowledge but the very place where the social code is continually dissolved and reconstructed. It becomes a space in which people literally "find themselves" caught in space and time and watching to see what happens, and yet it also makes them irreducible subjects encountering a world. It places the storyteller on the same plane with the story and produces not meanings per se but points of view, voices, and tropes. It implies both the contingency of subject positions and the reversibility of things, the ability to turn time back on itself and to reinscribe events in distinct voices. In such a space, culture itself can be seen as nothing more, and nothing less, than "what people say."

One day half a dozen strangers waiting for a new batch of chili dogs at the Rhodell volunteer fire department bake sale started in with talk about the weather—talk that quickly spiraled into idioms of roads and bodies, dangers and sicknesses. Then Miss Lavender slowed the talk with a story that focused on the lyrical image of her trying to paint her porch, which had been "ruint" by rain. Every time she brought the bucket of paint out to paint the porch, it would start to rain again and would not quit until she had taken the paint back inside. Then it would stop and she'd carry the paint back out and it would start up again and she'd carry the paint back in again, grumbling to herself:

Why don't it **quit?**
If it wouldn't rain right up **on** the **porch** I wouldn't **have** to paint it,
It don't rain on nobody **else's porch,**

I got **better** things to do than carry **paint** back and forth and wait on the **rain**. Buddy, I'm a **tellin' you**, I been so busy carryin' the **paint** back and forth I ain't had **time** to **paint**.

The others then spiraled off into talk of the bizarre and the uncanny in stories of storms where lightning traveled over the tops of the mountains in a string of flashes that went on for miles, ghosts that were seen in one flash and gone in the next, trees split just exactly down the middle and one half shriveled and died and the other half lived and bore a strange new fruit. Finally, by way of closing, they gave a litany of things "people say."

> ROSE: **Well**, you know, I got me a **walnut** tree right up agin' my place an' **they say** trees carry **lightnin'**.
> DREAMA: Oh yeah, **hit will, too**.
> KRYSTAL: But now **they say** if you tell a **lie, lightnin'** will strike you.
> LILLY: **Well**. That might **be**, I don't **know**, but they used to say if a baby **girl** is born in a **lightnin'** storm, why, she'll have her a **forked tongue** an' if hits a **boy**, why, he'll talk out of the both sides of his mouth at **once**.
> DREAMA: Well . . . They **used** to say a **lot a thangs**.
> LILLY: Oh, **Lord**, you **know** they **did**! Still do.
> ROSE: Ain't **that** the **truth**, now.

An Ethnographic Space

My own ethnographic space, here, like the space on the side of the road, grows dense and is given to excess. It takes as its "objects" of analysis the "Other's" mediations, following in the wake of modes of engagement, encounter, and agency and the texting of sociality in speech genres, positioned voices, and performative styles that bear the weight of cultural identity. In the effort to track something of the texture, density, and force of a local cultural real through its mediating forms and their social uses, it tears itself between evocation and representation, mimesis and interpretation. Faced with the daunting task of cultural translation, it interrupts itself to rail, as Agee did, against the theoretical and ideological foreclosures that disallow the needed room to maneuver. Then it doubles back on itself to pick up the track of the "Other's" moves.

Contingent on the re-presentation of local social and discursive practices, it grows unrelentingly discursive in the effort to lead with the "Other's" stories, to clear a space in which they might have not the last word but an Other word pointing to an Other world. It catches itself up in the dream of an Othered place and grows partial in both senses— motivated and polemically charged and yet always incomplete, con-

tingent, subject to interruption and displacement. It finds itself sifting
through signs and piling up details to "study on thangs"; it dis-members
and *re-members* things, gathers things into the states of intensification
people call "big meanings," launches rhetorical strategies to make a point
only to be reminded of the forcefully discontinuous effects of the local
cultural real, drifts off into its own concerns and associations only to be
reminded of everything that is still undisclosed or, worse, displaced or
obscured by its own line of argument. It dreams of translating the
"Other's" world only to be reminded of its own complicity in practices of
othering.

The effect is an ethnographic/theoretical discourse that shifts nervously
back and forth between story and exegesis. At times it performs a sharp
disjuncture between discourses—mine and theirs—and enacts the politics
of the dialogic, or diacritical, contest between them. At other times it
attempts a hybridization as if the two discourses could be simultaneously
evoked, and their effects performed, in one heterogeneous text.

At times it uses the free indirect discourse that both retains the gram-
matical signals of the observer and cultural critic and emulates some of
the phonetic, semantic, and syntactic structures of the "Other's" reported
speech (Gates 1988).

Its effort is not to find an answer to the problem of cultural re-presentation but to deflect the very search for quick solutions long enough to
remember that culture itself is a mode of questioning carried out in local
ways. Its own voice, then, remains double-voiced, its "thought makes its
way through a labyrinth of voices, semi-voices, other people's words,
other people's gestures . . . [it] juxtaposes orientations and amid them
constructs [its] own orientation" (Bakhtin 1984:95). Its task is, of necessity, an ideological one—partial in both senses—so that what unfolds
before it "is not a world of objects, illuminated and ordered by [a] monologic thought, but a world of consciousnesses mutually illuminating one
another, a world of yoked-together semantic human orientations"
(Bakhtin 1984:97). Whatever its plans and ideals, it finds itself caught in
something like a space on the side of the road, scurrying back and forth
looking at one moment for illumination and at the next for cover.

2

Mimetic Excess in an Occupied Place

An "Other" America

Driving back from California to Texas after a year at the Center for Cultural Studies in Santa Cruz, Danny and I stayed on the Hopi and Navajo reservations and I was reminded of the camps in West Virginia. Part of the resemblance was in those places here too, not unlike all those "trashy" pockets of life across the American cultural landscape from backwoods Maine to "Okie" California—the places piled high with collections of used-up things still in use, the chairs outside where people just set, the distant smell of food cooking across the expanse of barking dogs. But the reservations, like the hills, also have the quality of a place-in-itself squeezed into the wide expanses of an American no-man's-land. There is the quality of a doubly occupied place—a place that was taken over and surrounded by an occupying force and then resettled to occupy THIS place HERE with a force of its own. These are the kind of places where the matter has already been settled that this is a place apart—an "Other America" defined within and against an encompassing surround and become an inhabitable space of desire.

Judging from the look of things, I could imagine that on the reservations, as in the hills, polarized strategies of walking the line and living beyond the pale live side by side and can shift nervously back and forth from moment to moment in a productive schizophrenia of desire: there are the neatly ordered houses and the wilder places that seem, as Agee (1941) would say, to have abandoned themselves to the currents of existence; there are the Christians and the Sinners, the still moments of just settin' and the times of wild excess, all the cases of the nerves and the dizzy, the moments of heroic self-assertion and the abject faint of a life got down. Here, too, it seemed as if family and place were all-important, and I imagined that the porch lights left on all night here, too, signaled both a welcome to visitors and a warning to intruders. Here, too, a swath of open space around a house seemed to leave it both unprotected and in a position to see what approaches. I imagined the same watching out of the corner of the eye, the unrelenting chronicling of daily events, the vulnerability to sudden contingencies, the gaps in "the real" tended in an offhand, distracted way as you might rip at tufts of grass as you walk through the graveyard of things that say "this place is occupied."

I imagine a resemblance, too, between these doubly occupied American places and the countless other tensely occupied places in other parts of the world like the Palestinian home deep in the heart of Israel as Said (1986) describes it: the crowded, inhabited interiors, the pictures on the walls that are too high or somehow "off," the focus on entrances and passage-ways, the excesses of hospitality with ethnic foods piled high on the table, the nostalgia for an occupied homeland, the restlessness, the fighting in the streets, throwing stones at guns . . .

It may seem strange that it is in these most marginalized, out-of-the-way places that place seems to matter most while the places lodged firmly in the center of things grow vague and interchangeable. Strange that these places so devastated by history retain the marks and memories of the past while in the suburbs the sheer timelessness of the straight line of prog-ress spreads like oak wilt from house to house. Strange that these pieced-together, re-membered places bear the weight of a homeland while the "master planned communities" at the center of things encase themselves in the picture-perfect simulacra of homeyness emptied of history and memory. Strange how things seem to proliferate and amass themselves in the margins while the centers with the power to create look to these "Other" places as a source of both nostalgia and threat . . .

In the two political imaginaries of center and margin there is a telltale contrast: the one, relatively self-assured and oblivious in its privilege, de-limits clean lines of will and action to leave its mark on the world, while the "Other" raids, poaches, stays at the ready to take advantage of op-portunities that come along (de Certeau 1984:xix), and sifts through signs of its own otherness and remainder for something of lasting value. The one might come to imagine itself as structure and order while the "Other," with no power to keep the surrounding other at a distance, sees itself in moments of engagement and encounter and the sheer nervous movement of contingency and indeterminacy. Where the one seeks sleek surfaces and finished objects, the "Other" amasses fragments into a sur-round that stands at once as prison and protecting cocoon. Picture it as a space of desire emergent in the tight squeeze of the order of things. Imag-ine how it holds to the dream of a homeland, how it gives rise to the desire to chronicle, to re-member, how it insists on the materiality of things that matter.

An Occupied Place

Imagine, then, the constant movement and scanning for *signs* and the "centering" in local ways. Imagine how, in the hills, place is everything yet a family's *place* is not where they "live" but where they "stay at" as

8. Old truck on the outskirts of a place, Tommy Creek holler, Odd. Photograph © Kathleen Stewart.

if the staying has to be marked, like a temporary respite requiring constant vigilance. I could tell you how sometimes clumps of coal mud explode into the sink and then the water runs black, or there is no water at all, for the rest of the day. Or how sometimes, when a house falls vacant, it disappears overnight only to reappear sometime later as an addition-in-progress to someone else's place. I could tell you that houses, like people and things, circulate and become abstracted into moving forms, that it is their dismemberings and re-memberings that seem to matter most, that things do not hold, that "thangs are not what they seem." It is as if the ownerly attachment to objects that makes them seem unmoving, substantial, and discrete is only a mirage. Yet re-membered fragments grow infilled with absent presence and bear the marks of a continuous agency.

Picture the strange agency of fashioning aesthetic effects out of things that are always falling apart or already fallen into decay. How every *place* shows signs of having been pieced together and *fooled with* and nothing is ever finished once and for all: someone is tearing off a back porch, someone else is building on a bedroom or jacking up a sag, another leaves a coal stove out in the front yard for weeks "for spring cleaning." Bud Caulley has had his house half repainted for longer than anyone can remember: "Hit's where he cain't tell whether he likes the **old** or the **new. Tell** you the **truth**, buddy, I cain't **either. Can you?**" Picture the fascination with combining things into new hybrids or shifting their contexts and functions "just to see what happens." How they use washing-machine parts as truck parts to see what will happen, graft strange hybrids of plants in the gardens to see what fruit they will bear, and push words into strange new metaphors and surprising disjunctions. How they pile up objects ceaselessly and without goal in an "insane collection" that values objects for themselves and not for their place in a systematic, "collectible" order of things (S. Stewart 1984:154).

In the continuous experimental activity of foolin' with thangs, the sutures between old and new, or one thing and another, are left visible rather than smoothed and painted over as if the sutures themselves marked the acts of *re-membering* and amassing an inhabited cultural space. Words, too, fool with thangs in stories, replicating the poetics of amassing and remembering things by tracking along in the wake of events in search of the intimate details of their composition and decomposition.

This is a poetics in which identities seem to grow immanent in things; the storyteller adopts the "worm's-eye view," nose sniffing at tracks to discover how things unfold, and is left marked by what happens. Tastes and identities touch in a metonymic logic of contiguity as people find themselves drawn together with things. The men fooling with trucks, they say, are *like* the trucks—scarred and welded together out of a history of accidents; the old women fondle the quilts they have stitched together out

9. A place up Tommy Creek holler, Odd. Photograph © Kathleen Stewart.

of torn fragments of their relations' old clothes. They say Miss Banks's canned goods have a special look and taste unlike anyone else's because she's the best neighbor in the camp—"there's just somethin' **about** her" and her canned goods. Miss Lilly is *remembered* all day by the constant sounding of the pie plates that hang on strings from her garden fence posts. They say people *take to* some foods and not others; a child takes after one parent more than the other; a woman takes to gardening but smothers in the house; one man "takes to the bottle" while another "takes to playin' the **guitar**" and another finds Jesus.

Picture the visceral power of the attachment to place referenced in the shorthand ideal that "people shouldn't get above their raisin'." Using local ways, people dig their way in and down as if into the very substance of the hills—"so far in they ain't never comin' out." Identity depends on the hills themselves and the local ways of life in the hills as people work their way deeper and deeper "in" and are impacted by events. They say mining gets in your blood. The union is a "body of men." Your kin are "just people you have" and the bloodlines carry the traits of a hillbilly agency—*orneriness, meanness*, and "there's no tellin' **what** they might **do**." The ecstatic religious discourse promises transcendence only through immersion; it places people in the tactile "worm's-eye view" of the sinner and then converts them into pure "vessels" awash in the blood of Jesus. They say you have to get all the way down before you can "see." Political action erupts as an automatic response to graphic depictions of innocents victimized by the big people—"You **see** somethin' like 'at and you just have to **do** somethin', you don't **thank** about it, that's just the way we **do** 'round here."

Local *ideals* of kinship, neighborliness, and Christianity erupt as a desperate negation of a world got down. Urgency mounts in the course of a constant litany of disaster and contingency and erupts in a line drawn between what is right and what is wrong, local ways and the ways of the city. Listen, for instance, to Jerry Graham's complaint about how thangs is got down in Iroquois since the mines closed down.

> Well, they're just like **cats in heat**, buddy, they're **crazy**, they're doin' everything you can **think** of and that's just gettin' **started**.
> They're sellin' **marijuana** over **here** and layin' out drunk on the road over **here** and they're beatin' **up** on each other like they ain't got no better sense, and **shootin'** and **robbin'** people, and breakin' into **stores**.
> Well the **police** was down here other night and raided a **house**, they said it was full a **guns**.
> Now what do you **thank** they're a doin with all them **guns**?
> I don't **know** buddy and, **honey**, I don't **want** to **know**.
> And that old **Verley Meadows**, they come and tuk **him** away where he was shackin' up with his **daughter**.

People ain't got no better **sense.**

Got all them **kids** by her, and that's the **truth** because you can see **that** for yourself.

Well, they found a old woman down there locked up in a **chicken** coop like a **dog,** and that's how **her** daughter done **her.**

Oh, **Lord, I don't know,** well they ain't nobody workin' and nothin' to **do.** People cain't figure what to **do.**

A bunch of 'm went down **No'th** C'raliny and they loaded 'm up in **buses** and tuk 'm **off.**

And I don't know, they just treated 'm **awful** bad down there and they come back worst off than they ever was.

Well they was a workin' way out in the **fields,** way out from the **town** and no place to **stay**

and nobody wouldn't give 'm no **water** to **drank.**

And no **toilets.**

And they had to stay in the **fields.**

They wouldn't let 'm in the **town.**

So they got theirselves some **tents** to **stay** in and **some** of 'm had some **trailers** and they got their **stuff** with 'm.

And a great big **storm** come and blowed it all **away,** ever' **bit** of it and all they **had.**

Tuk ever'**thang** they **had** and they come on **back** and moved in with their mommy and daddy all piled up like cats and dogs.

And Reagan talks about how thangs is gettin' **better** all the **time** and that's **right,** they're gettin' a **whole** lot better for the rich people and the politicians and the **pore** people is a layin' out in the **fields** and fightin' like cats in heat.

That's what it's **come** to. Well, you cain't **trust** 'm, that's what **really** hurts, buddy.

And you hear about where all these people is on the **starvation** and the old people a dyin' in the cold of the night and eatin' **dog** food out a **cans.** And it ain't just **here neither.** It's in them cities down in South America.

They got whole **countries** full a people, **millions** a people livin' out in the mud. And in New York they're a dyin' on the **sidewalks** and people walk on **top** of 'm.

They walk on **top** a them, buddy, **don't** nobody **care.**

Reagan ain't nothin' but just **talk** is all.

That man ain't nothin **but** talk.

Well, any **fool** can see **that.**

In the litany of complaints, *anymore* people treat each other like dogs and the old people have to eat dog food out of cans, and people don't visit like they used to, and people don't **talk** like they used to, and there ain't nothin' **here** and nothin' to **do,** don't nobody care about nobody but their own self, and the mines is shet down and the young people is havin' to leave out—well, there ain't nothin' here **for** 'm, you cain't **blame** 'm. *Ways* and *ideals* and fundamental attachments emerge from out of the ruins as a space of desire resonant with nostalgias, heroics, and dreams of reversal.

It is among these ruins, then, that the storyteller stands; this is the *place* from which she speaks. A place from which there is no other place to go "in this world," no future of assimilation into America, no need for an abstract notion of progress. Yet it is also a place that in its very abandon to the performance of a world got down includes a utopia of latent and *remembered* possibilities. Litanies of conflict and abjection end in a seemingly inexplicable surge of pleasure and hope. Countering any positivist reading of a "dying culture" (as seen, enclosed, from a distance) or any "realistic" assimilationist claim to the necessity for change and adjustment, the melancholic litany of how thangs is got down begins and ends in a negative, reversible logic of an ultimate hope emergent in storied openings. They say, "Well, b'lieve thangs is gonna git back **up**, don't **you?** B'lieve the mines is a gonna **come back** and the people will git to go back to **work**." Or they say, "But **you know, I love** these people 'round **here, ain't** no better people in the world." Or they say, "But you know this is **home** to me and I wouldn't never want to **leave**." Then talk will move into the lighter, contentious voice of relating what happened on the way to the post office this morning or what Miss Lavender said when Bobby Johnson found her hauling fifty-pound sacks of pig feed up the railroad tracks because her neighbor, playing out their long and bitter feud, had driven pilings into her access road to prevent her using her truck and then skipped away singing. Miss Lavender—an elderly African-American woman—spreads the rumor that she will use witchcraft against him (K. Stewart 1988).

The attachment to place in the hills depends not on realism and normative judgment but on what Lukács (1968) called social realism—a cultural fabulation that places people within the entire historical dynamics of their society in such a way that "reality" is revealed as a process in concrete social experience. Piecing stories together without recourse to ideological transcendence, they construct a cultural space in which the impacts of history lie immanent in forms of action and story and in practices of fragmentation and re-membering, the opening of gaps and the moment of transgression. Forms of cultural agency emerge out of powerful lyric images of a world got down so that when the young people are sent off to the city with the words "there ain't nothin' here **for** 'm, thangs is **got down**," they are sent off with the weight of the place behind them. Then the others follow their "progress"—the drifting back and forth from the city to the hills via heartbreak and windstorms—in stories that are not so much assimilationist as they are revivalistic. News of the

10. Ralph Pendry, Tommy Creek holler, Odd. Photograph © Em Herzstein.

migrants passes through the camps like the waves of falling-down spells that now, on some days, wash through whole camps and leave people talking (K. Stewart 1988).

Picture the enchantments and investments in these hills as a lost and possible world. There are all the stories of those who found themselves adrift out in the world beyond the hills and dreamed of return. There was Ray Meadows, stationed in Germany in the seventies, who caught himself staring out the kitchen window at a lone dandelion in the yard and, hillbilly that he is, it was all he could do to keep from *showin' hisself* by running out and plucking it to eat. There was Bobby Lilly who was too *backward* to get anything to eat on the train coming home from the Korean War and who arrived home so weak from the starvation that he fell sick and had to be nursed back to health on a diet of beans and corn pone. There was the day that Jimmy Cunningham started back from Baltimore but was stopped by a feeling and turned back. He started out again the next day and made it back all right. "I ain't **superstitious**. I don't believe in **black cats** and all **that**. But a **feelin'** is somethin' **different**. A **feelin'** ain't somethin' you **ignore**." And one night Helen James had a dream. She dreamed that she was driving away in a big slow luxury car, drifting past beautiful pastoral mountain scenes filled with color and sound. She was coming up over the top of a big hill and she felt something "big" was going to happen. But then there was nothing—the terrifying annihilation of free fall. She woke up smothering. "It makes you not want to go nowhere."

Picture a world in which there is something wrong with the everyday and an "Other" world—more real than "the real" and resembling dream or fiction—rises as a sign of unrealized possibility. In the daily, lived conflict between what is and what might have been if people had not lived the lives they were forced to live or chose to live, there is a double vision of two lives (caught and free, *used to* and *anymore*, the city and home) differentiated by a lived experience of loss and the dream of redemption. The world grows texted with stories that elude simple characterization but highlight enigmas and the secrets of half-hidden dreams and nightmares. Imagine a world where texts are not just symbols of something else but acts of negation and excess that indicate the power of a doubly occupied place to exceed the space allotted to it by its own history.

The Hills as a Social Imaginary

Imagine the stubborn occupation of a home place always subject to encompassing forces and the vicissitudes of history yet stuffed full with the countervailing force of a local social imaginary. There are all the named *places* in the hills that *remember*: the empty *mouths* of the mines lying gaping on the sides of the hills, the remains of the big white *operators'* (i.e., mine managers') houses looming over the camps below, the lonely chimneys of the old family farms, the graveyards and rusted train tracks and mining tipples that remember accidents, strikes, and other striking scenes like the prayer services held underground at the start of a shift when hundreds of miners would crouch on their knees in the water under the painfully low thirty-inch ceilings in the dark listening to the bloody preaching of death and salvation, or the place where the union organizer was shot dead and his blood run out in the coal dirt and was lost, or the strip-mined hill that collapsed in on itself and slid down to cover the Graham family graves, or the *places* of hunts, suicides, murders, and car accidents, of children electrocuted on old mining wires, of fires when the people trapped inside cried out for help while the others stood outside and listened, helpless . . .

Picture all the places where people just set at odd times of the day—the chairs left out in the middle of the kitchen floor or on the porch or in the yard, the favored stumps or rocks out in the hills. Picture the ever-audible smothering breath of all the old men slowly suffocating with black lung who dream only of going back up into the hills once more—to a place "far in" where they could just set. More than once I have been persuaded to take them, pushing their wheelchairs over roots and wet leaves to a clearing and propping spare oxygen tanks around them.

Picture how such a space, once inhabited and held onto with the fierceness of necessity and choice, in-fills with the desire of remembered loss, how the real becomes a resistant surface scanned by wishes and regrets, an absent presence detectable only in its effects and disclosed only by desire, a collection of phantasmic fragments through which things appear obliquely yet powerfully as what they are and what they can be.

Imagine the hills as a phantasmagoric dream space—a wild zone beyond the pale that is filled with things dangerous, tragic, surprising, spectacular, and eccentric. Imagine how danger and promise mark the space of the hills as a dream world born of contingency and desire.

. . . They say there are snakes up there and wild young men who lie in wait or come in the night to rob and maim. Once there were hippies (demon worshipers) who lived out there under a rock. There are eccentric hermits living on nothing and *white trash* families filled with trouble. There are criminals in stolen-car rings drifting back and forth to Chicago and hiding out from the police.

. . . They say people are crazy and there's no telling what they might do. They keep guns loaded by the bed and at the door and shoot at the sound of noises in the night. They say that in the dog days of August when the snakes are blinded by their shedding skins and trapped in a frantic fury, the smell of snakes is strong enough to make you sick.

Yet imagine how fabulated danger and dread only fan the flames of

11. Abandoned hot rod. Photograph © Harriette Hartigan, Artemis.

desire. Picture the posses of women armed only with their garden hoes who go up into the hills to find the snakes in their dens and chop off their heads. How people make plans to go up into the hills to harvest the laden orchards of the old family farms or to gather wild berries or *greens*. All the old women who venture out in packs, salivating over dandelion greens, ramps, and a dozen named varieties of weeds as if they embodied desire itself. Or how Lacy Smith talks of a place up in the hills where a tiny hole opens into a great big room full of Indian things. He and Bud have looked for it but they never could find it again "where the hole is s' small."

Picture all the scavenging and looting. How people loot coal from the worked-out mines. How they scavenge for checks as they scavenge for meat or wood—food stamps, social security, black lung compensation, disability, welfare. How they carry away booty under cover of darkness. Remember all the unoccupied houses that disappear overnight or the night a group of striking miners sitting at the doctor's office spun a collective fantasy of how they would scale the big brick walls of Governor Rockefeller's mansion and loot it for all it was worth.

Picture all the restless coming and going, people *running their mouths* all day, how the young men *run the roads* all day and night until they run out of gas and money or until they are stopped by the force of accident.

Then picture them still roaming up and down the hollers in their wheelchairs. And on the side of the road, at the head of a treacherous hill, the
hand-painted traffic sign warns, "ETERNITY AHEAD."

Being Caught

Imagine yourself always already caught in the constant, prolific narration
of events people "cain't he'p but notice."

> . . . June 24, 1982. Kitty passes my place to see Sissy about the girls' fighting.
> Sissy goes to see about Miss Banks who has had an operation on her knee. Kitty
> comes to see if I think Sissy's mad at her "for saying anything to her"; Sissy, she
> says, has been acting funny with her. Anna Mae, out hanging her rugs, yells to
> Lilly to come out "if you want to" and they stand talking over the fence that
> joins their places. Kitty, still with me, wonders what they are talking about,
> "not that it's any a my business." She says they say Anna Mae's daughter has
> cancer and this leads to stories of the grotesque—cancers, bizarre accidents of
> mothers rolling over on their sleeping babies, bloody childbirth in the truck on
> the way to the hospital, babies born with the mark of the beet or the hamburger
> or the apple that the pregnant mother craved—"looks just like it." We say it's
> a shame that Kitty's daughter Julie had to find out from the other kids on the
> school bus that she was adopted, that Kitty should have told her herself. This
> leads us to talk about the danger of things left unsaid; Mr. Walker in Rhodell
> shot himself to death because he kept things to himself. I remember the look in
> his eyes the last time I saw him—at the public auction of his store, which he had
> neglected more and more over the years as his drinking got worse until finally
> people got tired of sour milk and bugs in their rice and "quit tradin' with him."
> I bring Sissy her cuttings and we sit out on her porch in the late afternoon sun,
> dangling our legs over the edge. Sissy says Kitty thinks she was the one who told
> about Julie being adopted, but she never would—"Ain't nobody's business."
> We watch the men on evening shift leave out, the men on day shift come in. We
> can smell Miss Murdock's greens cooking ("She's sa hateful she won't tell
> nobody where she got 'm"), Dreama's pork frying ("You reckon Bud's back
> workin'?").

Imagine a vigilant scanning become automatic, relentless, compulsive.
Picture people sitting on porches, standing beside fences, clumps of men
gathered around benches at the gas station or the stand, how they stare as
you pass, keeping track. Imagine that passing trucks can be recognized by
their distinctive sounds, that people track and time their comings and
goings to figure where they have been and how long they have lingered
there. Imagine the scanning for signs . . . how everything depends on
things overheard, overseen, on the effort to make somethin' of thangs.

Imagine how, in such a heavily occupied place, sociality is not a distanced "social context" but a pressing, all-encompassing force field.

Imagine how when someone falls sick or dies the others quite literally miss seein' 'm. How, when Riley Meadows *holed up* after his wife died his neighbors watched for him.

> And they say he's got a calendar in there on his wall and every morning he gets up he marks a **X** through another day gone by without her.
>
> He counts the days she's **gone**.

He's gone mean. He won't **talk** to anyone. He won't get **out** and **go**. He'll aggravate you to **death**. Picture those who watch for Miss Graham when she drops out of sight for a while. They "figure she's in there a **drankin'**. Hit's just a matter a time 'fore somethin' **happens**."

Or, on the other hand, picture the aggravation of keeping track of those who run their mouths and run the roads all day enacting an idiom of restless action and sheer momentum. Picture all the *roaming*, the *trading*, the *visiting*. How people holed up and studyin' on thangs *git squirrelly* to where there's no telling **what** they might do. Like Cab Atkins who went on a drunken spree breaking windows and felling telephone poles:

> At the **time** I didn't even know I was a **doin'** it.
> Now, somethin' **wrong there**.
> That's when I give up **drank**. **Had** to, really.
> You cain't **act** like 'at.
> Next thing, you **kill** somebody or they kill **you, one**.

. . . Or the night that some of the young men, caught in the trap of alcoholic roaming, made the trip to Chicago as a bold, spontaneous adventure, drinking all the way. They woke up in the city, in the noise, the traffic; they got lost; there was trouble with the **police**. Then again a drunken, dreamy night and they found themselves back in the hills, dreaming of losing themselves in a place "way back in" where they could never find their way out again.

. . . Or how one night Frankie, a Vietnam vet who they said had been living under rocks at a place on the side of the Odd road, went on a burning spree that took out five barns and shacks in the hour before dawn while volunteer firefighters raced from one call to the next, unable to track him down.

Picture how people literally keep moving as if to occupy this overfilled yet emptying space. Picture the overcrowding of effects in the cramped, reconstructed space of an encysted culture. How people smother in the face of the excesses of action and talk—people runnin' their mouths, *cuttin' up, tearin' up*. How people are given to ecstatic trance, visions, and

12. Porches lining the road, East Gulf. Photograph © John Hartigan.

signs, to *spells* of the nerves and the dizzy and *falling out*. How action for the sake of action is dangerous—nothing but foolishness and *ignorance*—yet it is a matter of pride to be mean, backward, and ornery, to run your mouth, to stand up against the company and the government or to stand up for the Lord. How when things aren't right people say they *cain't see it*—"I don't **know** no better, I have to git in there, try an' **do** somethin' **about** it." They say the working class of people has had to fight for everything they've ever got and they have to keep on fighting to keep it. Things do not hold.

Picture how the hills grow in-filled with the excesses of a place reacting to the threat of a world got down. Picture the shifting *satisfactions* and aggravations of those who sit on their porches in the gathering dusk to re-collect a barrage of images that have an impact and leave a trace as the hills come in to darken the sky at the end of the day.

The Spectacle of Impacts

Imagine the lived effects of such a nervous system of signs and agencies. The sense of being at home in a place caught between a rock and a hard place—at once protected from a threatening outside world and smothering in the excesses of reaction and fabulation. The sense of groping along in the midst of a minefield of forces, tracking the traces of impacts. Imagine a subjectivity located not in the power to name and evaluate but in the memory/imagination of events and images that *just come* and stand as intensely mimetic reminders of things uncontained by an overarching "order of things." Imagine a system in which the overarching desire is to relate an impact, "to incarnate oneself, to become more determined . . . a sudden narrowing of horizon" (Bakhtin 1979:352 as quoted in Todorov 1984:106). Imagine yourself surrounded.

Picture Sissy who sits on the stoop with her coffee in the early morning watching the blanket of mountain fog rise in floating, ghostly shapes. Or how people give directions by moving, as if in body, from one *place* to the next, drawn along by digressions into a space of mimetic excess.

> **All** right now, you know where Miss **Banks** stays at up there, don't you?
> All right, now, go on down Miss Banks's place past that **big ol' bridge** where that **McKinney** boy went over and hit looks like you might go in **after** 'm if you ain't careful, buddy.
> **Yeah BUDDY.**
> **All** right, now, you'll see a **bridge** what's got one side **down** and the other side 'bout covered up in **briars**.
> Keep on 'til you see the **Black Eagle** post office.

That's where the **snake** handlers **stay** at and Bud says **he's** skeered to deliver the **mail** down there where he might put his hand in a mailbox and there's a **snake** in there.

I don't guess they get much **mail** down there, do **you**?

All right, now, **keep** on, **keep** on, pretty soon you come to that place where they shot up that **boy**. **What** was that boy's name?

You know that one **kilt** his **wife**.

Well, really, I don't believe it **was** his **wife**, but they was a **livin'** together and **I** don't know **what** all.

Well they was **in** to it and he **kilt** her **there**.

They said there was blood all over the walls and never could get it out of the carpet because Sissy went down there right after it happened and **she** told **me** it was **bad**.

All right, now, you know where that old **woman** stays, there's a **washin'** ma-chine out front, well it's just past the sign for "free coffee."

. . . and perty soon you come to a big ol' **red**-colored house up on the hill. . . .

Imagine the kind of place where, when something happens, people make sense of it not by constructing an explanation of what happened but by offering accounts of its impacts, traces, and signs.

. . . Once there was an underground explosion that shook camps in a radius as wide as thirty miles. No one (but me) was interested in identify-ing what it "was"—what had "happened" to cause the ground to shake. Instead there was a flurry of talk about its placed effects—in Winding Gulf they said it knocked all the plates off Kitty's shelves; in East Gulf it knocked old man Graham out of his chair and he's got a *place* on his arm to show for it; in Helen it knocked a bucket of coal out of Julie's mommy's hands and spread a blanket of greasy coal soot over her kitchen floor—"seems like she never **could** git that **flo'** clean agin' after that." In the end, we have the graphic, culling images of the plates being knocked off the shelves, the *place* on the old man's arm, the spooky, ever-greasy floor.

Another time, in the spring of 1981, a forest fire burned in the hills surrounding Amigo, slowly working its way down to the camp. For days the air was so thick with smoke that all you could see beyond the alleys of the camp were bursts of blue and orange flame. At night the sight was spectacular, and people would sit on their porches and comment on its beauty and force and its chilling resemblance to the pits of hell—a world on fire. In the days there was a feeling of aggravation. There were dra-matic stories of people going up into the hills to fight the fire and conten-tious/nostalgic claims of how used to a forest fire meant **everyone** worked day and night to save the farms unlike **some** anymore. Finally, the fire threatened to jump the creek. Its presence grew more pressing and the houses closest to the creek began to steam. The atmosphere in the camp grew more watchful and calm—more satisfied—as the threat of fire grew palpable. All afternoon we carried buckets of water from the creek to throw on the threatened houses, and people noticed everything that happened as if out of the corner of their eyes. Later, there were hilarious comments. They were *tickled* by the look of old Miss Henson running back and forth from the creek with a rusty bucket full of holes. They noticed that Bud Smith would walk right by the Grahams' place to dump his buckets on some other place where he was still speaking to people. They noticed how the smoke just seemed to gather 'round that *no account* hypocritical Preacher Cole, the flames licking at his heels.

Such moments are moments of "mimetic excess" (Taussig 1993) in which an image flashes uncontained by a meaning; subjects, objects, and events become performers in a spectacle, and the act of mimesis rises to importance as a local "way"—an epistemological principle in its own right that exceeds the rigid discipline of cause and effect or truth and lie. These are moments, in other words, that enact the cultural poetics of being at home in a place that actively surrounds, impacts, and remembers, waiting for something to happen. They are moments of occupying an always already occupied place.

Picture how, in a world of loss and unreality, people tell stories first of all to bear witness, to leave a trace, to confer form on life and so survive (LeGuin 1981). How narrative rises to importance as the phantasmal rehabilitation of all lost frames of reference (H. Foster 1985:90) and fashions a mimetic representation out of graphic re-presentations. How, in story, events are temporally ordered and dramatized in the mode of things that happened, that could happen, that threaten to erupt at any moment. How narrators literally "find themselves" located in space and time and watching to see what happens. Imagine the sense of being caught up and carried along in a poetic movement, how meaning lies emergent in the unfolding of events about which there is always something more to say, how stories not only allow but actively produce an excess of meaningfulness, a constant searching (Chambers 1984, 1991; Sperber 1975; Strathern 1991). Picture how stories grounded in an overplus of meaning—a barely controlled semantic richness—take on a life of their own and index an extra-ordinary "real" above and beyond the people who tell them, the events they describe, the situation of the telling. Remember the roaming yet visceral operations of makin' somethin' of things that just come. Picture how narratives of and in such a place effect a mimetic reenchantment of a world got down.

Picture my introduction to the place one night in January 1982, shortly after I had moved from Odd to Amigo, when the camp's water main burst in the alley in front of my house.[1] When I heard the water rushing under the house and went out to see, the yard was already covered in several inches of water and the neighbor women—Sissy, Kitty, Dreama, Anna Mae, Miss Lavender, Miss Murdock—were standing in the alley admiring the small geyser and telling apparently hilarious stories of other Amigo disasters. They yelled, "Well, **welcome** to 'Migo. Now you're **really** here. How do you like **West Virginie?**"

They decided to dig a trench in the frozen ground to divert the water into a culvert (which had been pieced together, from scraps, in another "situation" involving a dispute between neighbors). They went off and came back with their garden hoes laughing about how they didn't know where the men kept their "shovels" if they even **had** any. Other women leaned out windows to comment on the "pitiful-lookin' road crew they sent down **this** time." Although it was below freezing, we worked slowly, stopping every few minutes to lean on the hoes and talk. Kitty and Sissy, who had come out without coats, ignored the cold.

Sissy went in from time to time to call the water company with more and more dramatic stories of floods and drowning and threats of suits if they didn't make it down tonight to fix the rupture.

I told em, said,
"You know people **down here's** got **sue** crazy anymore and you cain't do nothin' **with** 'm if you make 'm **mad.**
And when you git **drownded** people
and you got **water** in your house
they **git mad.**"
Said, "You **better** git on **down** here 'fore somethin' **happens.**"
Told 'm, "Don't be stoppin' for no **coffee, we** got **plenty.**"
Said, "**We** got somethin' **goin' on** down here and you just better just come on and **see** about it."
They said, "**Where'd** you say you're a **callin' from?**"
I said, "**'Miga.**"
They said, "**Oh yeah.**"
I said, "**You** know 'Miga, don't you?"
"**Oh yeah,**" they said, "we been **there** b'fore."
[Laughing.] Hah! Ever'body knows 'Miga.

When the trench was dug, we stood around for another hour talking over the fence and watching the water flow into the culvert. A redheaded woman living in the next county had murdered her husband and there was blood all over the walls and just **soaking** the carpet. "They said she blowed his brains out and they had a **time** of it cleanin' it up."

Now which one **was** he? Was he one a them **McKinneys** up **Basin Mountain? Basin Mountain!** There **ain't** no McKinneys up on **Basin Mountain.**

Oh **yeah**, because Jimmy worked with one of 'm, and one of 'm—and now **he** had **red hair**—he was up at Doctor Ross's last week where Bobby and them seen him. Said he was all **cut up.**

Well, I don't know, it might a **been** him but now I don't b'lieve I've ever **seen** him.

Finally, when they were ready to go home, they said: "**Well, welcome to** 'Migo. How do you **like** it?"

Imagine a world in which normalizing discourse is not a norm that people *take to* but an occasion for restless *back talk*. Picture Eva Mae.[2] Poor, black, and *crazy*, she spends her days walking back and forth along the road between Amigo and Rhodell, mumbling to herself and waving a gun or a butcher knife at any car that tries to stop and give her a ride. She acts "the wild mountain woman." Where other women threaten to go *crazy*, Eva Mae enacts the threat and fashions herself in its image to make herself a walking allegory. Her words are her weapons, and she aims them carefully at the fictions of a social order being bandied about in the camps—fictions that delimit "black" and "white" sections of camps and associate men with the roads and women with their houses. They say women out walking on the side of the road are either in need of help or looking for sex. Yet the women do walk, in pairs and for exercise, and as they walk they dare the others to *talk*. Eva Mae pushes the always already challenged limits of the normal by dressing in a shimmering red dress, huge rhinestone necklace and earrings, and a red wig sitting askew on her head.

> That'll give 'm somethin' to **talk** about.
> They say I **prostitutes**! **Hah!** I don't want no old man sweatin' over **me**, honey. You know they **talks**, but I sees 'm out there a layin' out of a night, they **ain't** foolin' **nobody.**
> Now **these people**, they'll try an **mess** with you, but they don' mess with **me**, honey, 'cause they **knows I knows.**

When she pauses at the house of "some snake" to openly proclaim the **talk** going around about him, the other women say they "get a kick out of her."

> You might think Eva Mae's **crazy**, way she **acts**,
> but now you stop and **talk** to her,
> well, **really**, she's **good** to talk to.
> There **ain't** nothin' wrong with her **mind**,
> she's just **crazy**.
> She don't **care**, buddy.
> She'll say **anything—and I mean anything**—and right to their face, you have to **give** it to her.

You could say that Eva Mae performs a transgression that transforms her otherness and marginality into the disruptive power of excess and social abandon. You could say that that is what the other women get such a kick out of. It is not a way out of the oppression, danger, and contingency of the hills but a way in through mimetic excess. It pushes into the matter of things, intensifies latent forces to the point of their visibility, and makes countervailing possibilities tangible by playing them out.

The women say they "get a kick out of" the occasional scandalous woman who *shows herself*, like Dreama's neighbor who blared her music all over the holler day and night and who drank and danced with strange men in her living room and shot at the utility man who came to shut off her lights and who bared her breasts against her window in the face of a nosy neighbor woman. Or the young woman on drugs who walked through the camp one day with no shirt on and embarrassed all the men—"an' you should a **seen** the look on his **face** when he saw her a **comin'**! I thought I'd **die**! That **tickled** me, it really **did**." Stepping over the line remains an always seductive possibility in a doubly occupied place where parameters were long ago set by encompassing forces and yet where there's no telling **what** people might **do**.

When she comes to rest on her rock on the outskirts of town, the stories of Eva Mae's life flood out of her, washing away what are to her nothing more than the infuriating hypocrisies of claims to Order and Truth floating on the surface of a world got down. In her stories of victims and meanness there is no line between heartfelt excesses of meaning and the outlines of history . . . She says she had a father but they worked him to death in the mines until one day his heart burst and the blood came up in his lungs and smothered him and got in his eyes and blinded him and he died. She says she had a mother but they raped and murdered her in her bed, split her face with an ax. She says she had a son but he laid down on the railroad tracks and kicked his feet raw until they took him away to an institution and she has never seen him since (someone else remembers the day they took him away). Her daughter, she says, went crazy and left out years ago, roaming from man to man and state to state and a few times she has come through town—barefooted, dazed, and you can't talk to her. She has a sister in the area but Illa drinks awful bad and when she drinks she gets mean and she'll kill you. Eva Mae says Illa has killed three men, and sometimes when I would give her a ride over to see her sister, Eva Mae would hesitate on the side of the road and then start back to Amigo—"B'lieve she's drunk up there."

The others listen not to decide which parts of these stories are "true" but to follow the poetics of a world got down into the tangible excess of what could happen if people were to take felt excesses of meaning into the realm of action. In a grotesque imaginary of extensions, excretions, and

13. Eva Mae on her rock on the side of the road between Amigo and Rhodell. Photograph © Em Herzstein.

abject degradation, stories fasten onto images of murder with blood all over the walls and soaking the carpets so the women could never get it clean, or old people treated like dogs and eating dog food out of cans and those who in their old age *turn* and spread feces on the walls and every word that comes out of their mouths is a swear word, or illnesses that work themselves out in huge boils or worms coming out all over the legs, or the dream of being washed in the blood of Jesus, the image of blood running out of the faucets in the *End Times*.

You could say that things in the fabulated world of the camps are as they were in the time and space of Rabelais's grotesque realism (Bakhtin 1968), or in the chronotope of Latin American magical realism, or in the world of the Luddites burning granaries and sabotaging industrial machinery, or in Michael Lesy's (1973) Wisconsin countryside at the turn of the century when country towns had become charnel houses and the counties that surrounded them had become places of dry bones. The land and its farms were filled with the guilty voices of women mourning for their children and the aimless mutterings of men asking about jobs. . . . The men burning houses and barns so that for ten years and more the countryside was an inferno of revenge. The old men who went mad with jealousy. The old women who jumped down wells. All those mothers: the ones who carried their children into rivers, and the ones who fed them arsenic and strychnine so that, if they had to die, at least it wouldn't be of epidemic disease. All those women who purified and punished themselves with kerosene and matches. All the men who cleansed the putrescence of their lives with carbolic acid. All the others who killed themselves with the same insecticide they used on potato bugs. . . . The hypnotists. The hydrophobes. The somnambulists. . . . The farmers who saw monsters pull squeaking pigs into lakes. . . . The men and women who received messages from the dead in their dreams. . . . All those suicides like litanies. . . . The stories of salvation and religious insanity. The accounts of berserkers who kept their villages at bay. All the wildmen who howled, naked in the winter nights . . . the rapt attention paid to coffins broken, bodies preserved, and people buried alive. . . . (Conclusion, unpaginated)

These are moments of disruption and displacement that gave rise to a wild cultural proliferation—the early Renaissance and the Russian Revolution that formed the context for Baktin's (1968) account of grotesque realism, the severe displacements of early industrialization that produced the Luddite reaction, the history of colonialism and the reigns of terror in Latin America that form a subtext to its magical realism, the wild impacts of industrialization and urbanization in the United States as the countryside emptied out into the city and left people at wit's end. They are moments of what Clark and Holquist (1984) call "a rip in the fabric of time" when "the commonest man was denied the luxury of believing that he could be a passive spectator in history's theatre, able to sit back and watch the kings and prophets who enacted the drama" (296). These are moments of dramatized, embodied spectacle, moments of the mimetic excess that comes of watching to see what happens in a world subject to eruptions of intensity out of the tension in things.

A Lost Homeland

Life in the hills, then, like life in so many other like places, finds itself caught in the prolific enactment of tensions that have penetrated to the very matter of things. A doubly occupied place collects itself in re-membered affinities and amassed effects and is tested in the experimental activity of foolin' with thangs. Culture becomes not a haven of ideas or a

fixed state of experience but a social imaginary erupting out of a storied
cultural real. Like the "space on the side of the road" figured in the stories
themselves, culture is ruminative and filled with density and desire; it de-
rails into magic and threat, trauma and melancholy, playful performance
and deep eccentricity. It imagines itself not as finished code but as a series
of encounters and sudden eruptions of signs and action out of a world got
down. It follows a logic of gaps in the naturalized order of things and
finds itself caught in latent force fields. And it is this that constitutes the
hills as cultural "home."

In conditions of cultural trauma, displacement, exile, and economic
collapse, the very negation of "home" constitutes its hold on people.
Those who have been expelled from the hills in times of economically
forced emigration *re-member* the time in the city as a time of exile.

> What is true of all exile is not that home and love of home are lost, but that loss
> is inherent in the very existence of both. They regard experiences as if they were
> about to disappear. What is it that anchors them in reality? What would you
> save of them? What could you give up? . . . only someone whose homeland is
> "sweet" but whose circumstances make it impossible to recapture that sweet-
> ness can answer those questions. (Said 1984:55)

Those who have been away and returned *disremember* Detroit or Dayton
or Chicago as if out of a perverse loyalty to the hills. It is the leaving and
return they *re-member*.

> TOMMY WALKER: Well, we left out back before Sammy—that's Madie's
> **baby**—was born and he was a **grown boy** when we come back.
> I remember the day we packed up that old **Ford truck** I traded **Wes Johnson** a
> hundred dollars for . . .
> and the **bed** was rotted through and we put down that old mattress we got from
> her **mommy's** place and that was our **bed** . . .
> **Buddy**, I never thought we'd make it **up** there.

They claim that in the city there was nothing—nothing but bars for the
men, the women cooped up in isolated apartments, no place to raise kids.
If pressed, the men may offer a string of strange, surreal stories of ethnic
fights, theft, disorientation on the city streets, a bizarre, miniature car that
a man and his brother built in his backyard out of parts stolen, piece by
piece, from the General Motors factory where they worked.[3] They may
describe the walk to work down city streets and cutting through yards
where things sometimes happened. The women often have less to say,
depicting a place of abject emptiness. Sylvie Hess describes her years in
Detroit as a litany of dead objects and constraining walls:

> There was **nothin'**.
> It was one room and a bed, a chair, one window,

we had a hot plate with two burners—one for the **beans** and one for the **coffee**.
Two **plates**, two **cups**, two **forks**, and four **walls**.
And there weren't no **garden** and no way to **git out** and nothin' to **do**.
And I'd set in that chair and rock and wait for Riley to git back.

Rocking only passed the time. Things had no immanent sense but could be inventoried as a lifeless collection of dead objects that stand as testimony to a terrifying nothingness. Sylvie would walk down the city streets every day with her niece but nothing ever happened.

The people was always **different**,
you never saw the same ones **again** and didn't nobody have nothin' to **say**.

Imagine how, to someone used to tracing the pressing presence of a place through the spectacle of vibrant signs, "nothing is more frightening than the absence of answer" (Bakhtin 1979:306 as quoted in Todorov 1984: 111).

In sharp contrast to her litany of dead objects constrained within four walls in the city, Sylvie recalled her childhood on Polk Mountain one day in a story that "just came" to her like a daydream from which she was awakened by the involuntary memory of a brutal accident of history.

Used to, up on the mountain, I had me some **sheep**.
Now I **love** a sheep.
That's my favorite animal.
And I had **two** of 'm, one called **Daisy** and **one** we called **Susie**. And they had a **big ol' stump** up there where they'd tuk down a tree and them **sheep**, they'd jump around and play on that stump all day **long**.
They was just as **sweet!**
And ever'where I **go**, well here come old **Susie**.
I'd go git the **mail** and here's **Susie**.
And I'd go out to the garden and here comes Susie right b'**hind**. She'd just **stay** with me all the time and come on back with me when it got **time**.
Well, just ever'where I went, here come **Susie**.
But they had some **dogs** up there and they **killed** Susie, killed them **both** one day.
Ripped out her **throat** and tore her all to **pieces**.
I hated to **see** it, Susie was all tore up on that stump and the blood all over.
I never heared **nothin'**, them dogs was already **gone**, and there was Susie a layin' there all tore up.
But that place was sa **perty!** And there was **flower** bushes all **in** there. And there's always a **breeze** that blows up there.

Here, home is a vibrant space of intensity where things happened and left their mark. Home is sweet not despite the loss of her favorite sheep but because of it. A place made present by an absence, Polk Mountain

14. Sylvia Hess and her mother, Nancy Taylor. Photograph © Em Herzstein.

grows tactile with the longing emergent in the memory of a violent tearing, an innocence lost. It becomes an occupied place re-membered as a site
of magical cosubstantiality linking a girl, the mountain, and the sheep
that stayed with her and left their blood on the flowers and in the breeze.

3

Unforgetting: The Anecdotal and the Accidental

I ENTERED the dense and haunting landscape of the camps on the words
of a social worker in town who told me flat out to just stay out of them.
She had moved to the area twenty-five years earlier when her husband
came to practice medicine in one of the five miners' hospitals in Beckley—
a town of 20,000 that is the service center for 150,000 people from the
hollers and camps within a radius of thirty or forty miles. Although she
had worked daily with clients from the camps, she had never herself ven-
tured out to this place that began five miles from her doorstep in a protected middle-class enclave. For her it was an imagined landscape beyond
the pale—a place given over to dirt and violence, lack and excess. In the
landscape of lack there was not enough money, not enough schooling, no
lawns, no police, no fire stations, no paint on the houses, no city water,
no cable TV, bad plumbing. It was unsanitary. There would be no one for
me to talk to. There was nothing out there. In the landscape of excess
there was the insanity of ecstatic fundamentalism, the danger of wild bars
where drunken men cut each other with knives, the filth of pigs and chickens, the smell of wildness and dirty bodies and unwashed hair, the piles
of junk on the porches and in the yards, the spreading junkyards of rusting trucks and washing machines, the excesses of talk and story, the obvious eccentricities of people, the bald stares of people who notice a
stranger passing.

Her words addressed the space of alterity itself—that process of always
approaching from without but never arriving (Levinas 1981), a state of
being in between where things are neither fully present nor absent but
linger and echo in a simultaneous lack/excess. But in the very process of
addressing the space of alterity, her words encased it in the prefabricated
code of a class defending itself against the contamination of a surrounding "Other" through the class-conscious phantasm of a life that would
somehow contain itself in coded norms of order, cleanliness, propriety,
safety, and self-control. In the mode of a shocked rhetorical query ("How
can people live like that? I just can't imagine") the diacritical construction
of self and other grew incarnate in the visceral look (and smell) of an
absolute "Other" as an object that contained lack and excess within itself
like a personal flaw. The hills were for her the monstrous unimaginable
locale of an "Other" that was not just overstepping its bounds but had

15. Cook Town. Photograph © Em Herzstein.

itself become somehow unbounded and contaminated—a place beyond the pale.

On my way out into the hills the next morning I too found myself caught in the space of alterity. The highway ended abruptly on the edge of town, and I found myself wending around a dizzying mountain pass trying to hold the road against the overwhelming density of the hills, the hand-painted signs, the porches lined with faces, and the yards piled high with things. I remember dismembered trucks and sagging porches and the texture of rusting metal box springs propped up against the sides of houses. I remember glimpses of neighbor women standing at their fence lines talking and clumps of men gathered around benches at gas stations staring. I remember a wild-looking white-haired couple hoeing their garden. I remember the sudden flash of a wildly careening car stuffed full of people flying around a hairpin curve on the wrong side of the road. And the more regular shock of passing drivers with eyes frozen straight ahead in fear, necks rigid, knuckles white on the steering wheel, who at the moment of passing would jerk the wheel quickly from side to side as if they, like the wild drivers, might also suddenly quit trying to hold the road and give themselves up to the momentum of a thing set in motion. I remember the desire to abandon myself to the surrounding texture and density.

For me, this first-glimpsed space of alterity was more haunting and sublime than monstrous, more thickly imagined than unimaginable. But for me too, as for the social worker, it was encased in a powerful code— an ethnographic code that deploys practices of classifying, mapping, and interpreting to imagine its object as a bounded symbolic whole with readable meanings and discoverable causes and explanations. Where the social worker's code expressed defensive disengagement from the hills, mine was expansive, engaged, appropriative. Where hers rested in visceral reaction, mine, armed with the spirit of adventure and a relativist chant, forcefully subverted visceral reaction in an act of transcendent self-reflection and the poetics of encounter. Yet, looking back, I wonder how deep the affinity goes between the social worker's class-coded signs of self-discipline and order and the safe distance of my own ethnographic "discipline." At the very least, both codes are moments like so many others in which "the West moistens everything with meaning, like an authoritarian religion which imposes baptism on entire peoples" (Barthes 1982:70).

I wonder if this "West" is nothing more, and nothing less, than that moment in which it becomes possible to isolate a subject with the power to postulate its own place and the exteriority of all targets and threats (de Certeau 1984). Nothing more, and nothing less, than that decontaminated mode of critique that inhabits a stable center of certitude by imagining itself above or outside its "objects" of study and privy to absolute

16. Coal trucks on the East Gulf road. Photograph © John Hartigan.

truths and original causes (K. Stewart 1991). I wonder if this is not what Heidegger (1971) called the certitude of forgetting—the origin of conceptual and representational thought in the act of forgetting that every clearing also conceals. It seems to me a kind of disciplined amnesia that replaces real space and time with a classificatory, tabular space (Fabian 1983) and re-members things only as fixed symbols or examples of ideas—as afterthought, illustration, ornament, or supplement. As Fabian (1983) argues, the result is a radically taxonomic model of culture that sees it as a process of selection and classification rather than a mode of creation and production.

The question, then, is how to "un-conceal" through un-forgetting (Heidegger 1971), how to arrest the progress of transcendent critique long enough to recognize the practices of concealment and forgetting inherent in all modes of explanation, description, and analysis. How to suspend the urge to Truth long enough to notice the nervous force and density of a lived cultural poetics caught in its own tensions of forgetting and unforgetting. It is an effort that leaves analysis and description caught in the space of alterity itself where the other remains exorbitant—an irreducible enigma that "refuses to be tamed or domesticated by a theme" (Levinas 1981:100) and opens into tensions, latent possibilities, and states of desire.

Unforgetting

What would happen, for instance, if I tried to unforget the whole series of accidental and contingent encounters through which I entered the dense landscape of the hills? Thinking back, I re-member some of these events as a fragmented series of anecdotes and luminous allegorical images. At the end of a long process of "writing up" from field notes, their particularity or texture lies buried under an apparatus of concepts and representations of "a culture." And yet their texture has also, in that very process, come to haunt the finished concepts, to stand as if in excess of any cultural "system" I might have conjured up.

What if I tried to arrest the progress of truth claims that reduce "anecdotal evidence" to a secondary and deeply suspect status? What if I tried to invert the hierarchy of "conceptual thought" over "data" and to take my own task of cultural translation as the supplement? What if in the place of a transcendent system or code there was only the anecdote, the fragment—insufficient and unfinished? What if the density of trash, porches, and hand-painted signs were allowed to disrupt intellectual concentration to a point where their material substance rubs against thought with a friction that generates cognitive sparks (Buck-Morss 1989)? What if, following Benjamin, I imagined my writing as a series of citations on collected fragments (1977:76–81) that, in the very search for an echo of the original, remain always charged with my own concerns and marked by the fleeting recognition of the myriad dimly known encounters buried in its scaffolding?

I can remember, for instance, a first "folky" trip to West Virginia in graduate school when Elizabeth Taylor and I ran a weeklong oral history seminar on the edge of the Monongahela National Forest for some private-school kids from Baltimore. I remember a "first day out" traipsing over the hills with a compass to chart our path (this charting re-membered from Girl Scout camping trips) and the eventual discovery of a deserted old farmhouse in a beautiful scene of rolling fields and rolling mists. I remember the way we marched right in in the spirit of adventure, how we gazed at the decorative stenciling along the walls, how I stood in the middle of the farm kitchen taking in the old timey furniture and utensils, the dozens of old calendars on the walls. The biggest find was a box of old letters in one of the upstairs bedrooms. I can barely remember them now but I do remember some mention of a bastard son and some payments that had something to do with him. I remember surrealistically banal postcards and strange little accounting sheets of the cost of nails, yarn, and buckets.

Now that I think of it, I can vaguely remember asking someone about this place later that day and he knew whose house it was. I think he said that it belonged to an old woman who had just weeks before (did he say two weeks?) moved into town and that her son, I think he said, had just been out there caring for the place that day, and I remember feeling relieved that we had not been caught. There had been a tragedy at the place in the months before—a suicide, I think, but I do not remember clearly. I may have notes on this somewhere. It may be that I was already, even at that point, taking notes.

There are only a few more traces of that week of roaming the edges of the forest: the old women who put on bonnets and played wooden organs for us, the old men who told ghost stories to scare the kids, the dredging up of superstitions like the one where people would put sharp knives under the bed and over the door at weddings (or was it births?) or the way someone with the gift to heal would lay hands on a wart on someone's face and it would disappear. I remember the dense texture of things— rusted metals and swollen wood. I remember the flat stares of children and an embarrassing encounter with a middle-aged man who was trying to tell me something with great animation and at great length until his elderly father finally said, "He wants you to see his dog. He's got snake-bite." I remember how the man stood in the corner of the room and watched as his father told the kids stories and then how he went out and waited in the yard when his father told him to. And how he watched and waved until we were out of sight. I remember the cook telling me about a ghost who came and sat in a rocker by her bed night after night until she moved out. And I remember a conversation with a social worker from the coal-mining area in the southwestern part of the state. Her father had been a miner and active in the union, and as we talked about the labor history of the area I began to imagine a "system" that was both "traditionalist" and "individualist," "hierarchical" and "egalitarian"— all categories from my qualifying exams. I remember deciding then and there to go to this place to do fieldwork; I remember how I began to imagine a dissertation and how the concepts began to snap into place.

Soon after that, I visited the coal-mining area with Susan, another anthropologist friend. I remember the pleasure of driving the roads, exploring. How we visited the exhibition mine in Beckley, how we stopped at every roadside place, admired the decor and bought trinkets—a cheap leather change purse decorated with a carving of a hillbilly Rip Van Winkle snoozing next to a *still* and an oversize made-in-Mexico bandanna of the rebel flag. I remember that one coffee shop that refused to serve us, though we never figured out exactly why. And I remember coming fast around a mountain curve, radio blaring, and the sudden appearance of a large colorful tent filled with people. How I screeched to a halt, gravel flying, radio blaring, and how we faced the faces turned toward us for a long moment as it slowly dawned on us that this was some kind of tent revival. As we sped away I had only the slightest sense of how strange, I now imagine, our sudden intrusion must have been.

The traces of these encounters, all odd fragments of first impressions, are now, as they were then, scripts of imagined alterity. They bear the ideological weight of previous uses and remain dangerously open to use. In the master narrative of ethnographic enlightenment, they can be trotted out to stand as prefabricated symbols of an initial ethnographic ignorance that is overcome, through initiation and revelation, by a deeper or more systematic ethnographic knowledge. Or they can be left cryptic to evoke the semantic richness of a barely glimpsed alterity or even the rich vitality of a "real" life beyond academic analysis. They can, in other words, stand as stages of mastering otherness or as embodiments of a desired otherness itself. If so, they will be encased in the endless replay of an othering that is contained and held at a distance—the closed loop that Said (1978) called orientalism, that Bhabha (1990) called colonialist ambivalence, or that Stocking (1989) called romantic motives. If not, they might be left to stand—if only for a moment—as graphic images of the pains and possibilities of unforgetting itself. We might find ourselves in something like the space on the side of the road—that nervous and ruminative space of intensity emergent in a tension between "meanings" and "just talk" in a world "got down."

As Clifford (1983a) has argued, ethnographic authority rests on two tensely related textual legs: the anthropologist's unique authority in having been there (the "my people" voice) and a scientific authority of data, method, and code. The two legs of ethnographic authority easily ally with a dualism of "subjective" and "objective" knowledge, and as Mary Louise Pratt (1986) has pointed out, they can be separated into two distinct texts that belie a hierarchical order of accounts; a scientific, self-effacing text becomes the "ethnography proper," while a secondary auto-biographical text that speaks to the experience of fieldwork takes on the status of the supplement. Ethnographic authority, in all its tension, re-solves into a hierarchy of modes of evidence and proper objects of cul-tural analysis: hard evidence over the "anecdotal," ideals and norms over implicit social knowledge and latent possibilities, unity over fragment, instrumental logic over unintended and accidental adjacencies of mean-ing. Yet despite itself ethnography remains always allegorical and "prompts us to say of any cultural description not 'this represents, or symbolizes, that' but rather, 'this is a (morally charged) *story* about that'" (Clifford 1986b:100).

Remember, then, the extent to which people in the camps build their own authority to textualize the world by in-filling the empty lines of an "objective" account with allegory and story. Remember, for instance, the process of giving directions by moving, as if in body, from one allegorical *place* to the next, drawn along by the materially charged fragments of *remembered* events and scenes. Such accounts displace the dualism of "objective" and "subjective" views with the haunting double vision of a subject who is simultaneously *in* a world and subject to it, and yet moving *through* it with the power to fabulate it and give it form. Views from the "inside" and the "outside" of events and characters constitute what Bakhtin calls the dual moments in aesthetic activity itself; empathy or identification and "exotopy" or the creative act of naming and textual-izing translated from Bakhtin's Russian coinage: *vnenakhodimost'*, liter-ally "finding oneself outside" (1979:24–26 as quoted in Todorov 1984: 99). The "extopic" position produces not objective distance but an excess of vision and comprehension, a watchful listening (Bakhtin 1979:357) akin to what Benjamin (1969b) called the "self-forgetfulness" of the storyteller. Standing at once outside and beside the world that is his or her "object," the storyteller re-creates "beings independent of himself, with whom he appears to be on an equal footing" (Bakhtin 1984:284). "The position from which a story is told, a portrayal built, or information provided, must be oriented in a new way to this new world—a world of autonomous subjects, not objects" (7).

The stance of these stories—a stance that displaces the rigid hierarchy of "subject" and "object"—engages a scanning reattention to events in the mode of unforgetting. In them the past is never quite past but reverberates in the present, and "things" are never quite set and contained but reverberate and echo in *signs* and excess significations. These stories are modes of representation that hinge on the accidental, the allegorical, and the constant promise of something more and other. They move with the doubled epistemology of one moving through a world that surrounds with a presence so pressing it haunts. Berger describes this haunting double vision in Seker Ahmet's nineteenth-century painting *Woodcutter in the Forest*.

> The attraction and terror of the forest is that you see yourself *in* it as Jonah was in the whale's belly . . . this experience . . . depends upon your seeing yourself in double vision. You make your way through the forest and simultaneously you see yourself, as from the outside, swallowed by the forest. . . . [The painter] faced the forest as a thing taking place in itself, as a presence that was so pressing that he could not . . . maintain his distance from it. (Berger 1980:81, 84)

The convention of "perspective" in the modern painting fixed a "point of view" into a single, centered focus as the individual became the "origin" of the object world. But in the narrativized world of the hills the perspective of the subject on the object world remains, or, more likely, it has become again, dual and haunting. Here, the practice of narrativizing things imbues objects with memory and haunting presence and catches up subject and object alike in allegorical scenes where things do not so much symbolize particular "meanings" as they stand as signs that literally point to a field of signification and illuminate it (Sperber 1975). It is as if these illuminated things have become a sign of unforgetting itself, as if unforgetting has been elevated in the hills to the status of an epistemology.

A Near Miss

I woke up that first morning in Odd to the sun shining and the sound of the long dry grasses gently brushing the windows in the morning breeze. My house rested on the top of a hill and commanded a beautiful view of rolling hay fields and half a dozen residual farms in varying states of order and decay. The men worked in the mines or collected disability or black lung compensation. I worked in the local health clinic, traveling the three miles down a treacherous winding dirt road to the Odd post office and stand at the start of the hardtop and then nine more winding miles past the inhabited remnants of Josephine, Lillybrook, East Gulf, Mead, and Winding Gulf to Rhodell.

Rhodell was one of three incorporated towns in the county, its one main road lined with four churches, three food stores of various descriptions, the post office, the county liquor store, the boarded-up movie theater, and a number of boarded-up or burned-out stores. Its four hundred residents lived in trailers and camp houses along the main road and two alleys running parallel to it. The two ends of town were still divided roughly into "white" and "black" sections. I spent several days a week at the clinic and going on home visits with the doctor to draw blood, pack abscesses, and help people with their papers.

Back at Odd I fixed up my house, painting and sanding to a fine finish, and raised a huge garden with some friends who no longer had any land of their own to work. They would build a bonfire under a tree at noon and roast "weenies." I visited neighbors, exchanged tomatoes for summer squash and eggs, canned green beans and corn in long afternoons in the heat of a neighbor's kitchen. Since I seemed to be interested in hillbillies and old timey things, people made sure to tell me about the wild families who lived way down the holler and ran shine and were said to fight and cut each other with knives and bite off the heads of chickens and drink their blood. They sent me to see Jimmy McBain—a hermit who many years before had walked away from the place on the hard road where he lived with his wife and eight kids and moved to his family *place* down a long unmarked trail that had to be walked. You could say he was a refugee from the tensions of the space on the side of the road or you could say he had adopted that space as his home, living as if there was a time and place in which that space was the world itself. I would see him walking the ten miles to and from the Odd stand like an apparition of a nineteenth-century man of the hills, his white hair and beard long and flowing in the breeze, a sack slung over his gaunt shoulder to hold his monthly supply of *commodities*—flour, sugar, salt, and coffee.

His *place* was one of the few two-story nineteenth-century farmhouses I ever saw in the coal-mining area and the only one I ever entered besides that first house on the edge of the Monongahela forest. It had the same decorative stenciling along the walls, the same old timey furniture and utensils, the dozens of old calendars on the walls, and Jimmy McBain's paintings—wild, luminous, violent paintings of spiritual revelations. We talked about his art, and then he ushered me into his museum rooms lined with glass cabinets filled with arrowheads he had dug and hundreds of his hand-carved canes—wild creations crawling with monsters and snakes and other creatures and splaying out at the head with as many as half a dozen grotesque faces and tongues. Everything was for sale, and although he seldom had visitors he would get up each day and carve the date out of a piece of prime maple or hickory and hang it over his door. He had me sign his guest book on the way out.

Slowly, over the course of a season, the strange, mythical landscape in-filled with events: the man in the trailer down the road shot his ex-wife and her boyfriend dead and then disappeared; the church I had been attending three times a week went into a time of *confusion* that ended in a violent schism and I was caught talking to some neighbors and not others; the house of a poverty-stricken family burned to the ground and the neighbor men worked nights to rebuild it and refill it with donated appliances and clothes; another family took up residence in the dark stone cellar of an old schoolhouse that had burned down years before so that all you could see above ground was the sheets of black plastic they used as a roof; a neighbor I was close to was brutally beaten by her husband but stayed with him and began to fantasize romantically about Jesus as the perfect man; another neighbor woman took to calling me complaining of terrible headaches and asking for drugs; people got their trucks stuck in ditches and were pulled out by neighbors; one man got drunk on shine one night and went crazy, ramming his head into a fence post until he passed out; a family's flock of turkeys were slaughtered in the night and they talked of killing sheep in retaliation; cows escaped from fences and I would go out at all hours to help round them up. Surrounding every event was a wide range of stories, and I began to feel both their pull and the *aggravation* of their constant proliferation.

Then I had a near accident. I was driving up the long, steep, winding road from Rhodell to Odd, going over in my mind the stories I had heard that afternoon. I remember the moment in that drive when I realized that these stories could be classified by genre, tone of voice, and mode of attention; there was, for instance, the "encounter with danger" story, the "empathy" story of shared identity, the "injustice" story that ended in back talk and people standing up for themselves, the stories of things strange and uncanny that tracked a mystical attention to latent meaning and force through the denaturalization of ordinary everyday life, the stories of what happens when people get *lazy* and quit noticing every little thing and then suddenly find themselves overcome by otherworldly forces. I remember the shock of pleasure, as I was driving along the road, at this discovery of "structures" and "contexts" in the puzzle of how culture works.

At the Odd post office there is a blind curve onto the one-lane dirt road that leads up and over the ridge. Three or four old men sat on the post office porch waiting for something to happen and they watched as I came around the curve and met head on with Leslie Meadows's big ol' Chevy truck. We were both going too fast to stop in time to avoid a collision but we both stepped on the gas and flashed across the other's path, ending up in the ditch on the wrong sides of the road facing each other. When I saw the pleased and satisfied look on his face, I realized that this was "something that happened" and I immediately wanted to go and tell my neighbors. Like the old man with the copperhead bite, I wanted to see the looks on their faces.

As I drove away, already sifting through the details for the right story for Miss Cadle (who, among other things, was an ecstatic fundamentalist) and the right slant for Buster Miller (who, among other things, thought he was the hottest driver on the mountain and vied with Leslie Meadows for the status of local hotrod), I saw that the old men on the post office porch had shifted the weight on their haunches to peer around the edge of the building at us, their faces long and serious but with a twinkle at the edges of their eyes.

By the time I got to my second storytelling stop on my way up the mountain, I had the impression that the Millers had already heard the story though no one ever said so or gave any overt sign. I don't remember how I realized this, though there may be precise observations in my notes. And it may be that I just imagined it, but what is the difference? All along the road I realized/imagined that the Lillys and the Walkers and Miss Cadle already had a version, or for all I knew, many versions of the near miss. I remember the strange, doubled sensation of being both subject and object of the story as "event" entered the space of retelling and was caught in the inescapable grafting of versions and voices.

A story is itself always already a retelling of events, and there is always something more and other to be said. When differing versions are amassed, the object of attention shifts from the bare re-collection of events to idioms of engagement and encounter expressed in particular genres and precise ideologies. Attention shifts from a search for the truth or for an authentic, original version to a more intricate, silent tracking of the meaning of voice, tone, and style. Language becomes neither transparent reflection of events nor container for ideas but a performative utterance (Volosinov 1986). Launched in the face of previous accounts and anticipated versions, it fills itself with citations and produces itself only by passing into other versions, inverting itself, contaminating itself, dividing itself (Ulmer 1985). Events become not fixed "objects" in the world "out there" but fabulations always already written through with the identity of a reproduction. What is central to the text in one story becomes context in another or is elided altogether; the line between figure and ground does not hold. Distinctions between things "objective" and "subjective" are deconstructed in an attention to objectivated cultural forms of mediation (Volosinov 1986). Storyteller and audience alike find themselves caught in the interpretive space of a cultural poetics, in search

17. Creed Polk. Photograph © Em Herzstein.

not of the signified event but of the event of the signifier itself as it is
fashioned into local ways.

What I am suggesting, then, is that in stories like these the hierarchy of
concept over event, or "idea" (with its metaphysics of the theoretical, the
internal, and the active) over "example" (connoting the supplemental, the
literal, the external, the passive) breaks down and is inverted in the attention to the sign as a graphic image in its own right.[1] In the hills you hear
this inversion repeated over and over like a mantra when people are asked
a direct question about what they think and they claim they "don't have
no ideal" and then move quickly into a story in which words and images
expand out of bounds to become a kind of theoretical model in themselves—a model to think with that centers on no particular "idea," ad-
vances no particular "meanings," and reaches no particular conclusion
but rests in the modes of attention, engagement, and encounter indexed in
the local identity of ways of talkin' and ways of doin' people.

I am suggesting that this kind of re-membered attention to events constitutes a form of unforgetting. Far from reducing remembered events to
illustrations of ideas, it uses them to interrupt the very progress of master
narrative codes and to displace the certainty of concept with a densely
textured interpretive space that follows a logic of digression and accidental adjacency.

In the work of unforgetting, then, it would be counterproductive to
encase the anecdote of my near accident in a master narrative of ethnographic progress where it would become an allegory of ethnographic initiation, conversion, and illumination. It would be counterproductive,
too, to use the story as a (merely) anecdotal example of a theory of narrative versions and the social and cultural life of discourse. The task, rather,
is to take story, anecdote, and allegory seriously as graphic theoretical
models in themselves and to locate the ethnographic task in the midst of
them.

The near accident was one of those things that happen in the hills. It
gave me the license to relate a story at the same time that it made me a
graphic object in a storied cultural landscape along with my car and
Leslie and his truck, and the blind curve, and everything else that had ever
happened at that particular place on the side of the road. It produced an
interpretive space of unanswered questions and amassed effects in which
there is always something more to say and people find it meaningful to sift
through graphic images of events. As a mode of representation that is
necessarily social and so given to surprise, interruption, and restarting, it
follows a logic of encounter into lines of contestation or agreement and
holds out the promise, or threat, of interrupting the great ideological lo-
comotive engine of the straight line of progress.

The Diacritics of Interruptions

Consider interruption as a two-way street in the diacritical relation of
"the West" and "the rest."[2] Take, for instance, the encounter between an
"Appalachian" man and a VISTA worker captured in the documentary
film *Before the Mountain Was Moved* (CRM/McGraw-Hill Films 1970).
Ellis Bailey is a man who finds himself involved in a nascent anti-strip-
mining movement after his house and car are covered up in a mud slide.
The VISTA worker is a law student who is trying to help organize the
locals. In the encounter, Ellis's critique of strip mining, which *remembers*
events in a litany of amassed and intensified effects, is repeatedly interrupted by the VISTA worker's efforts to propose models of "self" and
"political action."

> ELLIS BAILEY: **Strip minin'**
> is the **cheap** way
> of the **coal operator** gettin' the **coal,**
> cuttin' the whole top of the **mountain** off,
> pickin' the **coal** up,
> and not have to goin' **underground** to git it.
> Pickin' the coal up by a **cheap hoe** and **git rich quick.**
> Well what the hillside is **left** is left barren
> and no **place** for a **prayer** to **go**
> **first rain come**
> a **slide** will start
> it will start them **rocks, mud,** and ever' **tree** will all pull ever'thang in **front**
> of 'm
> there danger in whole **towns** to git hit
> whole **towns** get covered up
> whole **roads** disappear
> whole **rivers** dammed up
> there's no way that I **see** to stop it.
> it's a **barren land** left to **work**
> for a man to pay **taxes.**
> They's all tied up with the **coal** comp'nies
> the **coal** comp'ny's in with the **insurance** comp'ny
> what the hell you gonna **do?**
> There's nothin' we **can** do I don't **guess.**

The VISTA worker interrupts him at this point, presumably in an effort to disrupt the coalescence of what she must read as the famous "Appalachian fatalism." Reducing the speech act to a referential and instru-

mental function, she asks him to pull himself out of his *talk* and come to his senses and act rationally.

> Well, the **first** thing we can do is to talk about it.
> We're having a meeting down at the church Friday night,
> why don't you **come**?
> You can talk to people who have some of the same things happen to their places that you have with yours.

To her thinking, general laws of organizing can and should be posited, and it is this mental map, rather than the litany of narrated effects, that she would follow in the effort to lead words into action. She pulls herself back from Ellis's narrative spell, and asks him to do the same, by interrupting the pull of intensifying aporia with instrumental discourse.

But Ellis's discourse carries its own epistemology of action embedded in discursive styles in use. His near preacherly style signals a formal, authoritative statement on ultimate moral and epistemological matters. Marked by long pauses between lines, extensive repetition, explicit religious themes (rivers dammed up and running with blood), and an apocalyptic poetic of "the end times," it reaches a point of intensification that fuses rhetorical claim to the state of things and provokes response. Religion and politics merge in a history of use of a rhetorical form. In the long history of intense conflict between the miners and absentee corporations and the state, the dramatic expressive style of religious and political rhetorics developed cheek to cheek in strikes and religious revivals, union meetings and religious services held underground, and a series of mining-related movements in the 1960s and 1970s including the Black Lung Movement, the Miners for Democracy union reform movement, and the Save Our Mountains anti-strip-mining movement. Both discourses center on the graphic repetition of images of suffering and injustice to the point of intensification that elicits the countervoice: "I just can't **see** it. When you see somethin' like that you have to **do** somethin', don't even **thank** about it." Stories of monstrous crimes against organizing miners in the 1920s and horrifying mass deaths in preventable mine accidents since are told to renew the spirit of the union. Religious revivals focus on the fire in "the end times" that both destroys the world and renews it. Hell and damnation preaching gives people a *blessing* and draws them to salvation at the altar, and God's word is realized in the end in an absolute reversal: the poor find mansions in the sky and the meek inherit the earth. Daily stories of injustice and meanness track along in graphic detail as helpless victims suffer at the hands of doctors, lawyers, social workers, and shameless relatives and neighbors until the narrator is moved to action to help them. Idea is moved to action through the intensification of effects in a world got down.

It is at just this point in Ellis's speech that the VISTA worker interrupts him with the idea that he should get together with people with the same problems and interests. Yet Ellis continues on his own track, picking up the thread where he left off, by responding not to her idea but to the concrete utterance that "people have the same things happen to them." In the local discourse, the claim that "thangs happen" elicits graphic stories of accidents, tragedies, and bodily illnesses that come unexpectedly, could happen to anyone, and are suffered.

Well, I've had a **broken back** all my **life**
I got my **broke back** in the **mines** down there at . . .

Again she interrupts with an instrumental idea.

All the more reason that you should **do somethin'** about it.

Ellis is silenced. The VISTA worker's speech, aimed as it is at direct referents in a fixed, objective "real world" of causes and effects, seeks out the certainty of the last word, while Ellis's speech remains situated and dialogic—dependent on questions of style, timing, and response. For her, a politics is lodged in ideal models of Self, World, and Action, while for him politics emerge in social performance and they take on the fragmentary and interruptive nature of the discursive process itself (Scott 1991). The VISTA worker ends the scene with a badgering mode of direct questioning that would be unthinkable in the hills except as an address to an outside enemy like the company or the state.

So the **coal companies** did it to you in the **mines** and you're gonna let 'm do it to you in your **own home too?**
ELLIS: [Silenced, looking down, embarrassed.]

I am reminded of what they call *confusions* in the hills—conflicts in which things reach an impasse and there is not only nothing left to say but the social order itself seems to fall apart; in a confusion people will disremember a family member or a church will split apart in schism. Confusions are an embarrassing topic: no one likes to talk about them; it is almost as if they are an embarrassment to society itself—an unthinkable faux pas. In this case, the VISTA worker's speech itself might be taken as an embarrassment—an instance of shameless, socially ignorant talk that is the object of political back talk.

Later in the film there is another scene in which Ellis's preacherly-political rhetoric plays itself out uninterrupted and you can see something of the force of its nervous trajectory through fits and starts, doubts and certainties, sudden reversals and overwhelming intensifications, into a mode of encounter. He is pictured walking up the long steps of the state capitol building in Charleston on his way, with others, to testify before the West Virginia senate committee on strip mining. He begins to moan: "I'm dreading it. They'll never listen to a pore man." He goes on in a poetic litany for a few minutes, while the man walking beside him as they labor up the steps listens politely and intently and then pauses respectfully before he says: "Well, we'll just have to **make** 'm listen." In response, Ellis switches instantly to a heroic speech: "Well, that's **right**, we'll stay here 'til they **do** listen."

Once inside, as the group is waiting in the cavernous marble lobby panicked at the thought of having to stand up and say something to the *big men*, Ellis remembers that he has forgotten his teeth. Again, he wails in an intense discourse on what the big men will think of an old broke down pore man who can't talk educated and doesn't have his teeth. One of the others—a schoolteacher—takes him over to a bench and sits with him saying, "Well, Ellis, **they** understand, **everyone** forgets their teeth sometimes." When he is still unconvinced, she offers to help him write down what he wants to say so he won't forget. She takes out an old envelope and says, "Now what do you want to **tell** them, Ellis, just tell them in your **own words**," and she takes notes while he thinks up a thing or two to say. Then she hands him the crumpled little piece of paper. In the last scene of the film Ellis's name is called by a page, and he walks into the large formal senate hearing room full of suits and slowly approaches the podium, the piece of paper shaking in his hand. He swallows hard, forgets to look at the paper, and launches into an eloquent impassioned sermon/organizing speech on how **the pore man** has been dumped on, **whole mountains** come **down**, and his property **destroyed**, and his streams polluted so he can't **fish**, and the **pore man** has no money to send his children to **school**, and the **pore man**, he has **his rights too**. The film ends with a graphic depiction of a gloomy rainy night in the hollers as people with anxious eyes and wringing hands keep a watch on the unstable strip-mined hills surrounding their *places* and the news comes over the radio from Beckley that the strip-mining Land Reclamation Act has passed.

An Other Interruption, or
an Interruption from the Other Side

One day Ralph Pendry, Sylvie Hess, and I were in Sylvie's hot kitchen talking drowsily. Ralph was standing at a window staring out at the hills when there was a scuffling sound outside. I asked him what it was. He said,

I don't **know** what it **was** [as if this was an interesting question].
I'll tell you what I **seen** was a pack a **dogs** in them bushes by the **flower** garden.
Tearin' up.
Look like they're **after** somethin'.
Might not a **been** them but now that's what I **seen.**

Rather than follow my lead into a search for finalizing cause and effect
and encompassing explanation to say what the noise "was," Ralph in-
serted a gap between the look of things and their "meaning." In the space
of the gap the storyteller is placed on the same plane with storied events;
when thangs are not what they seem and the point of story is to make
something of them, memory and relating take on the full weight of unforgetting.

What followed was an exchange of dog stories. We talked about these
dogs that he had seen (whose they were, what they might have been hunting), and then the talk moved, through intensification, into the more
graphic, arresting images of retold stories. I remembered the day that my
neighbor Bud's dog died, and tried to relay some of the graphic detail of
his words on that morning when I found him standing in the middle of his
yard replaying the shock of discovering the dead dog.

I got up and got **dressed** just like I **always** do,
and I went out **first thang** to **see** about him,
just like I always do,
and there he **was.**
He got his tongue kindly **twisted** in his mouth and his legs **stuck out** from him
stiff.

I *re-membered* Bud's multiple explanations for the death, how Bud
thought the dog must have had the mysterious disease that had been killing all the blueticks in the area, how the dog must have had *the mark* on
him as Bud's wife had always claimed, how the dog must have been poi-
soned by a *hateful* neighbor and Bud had a pretty good idea of who it was
but wouldn't say. Then I ended the story the same way Bud had—by
repeating the graphic description of how the dog had looked when Bud
found him and how he had looked just fine just the night before his death.

Ralph retold the story he had heard from Bud Graham about some
dogs who had run themselves to death. I too had heard this story from
Bud one day when I was asking him about *places* in the hills.

BUD GRAHAM: Yeah, **buddy!** I been all **over** these here **heels.**
Used to, we'd go up a huntin' and **them dogs'd** run all up Devil's Fork clear up
to the old **Graham** place, crost Tommy Creek and way over yonder to **Made-
leine,** and them dogs **a mine** was as good **coon dogs** as you'd ever wanna

18. David Bolen and dog, Ralph Pendry at the window, staring out. Photograph © Em Herzstein.

19. Clemmy and Pete Acres with dogs. Photograph © Em Herzstein.

see and couldn't nobody else's dogs **catch** '**m** and buddy they **tried, too.**
[Laughing.]
I remember the **time** that Bud **Henson** fella useta stay down here at '**Miga,**
awful bad to **drank**
and **one night**
he was out here a layin' out **drunk** and his **dogs** got after them dogs a **mine** and
I said, "**Buddy,**" I said, "you better **git** them **dogs** 'fore they run **their**selves t'
death."
"**Well,**" he said, "**my** dogs can outrun **anythang,**" and I said, "Well all **right**
then, I guess you know your own **dogs** better'n I do," and them dogs run all
night and in the mornin' they was ever' one of 'm **dead.**
We hadda go pick up them **dogs** and brang 'm on **back to** '**m** where he was sa
tore up an' all.
Well, he jest set there and watched 'm come and we hadda bury 'm for 'm,
we buried 'm right there by that big ol' overhangin' **rock** looks out over
nothin'.
They say that's where that old feller jumped off that time after his **boy** got kilt
in the **mines.**
And there was people **skeered** a that place, claimed the old man's **h'aint** was
still up there.
Well I can't say nothin' 'bout **that,** but now we buried them **dogs** up there, sure
did.

Yeah boy! Them days we hunted **coon** and **rabbit, possum,** and just **ever'thang, buddy,** and we'd brang it on back and **skin** it, cook it **up** and we'd eat it.
Anymore, people's got to where they won't **eat wild thangs**
but they're **good** t' **eat.**
You have to know how to **cook** it, is **all.**
First you let it **cool,** you have to cool the **wild**ness out of it and then **parboil** it, and cook it and **eat** it.
People don't know t' **parboil** it.
People don't know thangs like 'at anymore.
But I been **all** over these here **heels.**

Ralph's retelling fastened onto the central arresting image of the dead dogs "gone stiff and their legs all stuck out."
And from there Sylvie retold the story from her idyllic childhood on Polk Mountain when the sheep who followed her everywhere were torn to pieces by a pack of wild dogs. Finally I asked Ralph if the dogs were still out there. He said,

Well they might **be,** Katie, I don't know.
But I stopped **seein'** em.

An exchange of stories like this one, then, begins and ends in the space of a gap between events and their meanings and fastens onto the meaning-fulness of graphic images of composition and decomposition. Fixed iden-tities and transcendent explanations decompose in the face of overwhelm-ing images that *just come* and that set off associations with other images of the same order. The result is an interpretive space in-filled not only with the dialogics of different voices but with the very act of unforgetting the tenuous hold of concept on event.
This reminds me, now, of a day in 1980 when I was walking in the woods with Lacy Graham and I saw that his arm was streaked with what looked like blood. I asked him what it was.

LACY: Reckon hit's where I come up agin' that old **huckle**berry bush back there.
Yeah **buddy,** that there's a **bright** red **ain't** it.
ME: But is that **blood** or from the **berries?**
LACY: **Well,** I don't know, honey, might be **blood,** might be the **berries,** might be some a **both.**
Yeah, boy, that's a **bright** red.

To dwell in the space of the gap between signifier and signified is to dwell in the space of alterity itself in which the names and meanings of things are never fully present but always still ahead and behind. It is to rob the hierarchy of paired oppositions—culture versus nature, order versus chaos, system versus accident, reality versus fiction, and original versus imitation/reproduction/repetition; to rob it of its metaphysical privilege to have the last word. Consciousness remains in a state of approaching but never quite arriving—a moving toward. A parallel order of animals and plants and the things that happen to them draws near to the human through the association of shared vulnerability. Things loom larger than life as the desire to capture the unknown in the known is displaced by an endless search for signs of alterity itself. Here, finished concept and past event enter the contingencies of speech as a social act in the present, and everything becomes a subject of remembrance and exchange in the constant fits and starts of the effort to unforget.

4

Chronotopes

> History is what hurts, it is what refuses desire
> and sets inexorable limits to individual as well
> as collective praxis, which its "ruses" turn
> into grisly and ironic reversals of their overt
> intention. But this History can be apprehended
> only through its effects and not as some
> reified force.
>   (*Frederic Jameson,* The Political
>   Unconscious)

Roaming the Ruins

> Places are fragmentary and inward-turning
> histories . . . accumulated times that can be
> unfolded like stories held in reserve, remaining
> in an enigmatic state.
>   (*Michel de Certeau,* The Practice of Everyday
>   Life)

Imagine history not as an accomplished fact or a formless tendency but as
an occupied space of contingency and desire in which people roam. Think
of it as a matter of re-membering, a process of being hit by events, an
aggravation that stirs a relentless scanning and chronicling. In the hills,
you could say, the effects of history lie gathered into a space of impacts
and remainders storied as a space on the side of the road. It is a space-time
littered with ruins and named *places* in which "history has physically
merged into the setting. And in this guise history does not assume the
form of the process of an eternal life so much as that of an irresistible
decay . . . the events of history shrivel up and become absorbed in the
setting" (Benjamin 1977:177, 179).

In the ruin that *remembers*, history and place, culture and nature converge in a tactile image that conveys not a picture-perfect reenactment of
"living pasts" but the allegorical re-presentation of remembered loss itself. The vacancy of a lot in Rhodell *remembers* the fire that burned
Johnny Millsap to death while he cried out for help and the others could

do nothing but watch; the exposed electrical wire in the hills above
Amigo mines #2[1] *remembers* the image of Buddy Hall, a nine-year-old
boy, hanging from it.

> And when hit finally dropped 'm it had blowed his heel plum off.
> Blowed a **hole** right through his **heel,** tuk the **meat** out of it. They said there was
> the meat on the ground next to his foot. (K. Stewart 1988:235)

Inexplicable or unspeakable events are culled into a living form capable of expressing feeling, movement, and vitality so that "the emotive
import belongs to the form itself, not to anything it represents or suggests" (Langer 1953:82). Here, you could say, history stands before people, as it does for Benjamin's famous Angel of History, as a pile of refuse
that is also the site of a dream of redemption. "His face is turned toward
the past. Where a chain of events appears to *us, he* sees one single catastrophe which relentlessly piles wreckage upon wreckage, and hurls them
before his feet . . ." (1969c:259). Turned with his back to the storm of
progress, the "pile of debris before him grows toward the sky" (260).

When people go out roaming the hills, whether in mind or in body, it
is this "refuse" and its illuminations they encounter. They come up
against *places* and are stopped dead in their tracks by a re-membered
image they cain't help but recall. Every time Tammy goes to the river now
she "cain't he'p but recall that pore man drowned." A young, strong man
was swimming out in the river with his friends:

> where it's just over your head even way out.
> And he started to go **down.**
> Well they tried to **he'p** him and they was all **around** him but they said hit was
> **just like** somethin' was **pullin'** him **down.**
> And finally he told 'm, said, "You better let me **go** and y'all get back to the
> **shallow.**"
> He said, "I'm a **goin' down.**"
> And they said they could feel him go down their **legs,** and they felt his hands
> down their legs like he wanted to **hold on** and then he was **gone.**
> Honey, that **haunts** me.
> And it **does,** too.

Named *places* become concrete models embodying not just the literal
impact of events but the local cultural epistemology of re-membering impacts by re-tracing them in graphic images that stand at once as refuse
and refuge. June 4, 1982. Sissy and I walked up Devil's Fork holler. As we
passed Amigo 2, stories just came of the people and events that once
surrounded the now-deserted shacks. The further we went up the holler
the more the talk drifted into a lyrical, melancholic rumination. At a

bridge Sissy recalled their old swimming hole here when the creek was still clean:

> But that was back before they got the **commodes** in and the **govermint** come in, told us a septic tank had to be so many feet **apart** and that's the **law**.
> **Well all right**, now, in **'Migo** most a them lots ain't **big** enough for the **law** and we **tried to tell** 'm but you just cain't **talk** to **them people**. They said, "You **have** to **have** 'm so far **apart**."
> So people started dumpin' in the **creek**.
> Honey, I hated to **see** it where that water was as **blue!** an' **used to** we'd swim here, the sun shined **down** on it, an all us **comin' up** then, we'd spend all **day**.

I noticed an overgrown stand of *ramblin' roses* in the middle of an empty field. Sissy said:

> Well, you cain't **see** it but there's a **chimbley** [chimney] other side them **blooms**, runs right up the far side of 'm, the grass is about covered it now.
> **Jake Catlitt**, he built that house, **big** house and it had a stone front to it and them **old timey** beams and big ol' **windas**.
> Well, Jake lived in it and then his baby **Pete, he** lived there **too**.
> An he'd just got **married** and they was livin' there and there was another young couple stayin' there with 'm to help pay the **bills**. There wasn't much **work** at that time but **Jake**, he was workin' down at that Joe's service station down **Black** Eagle and he was off at **work**.
> And the two **women** were home **alone** and it was where they didn't know how to make the **fire** in the **stove** and reckon they got it too **hot** and they said it musta **caught** on one of them old beams.
> Well, they run out with the **baby**, 'cause one of 'm had a **baby**, an' pore old **Petey**, he was a comin' back from work, an he **seen** it and come a **runnin'** and a hollerin', **buddy**.
> And the **Reeds**, they stayed right down here, **they** come **on** and them other people down 'Migo 2, they seen the smoke and **they** come **on**. Ever'body come a runnin' but there weren't nothin' they **could** do.
> The fire bust out a them windas and burned them old timey beams and it tuk that **whole house**, burned it right down to the **ground**, buddy.
> **Petey** an' them went down to **Viper** to stay, and I never **did** hear what happened to them other people.
> But that's where them **roses** bloom 'round that old **chimbley**. It's a **perty** place, but it's been **lonely** too long. They oughta get somebody **in**, come **stay** out here.

A rambling rose vine entwined around a crumbling chimney remembers an old family farm, the dramatic fire in which the place was lost, and the utopic potential still clinging to the traces of history. Objects that have decayed into fragments and traces draw together a transient past with the

very desire to *remember*. Concrete and embodying absence, they are confined to a context of strict immanence, limited to the representation of
ghostly apparitions. Yet they haunt. They become not a symbol of loss
but the embodiment of the process of remembering itself; the ruined *place*
itself *remembers* and grows lonely.

Ruined objects take on a meaningfulness or presence more compelling
than the original; just as a person's things (notebooks, saved letters, photographs, knickknacks) take on an added aura after death, so the ruins
become the collective presence of the place and are read as *signs* to be
plumbed for significance. They stand not as a specifiable meaning but as
a landmark or sign in which life trembling in a scene appears petrified,
spellbound (Nägele 1988). Through them, a setting speaks to people,
haunts the imagination, whispers an audible lamentation, trembles in
expectation.

Ricoeur (1984) asks what kind of representation emerges from the intersection of trembling and petrification in the sign. It is a representation
like these shaken yet irreducible ruins that speak and remember, a representation that is unforgettable and stands as if transfixed on the landscape yet is structured by an inner trembling. It is something like this that
Kristeva (1980) referred to as the foundation of poetic language in the
intersection of the thetic with the chora, or the place where the phenomenon of organized and conventional signs and symbols meets the phenomenon of a signification that is receptive, uncertain, undetermined, and
inconclusive.

We find it again in the hills in that narrative moment when the roaming
movement of following along in the wake of events stops to cull itself into
an arresting lyric image that haunts. It gives rise to a state of attention that
Benjamin identified as a state of mourning "in which feeling revives the
empty world in the form of a mask. . . . It is determined by an astounding
tenacity of intention . . . capable of a special intensification" (Benjamin
1977:139). In it, space and time converge in a chronotope in which "spatial and temporal indicators are fused. . . . Time, as it were, thickens,
takes on flesh, becomes artistically visible; likewise, space becomes
charged and responsive to the movement of time, plot, and history"
(Bakhtin 1981:84).

Encountered as a visible object while one is out roaming the hills, the
chronotope of the trembling space/time—the arrest of the sheer flow of
time in a lyrical scenic image—fuses the mythic with the everyday, the
fated with the accidental, the concrete with the symbolic, the storied with
"the Real." The notion of History itself lies captured in the concrete sign,
and the abstract notion of "the course of a life" is fused with the experience of wandering from *place* to *place*.

20. Ruin. Photograph © Harriette Hartigan, Artemis.

It is here that a mode of social critique grows immanent in encountered objects and scenes. The collection of ruins and *places* becomes a social text where a collective and political unconscious becomes readable (Jameson 1981). Fragments of profane life are transformed into emblems of salvation (Benjamin 1977), and lamentation finally becomes an accusation (Freud 1953). Sissy's nostalgia for the lost swimming hole aims an accusation against the commodes of progress and the crazy human effects of the state's irrational rationality of abstract laws. The lost *used to* embedded in the ruins accuses the cruel, unrelenting flow of naturalized time.

In the camps, where "life in the hills" is always already a re-membered life pieced together in memory and by roaming from place to place, moments of melancholic rumination cull rambling rememberings into an image with duration and haunting force that not only slows time but provides a space in which to dwell in time (Trinh 1991). They give pause for an interpretation—an intensive activity fashioned out of stasis in which the spectator turned melancholic subject falls under a spell, displacing an observer's distance with what Chambers (1991) calls the melancholic consciousness of a subject who produces herself only in passing into her other. As she is roaming the hills, the image of a *place* hits the interpreting subject like a tactile event, drawing her into an interpretive space in which "meaning" lies as much in the objects and spaces of observation as in the body and mind of the observer (Taussig 1991). The "self," like the ruin itself, is divided between a wandering self, homeless in the temporality of the present, and a nostalgically re-membered but unattainable center of stability and selfhood (Chambers 1991:107–8).

In the image of a trembling space, then, a reality that exceeds the constraints of history is born of the very *remembering* of unfulfilled possibilities. The arresting image provokes the participation of an audience as if collective survival depends on the contagious spread of a melancholic poetics of place. History seems to literally weigh on the lonely chimneys of the old family farms; the decaying orchards and graveyards sag under the weight of memory like bodies sagging and imploding under the weight of a lifetime of work too hard to bear. The nights breathe with the ever-audible gasping of all the old men slowly smothering of black lung. And all the old roads, now no longer passable, mark the space of past, but still remembered, itineraries.

In the ruin history itself is brought into the present as a narrative text. Luminous fragments of things in decay mimetically demonstrate a partially excluded but re-membered real. Wrecked material becomes a sign, at once, of the power of a history on a place and of the transitoriness of history itself. It fashions itself into an allegorical image—a representation attracted to the fragmentary, the imperfect, the incomplete, the decayed. It says that things are not what they seem, that meaning is not self-evident but emerges in the gap between signifier and signified. It proposes "a double attention to the descriptive surface and to the more abstract, comparative and explanatory levels of meaning . . . what one *sees* . . . is connected in a continuous double structure with what one understands" (Clifford 1986b:101).

In searching for a redemptive critique of history, Benjamin (1977) argued for a strategic inversion of the hierarchy in cultural theory of "symbol" over "allegory." For him, the humanist symbol was a self-satisfied fantasy of the mystical fusion of sign and referent, while allegory could plumb the depths of doubt, dread, and the dream of redemption in a world got down. There is something of this sense of allegory in the stories of the ruined and the trashed. They begin at the end of things, overwhelming the "ordinary" flow of time with inescapable memories and desires. A narrative suspense "forward" through events to discover what will happen next is overwhelmed by a spatial scene and frozen in the involuntary repetition of a haunting image, an unresolved consciousness that is "home." A melancholic epistemology of loss, unavailability, episodicity, and deferment throws "truth" and "objectivity" into question (Chambers 1991:117) and draws attention to forms and signifying practices made palpable as things in themselves. Physical objects, imaginary events, social relations, and moral and supernatural forces are united as aspects of a single poetic effect gathered into a scene. Master narratives of history as progress decompose into the tense confabulations of a continuously re-membered past that hits the present like a nervous shock.

Remember, once again, how Sylvie Hess's reverie of her childhood on the mountain turns on the shocking image of the sheep with their throats torn out. Here, as in the remembering of ruins, allegory has been fashioned into a dialectical image. "Where thought comes to a standstill in a constellation saturated with tensions, there appears the dialectical image. It is the caesura in the movement of thought . . . it is to be sought at the point where the tension between the dialectical oppositions is the greatest" (Benjamin 1972:595 as quoted in Buck-Morss 1989:219). An anti-progressive temporality of repetition and rupture, the arresting image interrupts historical continuities to grasp the monads or fissures in which time stops and prophetically restarts (Benjamin 1969a). A dialectics at a standstill, it presents the historical object within a charged force field of past and present, tragedy and utopic desire, in such a way that what is "lost" is illuminated and redeemed in a sudden flash (Buck-Morss 1989: 219). It asserts the discontinuity of those rough and jagged places where the myth of history-as-progress breaks down and impacted objects reveal the cracks in its construction (Buck-Morss 1989:290). Countering any dream of transcendence, the dialectical wish image superimposes the *used to* and the *anymore* in the concrete image of a form that is always decaying. The trash that collects around people's places, like the ruins that collect in the hills, is imprinted with a life history (and death) and embodies a continuous process of composition and decomposition. They become compelling *signs* of a past, like the present, where things fall apart and where everything, including power itself, is constructed and transient. They become objects for the imagination's ceaseless effort to wrest a local "real" from the tragic and senseless evolution of an extractive industry.

This, then, is history with a difference. Located in the tortured machinations of a local cultural poetics in social use, it lies in a space uncaptured by master narrative searches for context, perspective, and the outlines of a linear truth. It arises out of moments of loss and threat without benefit of hindsight, and it draws close to its objects, fragmenting master narratives into images, "meanings" into haunting *signs*. Where a master narrative cuts through a swath of extraneous detail and gathers the "objects" at hand to the broad outlines of History as a sequence of events, local practices of re-membering follow the dense fabulations of luminous fragments and ruins that hit the place and leave it reeling.

The Shock of History

> To articulate the past historically does not
> mean to recognize it "the way it really was."
> It means to seize hold of a memory as it flashes
> up at a moment of danger.
>   (Walter Benjamin, "Theses on the
>   Philosophy of History")

Master narratives speak a war of positions. In this case, in this doubly occupied place, there is first the perspective of industry and the status quo that would write the history of this place as an inevitable progress of events. In response, a critical voice claims events as evidence of the forceful exploitation of a people and the tragic death and destruction of a culture. Both are powerful stories that script hope and mourning into the very meaning of History for us. Both lurk in the wings of the political unconscious waiting to make a move in the search for causes of blame or celebration. Both, in their own way, attempt to finish the question of History in heavily scripted chronotopes of their own that would close the very gap that gives rise to the local chronotopes of haunting places and the need to constantly re-member things.

In this case, the story of History might begin, for instance, with the moment in 1902 when two capitalists from the U.S. Coal and Oil Company visited the "wilderness" town of Logan, deep in the mountains of southwestern West Virginia. It was reported that the capitalists were "undaunted," and after walking around the "property" they were buying up, they "retired to their tent, donned dinner jackets, and, gentlemen to the core, ate dinner in isolated elegance" (Salvati 1957:9 as quoted in Eller 1982:135).

A master narrative might take such a moment as a symbol that initiates a line of thought and gathers events to it; launched from such a perch the story of history snaps into place as a litany of events in which one thing leads to another. It could be written as the beginning of progress in the hills—the opening of the place to development, change, opportunity. Or you could take it as the beginning of the end.

I could tell you, for instance, that in 1880 the southern mountain region was an agricultural area, with an average farm size of 187 acres, and one of the major hog-producing areas in the country, and that forty years later the railroads had been built, 80 percent of the forests had been lumbered, leaving barely a single tree over twelve inches in diameter and no rich mash of nuts for hog raising, and 80 percent of the land in the, by then, "coal-mining counties" had been bought up by oil and mining

companies and the holdings consolidated into the control of a few dominant firms. By 1920 farm size had shrunk to 47 acres, and in the face of
forest depletion, growing property values, and rising taxes, 30 to 50 percent of the farmers in these counties had become tenants and large numbers of them were being drawn down to live and work in the coal camps
being built in every holler. By 1925 company towns outnumbered independent towns more than five to one and the population in the nine coal-
producing counties in southwestern West Virginia had increased more
than fourfold, and in some counties more than ninefold, as additional
"labor" was imported from neighboring Appalachian counties, the deep
south, and straight from Ellis Island (Althouse 1974; Eller 1982; Shifflett
1991; West Virginia Land Task Force 1980).

Then came a century of displacements and diasporic migrations as
people and place found themselves subject to the vagaries of the coal industry.[2] There were the violent events of labor organizing and its repres-
sion in the twenties—the armed battles with federal militia, the armed
march of thousands of striking miners across the state led by Mother
Jones, the Battle of Blair Mountain where the National Guard dropped
bombs on the miners from airplanes and the people scattered into the
hills, the company thugs who carried sawed-off shotguns and policed the
trains so no one could leave the camps, the killing of labor organizers
during strikes and the people evicted from their company houses, the
charges that the Mellons and John D. Rockefeller, Jr. were conspiring to
destroy the union (Corbin 1981; Lane 1921; Savage 1990). Union bust-
ing and the introduction of scientific management and mechanization in
the twenties led to dramatic pay cuts and layoffs (Dix 1988:170) and set
off the first great exodus as over 200,000 miners from central Appalachia, or an estimated 25 percent of the population, left to find work
in the northern cities. During the Depression people returned to abandoned cabins on worn-out farms to live off relief, and the hills suddenly
became a wasteland of the unemployed with as much as 75 percent of the
population living on welfare and Social Security Disability (Erikson
1976:69). When the National Industrial Recovery Act (NIRA) finally
guaranteed the right to organize unions, a labor organizer in southern
West Virginia reported that within a week virtually every mine in the area
had joined the United Mine Workers of America (Dix 1988:189).

I could tell you how the UMWA, with John L. Lewis at its head, became a pioneer industrial union and the most militant wing of the Congress of Industrial Organizations (CIO). Then union-sanctioned mechanization of the mines in the late forties disemployed three-quarters of the
miners, and the mass migrations of the 1950s and 1960s began. The company stores were closed and the camp houses sold to miners, they say, for
five hundred dollars apiece—"cain't get no kind a house for that now

21. Tipple at East Gulf. Photograph © John Hartigan.

[laughing]." In the mining counties the rate of population loss was close to 40 percent in the fifties and another 25 percent in the sixties (Philliber and McCoy 1981); as many as 65 percent of the people who were between the ages of ten and nineteen in 1960 had left by 1970 (Erikson 1976:100). I could tell you that it was then, in the fifties, as "the trouble" of mass unemployment and migration took hold, that the signs of the spirit exploded in the churches in the proliferation of expressive forms— trance states, speaking in tongues, the laying on of hands, snake handling, and drinking strychnine.

I could tell you, too, that with over 100,000 dead in the mines since 1906, the place became a war zone.

> If coal mining were an American war, it would rank third in number of deaths behind World War II (407,316 dead) and World War I (116,708 dead). Between 1930 and 1976, coal miners sustained more non-fatal disabling injuries than have all of America's soldiers in all of America's principal wars between the Revolution and Vietnam. Coal mine injuries in the 1930–1976 period numbered 1,647,994. Nonfatal wounds in American wars are estimated to total 1,580,000, according to the National Safety Council. (Health/Pac Bulletin 1977)

Daily roof falls killed an average of three miners a day (Eller 1982:180–82), and then there is the litany of mass deaths in major disasters every year: 1884, Pocahontas, Virginia—114 dead; 1895, Dayton, Tennessee—28 dead; 1900, Fayette County, West Virginia—57 dead; 1902, Coal Creek, Tennessee, 184 dead; 1907, Monongah, West Virginia, 358 dead, and so on.

In 1968 an explosion at the Consol mine in Farmington, West Virginia, killed 78 miners and set off a series of movements for mining health and safety including the West Virginia Black Lung Movement, which won compensation for black lung in the 1969 Black Lung Law. A union reform movement—Miners for Democracy—was formed in 1969 at reform candidate Jock Yablonski's funeral after he and his family were killed in their beds by the hired men of incumbent president Tony Boyle (Hume 1971). The movement eventually won a partial democratization of the union, shifting power from the central union headquarters in Washington to the locals. In 1970 Save Our Mountains and the Appalachian Group to Save the Land and the People were formed to fight strip mining, as anti-strip-mining heroes (Dan Gibson, Jink Ray, and others) "stood up to" the strip miners, in some cases (the widow Combs, Warren Wright, and others) by literally lying down in front of their bulldozers (Carawan and Carawan 1982; Whisnant 1973). The Retired and Disabled Miners Organization formed in Rhodell in 1970.

> GRADY LILLY: East Gulf was where we first organized for **black lung**.
> I'd heard a doctor come in from **England** or maybe **Wales**.
> He had a human lung with him from some miner out there who had died.
> He'd take a piece of that lung and smash it in his hands and show you how it just turned into nothing but **dust**.
> **Black lung**.
> That's the **common** name for it.
> And I went back to **East Gulf** and told the **rest** of 'm about it where bein' there so long I had a lot of influence with the men and they **come on** with me.
> And we went on up to **Washington** and talked with Congressman **Perkins** from Kentucky and **his** daddy and granddaddy died of black lung and suffered **awful** bad and he'd get up in the middle of the night to **turn** them.
> But these tests are **hard** on people.
> I've heard of guys who'd **fall out** after them.
> They shouldn't have to have any of those **tests**.
> They should be a presumptive clause in the bill and a full and total recognition of black lung.
> BOBBY MEADOWS: The **black lung**!
> Buddy, we went all the way up to **Washington** for that one and they tried to put people in **jail**!
> We said **go ahead buddy** and you can take all the **rest** of us too and we'll go stay in your jail and try your **Washington food**.

22. Roof on the side of the road proclaiming the names of "Scum Suckin Scabs."
Photograph © Harriette Hartigan, Artemis.

But they let us **go**. I don't believe they **wanted** us up there [everyone laughing].
But we had a **good** time up in Washington.
But now the union don't **b'long** up there in **Washington**, it don't **b'long** up
there a'tall.

In 1971 people staged a general March for Survival against Unfulfilled
Promises.

The oil crisis in the seventies set off a final boom in coal and saw the
return of an entire missing generation to the mines. Between 1970 and
1976 there were over a thousand wildcat strikes a year in central Appalachia over a wide spectrum of issues including gas rationing, the right
to strike, school textbooks, and road conditions, as well as seniority,
safety, job rights, union politics, and benefit cutbacks (J. Green 1978). A
strike could be started, and spread through roving pickets, if any miner
simply turned over his water bucket.

CREED MEADOWS: Yeah, buddy, we had us some **strikes** in that time when
the union was in its power again.
Ever' time you turn around there's somebody knocked over their **water bucket**
and we're **out** again.
We might not even find out what it **was** until we had a meetin' and then we'd
find out.

Well, most time it was **right** and it was over some kind a **safety** thang and we'd make what they called **rovin' pickets** and just go **all** over ever'where and pull 'm **out**.

You got **one man** come out where the boss man told him **hurry up** and don't bother with them old **pins** in the roof, **you know**, and that whole **place** was out a there before he could finish his **thought, you** know.

Because, you know, ever'body in the **mines** is in just about the same **place** and so they know to kindly **stick together**. Well, **I'll** tell you **what**, buddy, we got a **lot a fishin'** done.

But **anymore** the company is got the union **down**.

And the **oil** companies is tuk over coal and they're strippin' in the west

and they're brangin' in coal from Japan and Germany

and they closed the mines **down**

and the people cain't keep up with thangs anymore.

In 1977 and 1978 severe flooding throughout the area was attributed to strip mining. In Buffalo Creek, West Virginia, an unsupported slag "dam" burst in the middle of the night, washing away seventeen towns and killing hundreds of people. When the coal company disclaimed responsibility, saying the flood was "an act of God," the local people were incensed at the (political and religious) sacrilege and sued, winning over $100 million in damages. And in Amigo, my neighbors Sissy and Bud still talk about how they went to the flood relief office when the waters came up through their house but were ashamed when they saw all those poor people who had lost their homes or never had nothin' to begin with and they were a lot worse off than they were and needed the money. They were about to turn around and go home when they saw a "rich woman" dressed in furs and enormous diamond necklaces pushing her way through the line, pushing the poor people down, and she was crying about how her furs got ruint and it was going to take the government a lot to replace them. Well, that made them mad and they just stood right back up in that line, backs stiff as boards, to get what they had coming to them.

I could tell you that in the seventies people started trading in the supermarkets in Beckley, and many of the stands and butcher shops in the camps were closed and boarded up or disappeared in fires or overnight dismantlings. Public spaces largely disappeared from the landscape except for the church and the post office and the occasional union hall, gas station, and stand. Church became the primary, and for many the only, place of public expression, and signs of the spirit reverberated in preaching, song, trance, dance, and testimony. I could tell you that the schools were consolidated in the seventies and the kids were bused to school in town where they were called dirty camp kids (and still are). I could tell you that parents still "strike" the schools, pulling their kids out of classes,

23. David Bolen, Tommy Creek holler. Photograph © Em Herzstein.

over any issues under state control—like bad roads and the lack of corporate taxes in the area.

The eighties saw the final mine closings, the painful hanging on, the unthinkable leavings, people being wrenched away.[3] I could say that there is an end of things here. That now, at the end of a century of boom and bust, most of the men are unemployed and those who still work in the mines are traveling long distances across the mountains to work nonunion and they complain of dangerous work speedups and seven-day work weeks. The women have begun to take work in fast-food restaurants in Beckley, and the young people who survive the drinking and reckless driving go off to North Carolina and Virginia to find work. A new idiom has arisen in the camps of preparing the children to go out into the dog-eat-dog world out there by taking them—boys and girls both—to Beckley for karate lessons. They say there are some **DANGEROUS** black belts coming out of those hills. They say that "by law" their hands should be registered as lethal weapons.

Here I might interrupt a story already coalesced around images of victimization and decline with a revisionist counternarrative against the notion of an isolated, bounded, homogeneous "culture" that was suddenly opened to the winds of change without ever knowing what hit it. I could tell you that in 1880 the area had already long been integrated into a larger regional economy and that from the earliest settlements there had already been considerable movement from farm to farm and holler to holler and many had migrated west in the mid-nineteenth century to Kansas, Oklahoma, Texas, Arkansas, and Nebraska (Eller 1982:15). Against the image of a primeval rural innocence, I could tell you that by the turn of the century, with the massive recruitment of labor, the area had one of the highest population densities in rural America and the conditions of life in the camps were urban—crowded, smoky, sooty, and grimy (Ayers 1992). The population was diverse, including a range of European immigrants and African Americans recruited from areas along the Norfolk and Western Railroad of Virginia (Ayers 1992:120), and the place was written through with internal difference and eruptions of violence as a forcefully localized culture grew nervous. Under the sign of miners gathered into the order of the camps, people said there was no "color" in the mines; miners of all ethnicities worked together, lived in identical houses, and received the same payment for their labor; their wives shopped at the same store and their children went to the same school (Corbin 1981:64–66; Eller 1982:165–72; R. Lewis 1987:130). Yet residential sections of the camps were segregated in an order of things, and signs of social *place* spread to encompass new distinctions as they were introduced. Daily social life was, and is, filled with performances of the distinctions of age, gender, race, religion, neighborhood, and kinship line, and transgressions could result in ostracism or violence. In the face of a weak state in the region, high rates of black population growth, and high levels of transiency between camps, the mountains soon reached the southern regional average in black lynchings in cases where violent racial hatred erupted over claims of the sexual transgression of an unknown black man (Ayers 1992:152–53).

I could tell you that the place shifted nervously back and forth in a mix of "centers" and "margins" and found itself torn between dreams of progress and return to the *used to*. I could tell you that at the turn of the century there were already-developed towns in the area and local entrepreneurs who acted as middlemen between poor farmers and outside interests, helping to locate land for sale, buying up mineral rights, and spreading the gospel of "progress through industrial growth" (Eller 1982:63–64, 65–85; Corbin 1981:7; Waller 1988). I could tell you that the hills were not "outside" the imagined community (Anderson 1983) of America but caught like other places in the dream of wage labor, modernity, and consumption. There was money to be made in mining, in cutting trees into railroad ties, in selling seemingly worthless mineral rights, and in raising crops for the new company stores in the camps.

By the turn of the century the log cabin had already begun to give way to frame houses; by 1900 nine of out ten new houses were being built from modern milled lumber, the walls bore the characteristic decorations of the period in America at large—photographs, tintypes, and prints from magazines—and people claimed to be proud to be as up-to-date as they could manage (Ayers 1992:118). I could point to evidence that there was already in the 1880s a pervasive desire for "progress" in the area. In the words of a dissenter from the time: "The people have been educated to believe that our immediate development must be obtained at any cost and regardless of sacrifices; the public mind has become saturated with an idea that progress means one railroad where there is no railroad, and two railroads where there is only one" (Mason 1884:3 as quoted in Eller 1982:64).

I could argue that the meanings of "kinship" and "place" arose out of the meanings of class (Brown 1951; Batteau 1982) and that the meaning of "home" grew out of the effects of industrial occupation. Picture Mr. Workman, a miner, testifying before the Senate hearings on education and labor in 1913.

SENATOR KENYAN: What do you say about people, men and women, becoming attached to that country up there?

MR. WORKMAN: They are to some extent. They seem to have the idea . . . that they are the men who used to own the land, a great many old settlers and their children, and they built up the mines, and they are living there, and have

lived there, and have their places of residence there, and they think they should
have a home there in time of peace or strike . . . They look on it as their homes
in the West Virginia hills. (U.S. Congress, Senate, 1913, 789–90, as quoted in
Eller 1982:197)

I could argue that people were not passive objects of history but active
subjects in it and that the local culture was not pristine and separate but
caught in the dialectics of class and race and gender (R. Lewis 1987;
Moore 1990; A. Puckett 1992; Shifflett 1991; Trotter 1990; W. Turner
and Cabell 1985; Yarrow 1991). I could tell you that the very image of
the *used to* could not hold as a simple nostalgia of origins, wholeness,
and peak times but was written through and through with violence and
tragedy. Or that the nostalgia for the family farm is a white idiom, not a
black one, and that African Americans clustered in towns when they
could and left in disproportionate numbers for the cities up north along
with the Italians and Poles who arrived from Ellis Island.

I could tell you that the place grew more, not less, "wild" as it formed
itself diacritically in relation to the "civilizing" efforts of the center of
things. That it was just at that moment when the bourgeois imaginary
was taming "nature" to a picturesque harmony of form, color, and light
and fashioning the disciplined individual subject into an image of fantastic proportions to encompass a miniaturized world (S. Stewart 1984) that
the hills found themselves caught in the wild swings of wildness and
order, stability and eruptions of violence, and the world loomed gigantic
over a subject that was subject to the accidental and contingent and
struck by unforgettable scenes and latent possibilities. I could tell you that
in the face of modernization and "civilization" the hills were scripted as
a site of a superfluity of "nature" over "culture" or the site of a potential
for a dangerous surrender to the disorder in "nature," and the place itself
grew restless and registered events in idioms of astonishment.

But this takes us not to a finally True History and a story straightened
out but back to the idioms of "history" as they are actively deployed in
the place itself. Aside from History as a sequence of events there are still
the chronotopes of *remembering* ruins, the state of mourning with its
peculiar intensification, the arresting image that provokes the participation of an audience in a poetics of space-time that traces the accidental
within the ordinary and the sudden eruption of the traumatic in the
course of daily roamings. Here history becomes a series of focal points
remembered in images that have been lifted out of once-told stories, fastened onto, and spread contagiously in the invention of an ongoing way
of life in the hills. In short, there is more to the "history" *re-membered* in
the cultural poetics of ruins, *places*, arresting images, and *just talk* than
any master narrative can tell us. There is still, in the tense fabulations of

local chronotopes, a history that lies collected in fragmented allegories of shock and remainder, hope and refuge, and in tactile *places* encountered in daily roamings and reveries.

In the local chronotopes, the image of the gentleman capitalists retiring "undaunted" to their tent might illuminate some of the tension of a place poised precariously on an edge. On one side there is the daydream of modernization and economic "takeoff," and on the other there is the space of alterity opened up between the "wilderness" of the hills and the capitalists dining in self-assured elegance in their tent. I could say that it is around this gap—this precarious edge—that the flood of history stories gather and dig themselves in. They coalesce in moments and spaces poised on dangerous brinks like the slag dams that threaten the camps below. Here, on this edge facing danger, master narratives give way to the more fragmented, situated stories of people getting around and making do, and to the excesses of stories that fasten onto moments of shock when endangered ways are suddenly illuminated with hypersignificance. Here the moves of master narrative give way, momentarily, to the movements of roaming and stopping to study on thangs. On the one hand, there is the roaming—the everydayness of moving through things, fashioning paths through contingency, and discovering new ways to get from place to place. And on the other hand, the melancholic rumination that gives pause to *remember* and culls impacts into unforgettable *signs*.

Take, for instance, the roaming, everyday stories of those who worked in the mines and then went home to work the farm, tracing daily itineraries over the hills. Bud Henson *remembers* years of walking across Tommy Creek and Barker's Ridge and down Walkertown Mountain to follow Devil's Fork holler all the way into Amigo. "You can't go that way anymore, the road's got so bad." Jethro Graham walked across Lillybrook and Tams Mountains and followed Soak Creek on into Winding Gulf and there was the time that . . . (and something dramatic or terrible or unforgettable is relayed). Or there are the bragging, heroic stories that surround the deforestation of the hills with the feats of men cutting railroad ties for cash and carrying massive loads on their shoulders over the hills: "Worked m'self to death, carryin' two-hundred-pound ties all day and go back to my place and start work. That's the reason I'm broke down today, didn't have no better sense."

For every roaming litany of agency in everyday life there is an arresting image of remembered trauma. The rhythm of history follows the stops and starts of moving with the times and being arrested by shock only to move on again. There is the traumatic image of how the old people sold the mineral rights to their land for twenty-five cents an acre to "go along with" the insistent buyers because "they never thought nothin' would come of it, you know. They didn't know no better." Or the tragedy of a young father dead of appendicitis despite heroic efforts of the neighbors to carry the sick man over the logging road to town in the dead of the night and the snow coming down, or the young mother dead in childbirth despite the efforts of the midwives and the other neighbor women to stop the bleeding, or the child dead of the pneumonia in a drafty cabin and broke his mother's heart. Yet each arresting trauma elicits memories of a way of life in the used to—of raising gardens and pigs and cows, of roaming in the hills and hunting, of orchards, flowers, and herbs. Old man Mills could graft a pear and an apple tree to make the fruit grow exactly half-apple and half-pear right down the middle and if one didn't come out right he'd get mad and start a whole new tree. People thought he was crazy but they said those apple-pears were good to eat.

The shocks of history cull themselves into traumatic images and then disperse again in the anecdotal flow of *just talk*. Stories of the trauma of people losing their *places* to taxes and waking up to find themselves crowded together in the camps move into the detailed, situated memories of the old paths down from the hills into the camps traversed back and forth at a walking pace over the course of decades. Stories of cutting wood for cooking and heating and railroad ties link the past to the on-going present; things happened in the woods then as they do now, and the woodcutter remains a doubled figure of victim and hero/outlaw. The past grows legendary in the story of John Henry who could lay ties just about as fast as a train could run and who died trying. The present in-fills with stories of outlaws outrunning the forest ranger now that there is a law against scavenging wood. Or there are the stories like Dreama's of her sister who got killed at the hand of her husband when he took her and the kids to cut wood on Sunday (the Lord's day) and the first tree tried to come down on her baby and Sissy ran to push her out of the way and the tree come down on Sissy's head and shattered her head to pieces and she lay under the tree. Out roaming the hills people encounter all the named places that remember traumatic events—Indian Flats, the Rhinehart stand, the stand at the old Meadows place, the exposed wire that electrocuted Buddy Hall and left him dangling.

There is the traumatic image of how people were forced to use company scrip and how the company would take the bills out of the pay day before you ever saw it so people came up owing the company for their work. Yet the memory also elicits reminiscences of extraordinary things like the large East Gulf mines that had 1,300 miners working three shifts and they had a chapel down there where they would pray at the start of the shift. There was one preacher they called "Brother Jackson" and he was a black preacher, came up from Georgia, and he could make a man's blood run cold. Following such talk there may be further talk of how some of the bosses were good men and some were mean (just like now) and some of the miners were good men and some were bad (just like it is now).

Even the traumatic images of violence and death during the labor organizing of the twenties elicit stories of an ongoing way of life. There are the images of the company thugs who policed the camps, the killing of labor organizers and the blood that ran in the streets and into the old coal dirt and was lost, the people evicted from their company houses during strikes, the tents that people stayed in and the thugs came in and set them on fire, the babies that lay upon the quilts and the thugs poured kerosene in their milk . . . But such images lead into stories of how as the thugs patrolled the camps from the tops of the hills at night the local shine runners made an art of slipping past them, and how the men went hunting, how they would call to each other with horns to gather at known places in the hills and the dogs would run the hills all night as the men crouched over the fire listening to their movement from one named place to another—Barker's Ridge, Tommy Creek, The Flats, Devil's Fork, that place where Bud and Henry always set—you remember them boys, their daddy worked with your daddy down 'Soco.

In the face of constant death and dismemberment, the miners speak of mining as a primal contest and bond of "man" and "the mountain." They point to the blue-black patches on their faces where they got hit years ago and the coal worked its way in. They say mining gets in the blood. They say they can "hear" the difference between the crack in the roof that comes just before a roof fall and the constant ordinary cracking of the roof settling and the mountain shifting. They object to *the miner* (i.e., the continuous miner—the massive machine that literally chews through the face of the coal and spits it out its back end onto a long belt that extends like entrails to the mouth of the mine) because it makes so much noise that they cannot hear and it kicks up so much coal dust that they cannot see. Used to, they say, when the canary died they knew to get out before the explosion but the mechanical gas gauges they use now often fail (and it is in the hands of the company to maintain them). It is only after the litany of deaths and dismemberments that a story moves again into everyday choices.

> BUD COALSON: Honey, I don't care **what** it is.
> You might be havin' trouble with your **old lady**, maybe you got a **baby** down **sick**,
> and honey ever'body's got trouble meetin' the **bills**.
> I don't care **what** it is, **it'll wait**.
> When you walk in that **mines** ever'**thang** goes out a your **head** or you ain't gonna come **out, one.**
> It's **that simple.**

Don't thank a **nothin'**, **buddy.**

I worked down **East Gulf** forty-two years and **ever'** day I walked in that **mouth** I put ever'**thang** out a my **head,** didn't thank about nothin' but **us** and that **mountain** 'til I got back **out.**

It's **fear** that kills in the mines.

Just like that **Reed** boy got kilt down here.

Well, it **weren't** but his sixth day **in** and they put him on the **miner.**

And that boy was **skeered.**

Well, he's a comin' in on the lizard and honey you got to recall where you **at.**

But he thought he **heared** somethin' and he picked his head up to see what it was and tuk the top of his head right off.

Sure did.

Lord, I hated to **see** it.

Weren't nothin' but a boy and his six day **in.**

Well, they shouldn't never have put him on the miner and they **knowed** it too.

Buddy we was out for **months** over that'n.

You gotta **watch** them people day and night.

You gotta fight to git ever'thang you **git** and **buddy** you gotta fight to **keep** it **too,** this old world we's livin' in.

And the **young** people comin' up **today, they** ain't got no better sense.

They don't know just exactly **about** the union.

Well, they're **in** the union, but they don't know just exactly about it. We fought to **get** the union.

And buddy they're down there a **smokin'** and some of 'm's **a drankin'.** You cain't **do** that stuff in the **mines.**

They're puttin' **their**selves and everybody else **in** there in **danger** and that's just the way it **is.**

Buddy over here went down **Red Jacket** to get him a **job** and he **come out** after one day.

An' that man **needed** a job, didn't you, Buddy?

BUDDY: Ah hah, sure did.

BUD COALSON: Been outta a work—how long you been outta work, Buddy? Tell her.

BUDDY: **Well,** let's see, it'll be two year next month, I b'lieve.

BUD COALSON: Two years and he went in there **one day** and **come out** because them boys in there was a drankin' and a smokin' and you just cain't get used to that, **can you Buddy.**

BUDDY: No sir, you cain't.

BUD COALSON: **Buddy's** out a **job.**

BUDDY: I said **well,** I'll just have to find me a place where I know the **people, you** know.

BUD COALSON: **Well,** hit's a **shame** how they're a'doin'.

Well, I wish 'm well, and I do, but them boys ain't a gonna live long that a way, that's all.

In the local poetics, then, time is gathered, on the one hand, into a chronotopic dream space of dissolution, disillusion, tribulation, death and decay, wandering and nostalgia. On the other hand there is the on-going way of life in the hills referenced in the social and aesthetic satisfaction that comes of litany and story itself. The arresting dialectical image culls the dialectic in social life between rumination and restless scanning, melancholy and agentic engagement, stillness and violent eruption into an image of a "real" haunted by catastrophe. The used to is haunted by history; the final resting place in heaven awaits the catastrophic violence of the End Times. The metaphysical lies incarnate in states of contingency, desire arises out of the moments that block it, and the hope of release becomes not an abstract end in itself but the very sustenance of the present times.

The shock of history, then, is not the end of the story but its ground and motivation. Things do not simply fall into ruin or dissipate in the winds of progress but fashion themselves into powerful effects that re-member things in such a way that "history" digs itself into the present and people cain't help but recall it. Stories grow graphic and promote a strange intimacy of subject and object, drawing them together in a melan-cholic consciousness that knows itself only in passing into its other. Then they move back to the task of chronicling what is at hand and making something of things. People watch each other and the place itself for *signs*, remembering things in a melancholic litany that moves from inten-sified image into the sociality of just talk.

MISS BLEVINS: **Anymore** don't nobody **visit**.
They got thangs easy and they spread and got **fat**.
An' they let thangs get **away** from 'm.
Well, the mines is got down and cain't nobody **work**.
And Mr. **Reagan** is tuk the old people's checks and the **old people** is on the **starvation**.
The old people is eatin' dog food out a cans and the young people don't know just exactly **about** thangs.
They've let thangs git **away** from 'm.
Buddy, I'm a tellin' **you**.
Well.
Seen Miss Lavender out here while back and she was a haulin' feed down the track for them hogs where that Buddy Bowens got sa **mean** and stuck them posts on the bridge so she cain't git out and cain't nobody git nothin' in to her.
Lord that makes me **mad!**

Well, that man don' own that **bridge!**
You cain' own a **bridge!**
Don' nobody own that **bridge.**
That's just a **bridge.**
Well, I'd like to go on up there and say somethin' **to him** because that ain't
right.
But I'm a tellin' **you,** honey, she was a **sight.**
Up past ninety year old and a haulin' **sacks,** buddy.
Well they **weigh** more'n **she** does.
And her just a **hollerin'** to ever'body all up and down the creek like she's on her
way to church.
And I said, "**Lord have mercy Miss Lavender** whyn't you git one a them boys
come help you?"
She said, "I got to get my **feed** in for my **hogs,** this here's for my **hogs,**
I ain't got time to **fool** with nobody."
I said, "Well, you're a gonna be **dead** if you keep up and you won't have time
for **nothin'.**"
But now you cain't **talk** to Miss Lavender, you might as well be talkin' to one
a them **hogs.**
Weeelll, she **kep' on, kep' on,**
drag one a them sacks up the tracks and 'fore you know it **here** she come **again,**
come back,
go back for another one
come back, **go** back
come back, **go** back
come back, **go** back
come back, **go** back
That woman kep' me aggravated all **day.**
I said well how many **hogs** she **have?**
Well, she's just the **sweetest** old thang, but she's **mean, buddy.**
She'll **aggravate** you to **death.**

Riley's Last Ride

History becomes a chronotope only through operations that orient, situate, and temporalize. Like a street that becomes a space for walking only
in the act of crossing it or a text that becomes an interpretive space only
in the act of reading it, the hills become a space-time only in the act of
roaming and reverie. Like a word spoken, "history" is an act caught in
the ambiguity of actualization, an utterance dependent on conventions,
situated in time, and transformed by shifting contexts (de Certeau 1984).
They say you have to get out and go and make somethin' **of** thangs.

In 1985 Riley Hess was dying of black lung. He had been confined to his place for two years and he longed to go out hunting once more. "I'd find me a place somewheres way out and set down." Unable to go, Riley was gettin' squirrelly and his storytelling was more and more limited to fantastic symbols of grandiosity, heroic action, and mystical connection. Stories of a year in Arizona featured ten-foot snakes, diamonds the size of goose eggs sparkling in the desert sun, and wildcats wrestled to the ground. Stories of the recent years confined to the house featured Smokey the cat who had come to Riley as a feral kitten lodged under the back porch scrapping with the chickens for food. Then he got to where he just followed Riley everywhere and slept on his bed.

> When he come that cat weren't no bigger'n the nipple on that **bottle**. Little **bitty** thang and I kep' him in a **matchbox**. And that was his **house**, I put him a little **bed** in there and I'd keep him in my **pocket** and take him out and look at him. Now he's a **wildcat**; that cat's big as a **bear**.

Riley's lyin' buddies were getting tired of this kind of talk, Riley's "'magination runnin' away with him" in the absence of everyday stories encountered while out roaming.

He wanted to get out and go once more, so one day he and Sylvie and I took a drive over the hills to the river—the place where people go to get away from nosy neighbors and the stifling overstimulation of the camps and they go completely crazy with drinking and guns and running around. As we followed the old roads they used to roam, they remembered places—an old shack hanging over a cliff ("and still ain't falled off"), a curve in the river ("looks like they moved it"), the statue of John Henry ("still there, ain't it"), a "yellow-color" house now almost bare of paint, stands of trees, precipices, bends in the road, and several suddenly haunting places like the pond.

> RILEY: That there **pond** is where that pore woman run off the road and kilt her **baby**.
> Little baby girl got **drownded**.
> And she got to where she couldn't come by **that pond** without thankin' 'bout her baby and what she **done**.
> Then they said finally one day she forgot and come on **by** here and she saw that **place** and they said she lost her **mind** and she still ain't got it back I don't believe, do **you**, Sylvie?
> SYLVIE [irritated]: **Now Riley**, I don't know **nothin'** 'bout it.
> RILEY: Used to, ever' time we'd come **by** here I'd thank about that **pore woman**.

Finally, at the end of a long afternoon of roaming and remembering, Riley said he was *satisfied*. An old hillbilly song on the radio reminded him that he had played it for Sylvie, with a banjo he'd borrowed from Bud Halsey, when they were courting on her daddy's porch.

> RILEY: And I couldn't hardly play that thang to save my life but I banged away on that old thang like I was on my way to **Nashville**, didn' I Sylvie.
> SYLVIE: **Oh yeah**, [laughing] you sure did. You thought you could **play** that thang.

We stopped at a Dairy Queen on the river and I went to order the food while Sylvie folded a stack of napkins—some red, some white—into quilt shapes and fit them into patterns all over the table, patting and smoothing them as she worked.

> SYLVIE: Used to I just loved to **quilt**, but now it's been years.
> ME: Why?
> SYLVIE: **Well**, what with **Riley** sick, and **mommy** to take care of and all, I **keep** thangs on my mind.
> ME: Well.

Someone said they used to paper the walls with newspapers and Sears catalogs.

> SYLVIE: Oh yeah, ever' time we got a paper we'd stick it up on the wall and that's what we had to read.
> And when they'd git dirty, why, we'd put us up a new one. We was all the time puttin' up new ones, just do a little bit at a time, you know.
> **Flour** sacks too. We'd cut out the bottom of a flour sack just as soon as we got it empty, and we'd stick **that** up **too**. They was s' **perty**, they had the blue flowers in the middle like on the old butter presses.
> Then they got the **panelin'** in in 19 and 39 and 19 and 40 and course ever' body had to **have** it and that was the end of the other.
> But you know that was all we **had** and we really **enjoyed** it.
> They'd make **patterns**, you know, you might put all **red** together over here and **blue** over here or mix 'm up and it would grow. Or they'd get tired of it and just start over on another wall, you know. Well, they **enjoyed** it.

After Riley died in 1986, and Sylvie's mommy died in '88 (at the age of ninety-six), Sylvie took to making quilts again in the winter. That's what keeps her going in those months when she has no garden and sometimes she can't even get out to church down the holler or even to feed her chickens in the coop out back where the ice is so bad. While some women say quilting **aggravates** them and gives them the nerves, many of the older women like Sylvie say it gives their hands something to do, keeps them from getting the nerves, and passes the time. She does it for hours and hours on end as if it were a job and gathers old clothes greedily when she can get out to a yard sale. She has a whole room packed from floor to ceiling, every inch of the floor covered, with discarded polyester, and she asks me to send her whatever I can find in Texas. Here, too, we find the chronotope of refuse and refuge, the intimacy of subject and object gathered together in the work of amassing and chronicling things, the trembling space/time filled with contingency and desire in which people roam, the aggravation that stirs a relentless scanning, and the allegorical re-presentation of *re-membering* itself.

Mr. Henry's Sticks

Mr. Henry was a retired black miner who spent his time making lamps and miniature furniture from Popsicle sticks. He worked all day in a shed out in the yard, and people would come by and visit him and look at his stuff. When visitors from the city were sent down to see him, he might sell them something they wanted or he might not. In the summer Mr. Henry would take his "show" on the road for weeks at a time, covering five states and selling things here and there as he went. He said he liked to get out and see things.

He began to lose his eyesight and to take dizzy spells. The doctors said he had fluid on his brain at the back of his head and they would have to put a shunt in to drain it. He said he didn't want to be cut. They sent him to a specialist in Virginia who took the time to try to convince him to have the operation. First the doctor thought he was afraid so he assured him that the operation was a simple and safe one, and Mr. Henry said well, he was ready to go any time the Lord was ready to take him on but he didn't need any operation. So the doctor tried to tell him that if he didn't have the operation he would lose his memory and his ability to plan for the future.

MR. HENRY: He said, "Now Mr. Henry," he said, "now I want you to listen to me for I've got somethin' I've got to **tell** you."
I said, "All right, doctor," I said, "go ahead. **I'm ready.**"
And the man says, "Well, if you don't get this shunt put in there you'll be gettin' foggy-headed and you won't be able to recall the past," he says, "and you won't be able to look forward to the future," That's what he said.
And I said, "Well, I sure thank you for your **time,** doctor, but I won't be needin' no operation right at the present time." And I went **home.**
Man told me I'm wantin' to look back in the past and up on into the future. I said what in the **world for?**
Heh heh. That ain't no reason to have no **operation,** now is it? But that **tickled** me.
Well, it got worse, and it got perty **bad.**
So I went back to see Doctor Ross and she told me if I didn't do somethin' with it perty soon time would **come** and I'd have to quit ma **foolin'** with them **sticks** an' all. So I heared that and I said well, all right, now **there's** a **reason.**

History, then, we might say, arises in the present. Grand causes and ultimate consequences gather themselves around the everyday in the trembling space/time where the question of "meaning" finds itself caught in a signification that is at once contingent and receptive, overwhelming and inconclusive, tactile and uncertain. The past, like the future, comes and goes, drifting in and out of vision, but it haunts things until there's no telling what might happen and what people might do.

5

Encounters

> It is one of the most powerful ruses of the
> dominant to pretend that critique can only exist
> in the language of 'reason', 'pure knowledge',
> and 'seriousness.'
> *(Peter Stallybrass and Allon White,*
> The Politics and Poetics of Transgression)

> Only to those who are excluded from the social
> nexus comes the idea of raising a question
> about the limits of human nature because they
> need a human that includes them.
> *(Edward Said, "The Mind of Winter:*
> *Reflections on Life in Exile")*

The Bourgeois Imaginary

In the seventeenth and eighteenth centuries the European bourgeoisie carved out a new social and discursive space of rational judgment and enlightened critique. Everyone was welcome for the free exchange of reasoned discourse in the new spas, resorts, and coffeehouses, but "immoderate elements" such as the "foul language" of the lower classes and the "high and mighty ways" of the upper classes were excluded (Stallybrass and White 1986). A new space of critique grew up side by side with the rewriting of social and physical space in the modern city through a threefold operation: (1) the creation of a clean space in which rational organization attempts to eliminate all physical, mental, and political pollution; (2) the displacement of particularized traditions by a totalizing classificatory order; and (3) the creation of a universal and impersonal subject (de Certeau 1984). A set of precise, strategically deployed discourses of moderation, transcendent rationality, and self-control was writ large as a naturalized, universalized order of things.[1] A cultural diacritics rooted in difference and social conflict was displaced by an internalized struggle for self-discipline, discerning judgment, and good taste.

The clamor of particular voices out of which the bourgeois order emerged was at once suppressed and suddenly illuminated as a prolific excess of hybrid figures, competing gods, and exorbitant demands; a bourgeois ethos of elective distance from the necessities of the natural and social world (Bourdieu 1984) wrote center and margin into polar oppositions between "high" and "low" states of mind, body, society, and nature (Stallybrass and White 1986; Terdiman 1985). Lowly and excluded elements took on a powerful symbolic charge and a new psychological depth as they became a threatening surround.

Yet the "Otherness" of the margins, filled with alter egos and "lower" freedoms and counterdiscourses, also marked the space of an other mode of critique. Here a kind of madness directly counterposed to the modern bourgeois madness for monitoring progress and order became not only possible but overdetermined and pressing. Here, the "excessive," fragmented, and "extraneous" gathered into a logic of graphic encounter with the center's order of things and its moves to exclude them. It addressed itself not to the nature of things but to the very forms of signification and naturalization lodged in the bourgeois imaginary. Its own logic, lodged in gaps and displacements, took on the symbolic charge of the fragment within the totalized, the particular within the universalized, and the degraded within the transcendent.

In the United States, "Appalachia" became one of these "Other" places and filled the bourgeois imaginary with both dread and desire. In popular literature from the 1830s to the 1870s, people from the hills were portrayed at once as tough pioneers ("our contemporary ancestors"), grotesque figures (vicious, bestial, extravagant, eccentric), and tricksters (wily, survivalist, con men who were as much victimizers as they were victims). By the turn of the century the local color movement had begun to portray them as picturesque or pathetic folk carrying on a tradition now lost to the modern world (Anglin 1992; Batteau 1990; Cook 1976; McNeil 1988; Shapiro 1978; Whisnant 1983).

During the Progressive Era from 1880 to 1920 difference came to be seen as cultural difference and "the other" became conceivable as "a culture." An antimodernist preservationist movement saw the hills as an enclave of culture that had been preserved against the ravages of time and progress. Professionals started settlement schools and folk centers that sought to preserve and elevate what were seen as the pure cultural forms of the hills and to suppress and exclude presumed degenerations brought about by contact with the outside world and the internal cultural decay that came of isolation (Whisnant 1983). "Appalachia," like the inner city, became a symbolic pocket of poverty in an affluent society and an unassimilated region in an otherwise united nation (Billings 1974; Harrington 1962; Mathews 1965; Pearsall 1959; Wigginton 1972–1980; Weller 1965). It was at once an absence that marked the gains of "our" material wealth, education, literacy, and sophistication and a living folkways that marked the hope of redemption lodged in culture or tradition itself.

Anthropology, too, emerged out of this period and enacted the drama of the transcendent discerning subject in the figure of the adventurous ethnographer who traveled to other cultures to witness and ponder their particularity without succumbing to it. Its classificatory relativism, like the bourgeois ethics of universalized personhood, enacted an enlightened self-constraint in direct contrast to the more naive suppositions and outright prejudices of its "Others." The superiority of anthropological knowledge, like the superiority of the discerning self and the reasoned critique, rested in the value attached to knowing that one's own "cultural values" were relative while those of the "Other" remained imprisoned in a particular culture (McGrane 1989). Yet Otherness stood as an appealing object of desire, as well as a threat, in its very situatedness.

In the social science literature, then, as in popular culture, the figure of the "Appalachian," or "hillbilly," remained tense and contradictory as it carried the weight of the "highs" and "lows" of a bourgeois space of desire. Contradiction came to be seen as an essential characteristic of the culture itself: people in the hills were friendly and suspicious, talkative and taciturn, fatalist and individualist, religious and antireligious, pathologically dependent and utterly self-sufficient, pathetic and heroic, loving and violent, and above all capable of living with contradiction (Erikson 1976; Ford 1962; Gazaway 1969; Howell 1973; Kephart 1922; Weller 1965). In the sixties, with the War on Poverty and the creation of the Appalachian Regional Commission (ARC), it became a distinct area marred by the culture of poverty. Trapped in its own contradictions and living within its own isolated ways it came to encode the "lowliness" of an intractable Otherness itself; under the signs of "rednecks" or "white trash" it became the site of a culture that was irredeemably white, poor, rural, male, racist, illiterate, fundamentalist, inbred, alcoholic, violent, and given to all forms of excess, degradation, and decay.

Spaces of Encounter

In the schizophrenic space of desire of the bourgeois imaginary, the "Other" literally embodies both authenticity and a degraded state of nature. "American" encounters with "Appalachia," then, come always already encased in a totalizing transcendent order that scans the surface of things for its own "highs" and "lows." Take, for instance, William Least Heat Moon's account of "Appalachia" in his best-seller, *Blue Highways*. He has just been denied tenure in an English department and his marriage has fallen apart. He sets out on a personal quest and a search for authenticity on the small roads off the interstates. The first place on the side of the road he comes to is "Appalachia."

> The highway took me through Danville, where I saw a pillared antebellum mansion with a trailer court on the front lawn. Route 127 ran down a long valley of pastures and fields edged by low, rocky bluffs and split by a stream the color of muskmelon. In the distance rose the foothills of the Appalachians, old mountains that once separated the Atlantic from the shallow inland sea now the middle of America. The licks came out of the hills, the fields got smaller, and there were little sawmills cutting hardwoods into pallets, crates, fenceposts. The houses shrank, and their colors changed from white to pastels to iridescents to no paint at all. The lawns went from Vertagreen bluegrass to thin fescue to hard packed dirt glinting with fragments of glass, and the lawn ornaments changed from birdbaths to plastic flamingoes and donkeys to broken down automobiles with raised hoods like tombstones. On the porches stood long legged wringer washers and ruined sofas, and by the front doors, washtubs hung like coats of arms. A cold drizzle fell as I wound around into the slopes of the Cumberland Mountains. Clouds like smudged charcoal turned the afternoon to dusk, and the only relief from the gloom came from a fiddler on the radio who ripped out "Turkey Bone Buzzer."
>
> At Ida, a sign in front of a church announced the Easter sermon: "Welcome All God's Children: Thieves, Liars, Gossips, Bigots, Adulterers, Children." I felt welcome. Also at Ida was one of those hitching posts in the form of a crouching livery boy reaching up to take the master's reins; but the face of this iron Negro had been painted white and his eyes Nordic blue. Ida, on the southern edge of Appalachia, a place (they said) where change comes slowly or not at all, had a church welcoming everyone and a family displaying integrated lawn decorations. (1982:24–25)

He constructs a totalized interpretive space, not unlike an ethnographic space, that pictures a complex whole made up of tensions and surprises (as in the church "welcome," the white-faced jockeys). The world becomes a symbolic text and the author effects a magical fusion of mind and world; his ideas make a fit with a detailed picture-perfect image and we imagine ourselves privy to something like the "gist" of the place.

But without the distanced reflection and stable interpretive space of a relativist frame, Otherness can grow larger than life as a threatening surround. The dark side of the bourgeois imaginary erupts, for instance, in James Dickey's *Deliverance*, which envisions a nightmarish, all too real encounter with mountain men. A group of city men take a trip down the river to get in touch with a way of life that is itself not out of touch—a place, they think, where the seasons mean something and a man can make himself in an encounter with the elements. They are given an omen when

24. Coal operator's house perched up on the hill overlooking Meade. Photograph © Harriette Hartigan, Artemis.

a local man asks them why they would want to go down the river in a canoe. They say, "Because it's there," and he replies, "It's there, all right. If you git in there and can't get out you're goin' to wish it wudn't" (1971:59).

The omen plays itself out in a sudden, horrific shift from a "good" encounter to a "bad" one as the men get further into the woods. The first "good" encounter enacts the idyllic fantasy of direct, unmediated contact with an ugly but harmless and magically lyrical "Other": the dueling-banjos scene in which two banjos speak melodically to each other, over-coming the gap of cultural hostility and mental and physical handicap. But only moments later in the film version a second encounter degenerates into a vicious and depraved male-on-male rape scene and subsequent murder. Caught in the encounter with wildness, the city men become their own worst nightmares of the wild mountain men; they kill a man and then hide the body rather than go to the law, digging through rotten mulch to make the shallow grave. They explain, "If you were in some-thing as deep as we were in, it was better to go all the way," and they are off into an "Other" mode of action, reason, and critique that takes them deeper and deeper into the life of the river and the hills. The othered culture, reduced to a state of nature, becomes dangerously seductive, and it is only through a series of more and more intense encounters with it that they are eventually able to redeem themselves and find their way out of the woods. At the river's edge they find a jaded and sinister semicivili-zation (in which degenerate wildness lurks). Safety, reason, and a renatu-ralized order of things lies in the city, though the foray out into the wilds has left the men themselves marked with Otherness (Hartigan 1992). Di-rect encounter is dangerous.

Now counter both the "light" and "dark" moments of the bourgeois encounter with Otherness to Sissy Miller's polemic against old man Hen-son when he complained about the kids from the camp running across his well-tended lawn.

> Why, I'll tell you what, if I had to live in a place where I had to have me a patch a grass like 'at and couldn't nobody git up **on** it, well, what good is it **for?**
> I'd just get me a **cement** truck—one a them **big** ones—ah'd cover me th' whole thang over with cement.
> That way people could park their **cars** on it if they **wanted** to, I don't **care.**
> **Buddy,** I'd turn it into a **parkin'** lot 'fore I'd git all high and mighty over some old patch a **weeds.**
> I tell you **what, buddy,**
> now when you git to where you gotta watch your **grass** for fear somebody'll come and git up **on** it, buddy that's when thangs is **really** got down. (K. Stewart 1988:237)

In the abstract, universalized order of things neighbors should respect tended boundaries and people should be "nice." But in the camps the *ideal* of neighborliness grows dense with the very signs of a localized sociality itself and stands as a metacultural claim to an "Other" mode of critique. Those who fail to recognize and engage precise, local *ways* are called *shameless*. Church people who act like they're better than other people are more shameless than the worst sinner. People like old man Henson who live in brick houses (read as imitations of the "big houses" in the city) are more shameless than those who fall into the faint of total abjection and hole up. People who brag (that is, claim to know something for certain) are no better than people who talk about other people behind their backs or people who are so backward that they can't speak at all. People who seem so nice and "keep things up so nice" might turn around and treat their mommy and daddy like dogs. Then people will say, "They ain't foolin' nobody." Things are not what they seem.

Sissy, encountering old man Henson, asserts local ways against what she sees as the dis-placement, or anticultural space, of city ways. She opens a gap in the closure of abstract codes of respectability and property with a performative poetics of encounter. In the place of Least Heat Moon's smooth visual evolution of lawn types "from Vertagreen bluegrass . . . to hard packed dirt glinting with fragments of glass," she deploys a loudmouthed polemic against the machinery of class cultural production. Using exaggeration and fantastical threat, she claims a slippage in the visual code of a "picture-perfect" meaning that "fits": smooth lawns hide a nightmarish invasion of the asocial; a parking lot in the middle of the neighborhood holds the promise of redemption. In the space of the gap, the "meaning" of things can be evaluated only within a local knowledge.

Where *Blue Highways* and *Deliverance* construct an encompassing symbolic order written through with the spin of idyllic and horrific otherings, Sissy directs her words against this very function of the "city's" symbolic code itself, fragmenting its magical syntheses with loudmouthed back talk. It is as if she is calling it out, encountering it, to make room for localized ways marked by eccentricity, inescapable closeness, and the contingency of social place. Here "meaning" lies not in an abstract order of images and beliefs but in the diacritical process of encountering alterity itself. It is a space of desire "centered," strangely, in the tense and shifting interface between movements of closure and rupture, finalization and transformation, classificatory order and poetic performance, authority and antiauthority, coherence and fragmentation.

Picture how in the camps the order of things is not a civilizing presence captured in well-tended lawns and balanced checkbooks, disciplined bodies, educated reason, and routinized careers but a conspiratorial

25. Peanut Lowe and baby, Tommy Creek holler. Photograph © Em Herzstein.

threat. Here there is no middle-class presence to embody a path of safety
and success through the battleground of capital and labor, no fire depart-
ments to save the houses that are constantly burning down, no police
except for the state police who occasionally come down to the camps to
set up sweeping roadblocks and stop and search everyone leaving the
camps all day and night. Here people complain about mean teachers and
the rationalized discipline of the schools, and parents "strike" the
schools, pulling their kids out for days or weeks at a time. Here lawyers
and judges are likened to vultures preying on the weak. Social service
professionals are mean, and there are stories of their shameless abuse of
the old people and the helpless. Doctors give people pills that make them
sick and subject bodies to humiliating probes and internal exams. TV
news is something to talk back to. Picture how, when they put in the
"new" mailboxes with combination locks at the Amigo post office and
people couldn't get theirs open, someone said, "Well, they're not 'new,'
I don't know where they came from," and this led to wild speculative
claims that there are actually two completely different versions of the
newspaper out of Beckley—one for the city people and one for the camps.
This had come to light in Amigo because the town straddled two counties. Two neighbors, they said, could be reading two completely different
newspapers. Some said they thought they had noticed something funny.

Encountering Alterity

If in the bourgeois imaginary there is a dream of a utopian public sphere where there can be a free exchange of ideas and where intercultural conflicts can be mediated to avoid violence and fissure, then its counterpublics in "unassimilated" places emerge not as empirical reals but as negations emergent in gaps. As a diacritical sign, they can be derived as that which is systematically negated by the ideal order of things in a logic of excess and remainder. But as a local confabulation of social and discursive practices aimed at encountering a foreign yet encompassing order, these situated counterpublics carve out an "Other" space of desire, deflecting desire away from the dominant enclosures in the very process of constituting themselves within and "against" them (Chambers 1991). They dramatize moments of slippage and emergence and embed things in a density of re-membered experience. They shut themselves in a cyst, fall into the faint of abjection, intensify, and propel themselves out in eccentricity, ecstatic expression, and sudden, violent conversions. They follow along in the wake of things and fashion a space in which particularity is everything and the forms of things matter.

There are times, then, when the camps become the kind of place where people say you have to get all the way down before you can get up, where backsliders have to hit rock bottom before they can be borned again. They become a space of desire like that of country music's sad songs of lost love and lost lives re-membered from a place got all the way down (alone, on the bottle, in the gutter, on the cold city streets, in prison, or from the grave). As in these country songs, the symbolic polarization of high and low states lends itself to a redemptive polemic of class that pits "lowbrow" sociality against highbrow anomie and self-interest, a nostalgic rural home of the south against the "cold" north and the empty city life, and a localized working-class code of desire-filled objects against the desired-but-defiling object—"money" (Fox 1992, 1993, 1994; K. Stewart 1993). In country music an inhabited, negating space of desire challenges the class codes of ideologically marked objects: Cadillacs versus pickup trucks, diamonds versus rhinestones, champagne in fancy glasses versus beer in the can, people who pay their bills by home computer versus those who get their coffee already ground.

In the hills they say people shouldn't try an' get above their raisin', and the status-coded landscape of "the cities" is displaced by an "Other" mode of reading things with an eye for the epiphany of particularity and the loose and shifting metonymic associations between things placed together in the course of a story or other social practice. The very practice of coding things as emblems of a fixed ideological order gives way to modes of address, encounter, and contestation and to evocations of motivating spaces of desire. The poetics of contingency and desire become a mode of address aimed doubly at an encompassing surround and the possibility of an "Other" future.

Listen, for instance, to the logic of encystment, graphic embodiment, encounter, and address in Nimrod Workman's version of the traditional song "The N and W Train," which he prefaced with a story about telling his son not to follow him into the mines.

> I remember a day that **my** boy
> he never **did** go in the coal mines
> but he followed me when he was a **little BIT** of a fella like 'at
> to the **coal mines!**
> There he **was!**
> I hadda take 'm **back home.**
> Oh, and I made him to **mind** along the **way,** you know, I'm a **huntin'** for **hounds.**
> But he was goin' in to the **coal mines!**
> Little **bit** of a fella!
> Ha.
> I begin to **thank** about that **boy.**
> I set that boy **down.**
> And I did, set him up on there.
> I said, "Thomas
> **Never**"—begin to try to **teach** him, **tell** him somethin', he wasn't old enough to go to **school**
> "Don't you **never**
> follow **me**
> into the **coal mines**
> or ever **thank** a stickin' your **head** in a coal mine.
> It's a **dog's life,"** that's what I told him.
> **"Go and get your education, son."**
> But that boy finished **school!**
> That boy never **did** go in the **coal mines!**

With this preface Nimrod embeds a discourse of opposition to work in the mines in the ideally intimate sociality of fathers and sons. Ironically, it is precisely this indexed intimacy that produces the effect Nimrod is trying to avoid—the intense continuity between generations in the camps that draws the young men into the mines after their fathers. They say mining gets in your blood. They say their fathers did it and their grandfathers before them. It is ironic again that Nimrod delivers the message to stay in school in the very tactile, poetically elaborated and positioned style that clashes with the routinized, universalizing modes of the schools themselves which the young people react to viscerally. They drop out of school to go back to the hollers almost as if it is a matter of cultural honor. In short, there is more going on here—more to attend to—than the referential message, and it is this "more" that people find themselves caught in and fashion a space out of.

As Nimrod moves into the song, he breaks into the shockingly discordant style of old timey singing that again indexes local difference—a slow, strained, disharmonious high-pitched wail.

When I raised my family in **Chattaroy holler**
coal train right **by my door**
now it's settin' in the yard all **rusty and empty**
and the N & W train don't **stop** here **no more**

When Thomas was a very small boy
set 'm up on my **knee**
Tommy go to school and learn your **numbers**
don't be an old coal miner like **me**

My children, they thought I's a **rich man**
had scrip to buy that **company store**
but I go down old Williamson town with my pocket all **empty**
Lord my **hair** as white as **snow**

That man that made that **big machin'ry**
he's takin' out all of our **coal**
he's leavin' children **hungry**
and he's robbin' your good land **pore**

I don't see what's wrong with our **govermint**
they won't protect my **place to me**
when Rockefeller gets all that **big machin'ry**
he's gonna turn it **over to me**
I'm gonna take it to the 'lantic ocean
I'm gonna dump it in the middle of the sea

The song, as Nimrod sings it, gives form to an immanent present by objectifying the state of thangs got down. He concretizes and literalizes metaphors to make them graphic and bodily and lingers on their impact in a lyrical poetics (the wrecks of progress embodied in the rusty train, the poor man with his pockets all empty, the worn-out worker with his hair as white as snow, the literalization of the idea that his son should not follow him into the mines in the command "Don't you never follow me into the coal mines or ever thank a stickin' your head in a coal mine"). He also weaves in the immanence of desire itself. In the dizzying simultaneity

of desire for the power of the "rich man" and the polemic against it, the
polarity of high and low states is first intensified in the image of the poverty-stricken broke down old man ashamed in front of his kids and then
transformed into a political critique of a world that is morally "got
down" ("leavin' children hungry and . . robbin' your good land pore").
The final image of expulsion and revolt gives form to the immanent
dream of escape and revenge:

> when Rockefeller gets all that **big machin'ry**
> he's gonna turn it over to **me**
> I'm gonna take it to the 'lantic ocean
> **I'm gonna dump it in the middle of the sea**

The song ends in the space of fiction and dream that is also the real
space of an "Other" epistemology in which wild talk performs a negation
of the order of things to expose the machinery of its construction as the
curtain is pulled to expose the machinations of the Wizard of Oz. In
heightened performances of semiotic action the logic of encounter in a
doubly occupied place is brought to the fore, pushed to extremes, and
made tactile in the search for the satisfaction that comes with fragmenting
a felt enclosure which excludes a local real.

The Sign of the Body

Forest Woods, who is illiterate, was getting out of his truck one day with
his arm bandaged and in a sling. When I asked him what happened to
him, he explained that he had had to go to court. I asked him what he
meant, and he explained that he had been lying awake at night for weeks
thinking about the day in court because he was afraid the judge would
ask him to read something and sign it.

> Well, then he's got me in between a **rock** and **hard place.**
> And that's just what **happened.**
> He told me, "Come up here and **sign** this if you read it and you thank it's **all
> right.**"
> But I was **ready** for him.
> I said, "**Judge,**" I said, "I'd like to **he'p** you but I cain't **do** it," said, "I broke my
> **glasses** and this here **arm's** busted up."
> Told that judge I needed **glasses!**
> Well, **that** way, the girl had to read it to me and I put down my **mark** [an X] like
> that was all I **could** do, **you know.**

Confronting his own very real inarticulateness in the face of the state
apparatus, Forest turned his body into a concrete sign in a field of
semiotic action. In a self-presentation both fully, and literally, caught in

the other's code and yet carving out a space of self-construction within and against it, he inscribed himself into a power relation that objectified and subjugated him. In becoming his disability, literally turning himself into a graphic allegory, he also demonstrated his ability as a subject to manipulate the signs of power and outsmart a shameless judge. Facing the possibility of his impersonal objectification as "an illiterate," he objectified his otherness as an "accident of history" (the broken arm, the lost glasses) and effected a shift in the politics of the transaction so that it was the judge, and not Forest, who found himself caught between a rock and a hard place.

In the camps, clerks in the stores or the post office take care to know who is illiterate or, failing that, they read the subtle cues that someone needs help in signing a check or reading a letter. It would be shameless to do otherwise. But in his official capacity as a functionary of the court the judge knows only to follow precise, universalized procedures; to the extent, then, that he could not be counted on to take account of the signs of Forest's illiteracy, he raised the terrifying specter of people being shameless, ignorant, or no account.

The local accounting of power reads it, as Foucault did, not as a homogeneous, abstract force operating from a place outside subjects but as an effect produced precisely through its investment in subjects and defined only by the points through which it passes. The subjected subject takes on the moves of power, "makes them play spontaneously upon himself . . . he becomes the principle of his own subjection" (Foucault 1979a:202–3), and yet it is through this embodiment that the effects of power become visible. "Power, after investing itself in the body, finds itself exposed to a counterattack in that same body" (Foucault 1980:56).

And so it is that Forest, feeling the dread of the court encounter, embodied his own "disability" in the face of power in a move that was at once self-objectifying and a plastic performance of lost glasses and bandaged limbs. On the one hand, he congealed his otherness into an object to be subjected to the examination of a normalizing gaze with the power to classify and judge (Foucault 1979a:184). On the other hand, he wore his signs of disability as an empty mask that expressed not his "identity" but a political performance lodged in the space of the gap between signifier and meaning and filled with double entendre. His signs gathered up the amorphous yet visceral effects of power in such a way that it would be impossible to read through them or scan past them.

Here, the body is not a simple embodiment of Otherness as the bourgeois imaginary would have it but a concrete performance of the self/other power relation itself. In performance, it becomes neither "subject" nor "object" but both and neither (Feldman 1991). As if as an object, it simulates the application of power on itself, but at the same time and in the same move it turns the effects of power into the fecund space of desire of a subject fashioning itself "within" and "against" the threat of subjection. The subjected body becomes a form of signification that has meaning in itself. By concretizing metaphor into matter it creates a space in which the subjected subject not only dwells but dwells on things and stages performative encounters. It becomes not merely a means for the expression of power and agency but the very ground in which a contingent agency can take root. As a subject of power/knowledge "power relations have an immediate hold upon it; they invest it, mark it, train it, torture it, force it to carry out tasks, to perform ceremonies, to emit signs" (Foucault 1979a:25). Yet in the same move it also exceeds itself and becomes a space of excess in which the physicality of cultural politics (vocality, tactility, touch, resonance) exceeds the rationalized clarity of "system" and transcendent understanding (Trinh 1991:44).

In the camps, where people are often enabled to stay in the hills through disability, and where they suffer the diseases of an economic and cultural double bind with nowhere to go and you can't stay here when "here" is constantly disappearing before your eyes, generalized states of the dizzy, the nerves, and spells of smothering become a kind of remembrance that brings forces and encounters to life concretely in the workings of the body.[2] "**Mr. Birdsong**, he's been bad with the nerves ever since his **boy got kilt**. He never could work no more his **nerves** was so **bad**." "**Miss Blevins**, she gits **the dizzy** where her baby died, **you know**." The body becomes an irreducible mediator of social forces—a gap, a space of friction, intensification, and proliferation.

People talk about themselves as bodies in ways that both concretize metaphors of social action into matter and clear a space in which anything can happen: "A body cain't **blow their nose** around here without somebody's got their **nose** in it"; "That **tickled** me"; "She got her **hind end up** about somethin'"; "A **body** would **think** . . . "; "If I stagger across any more of your **mail** I'll brang it on **by**"; "You haven't been **stirrin'** much, I **pecked** on the **door** but I couldn't **raise** you"; "**Buddy**, I'll tell you **what**, if **looks** could **kill** I'd a been chopped up in **little pieces**." The flood of daily stories amass graphic images of a world enacted from within the body and felt as impacts on the body, as when Sissy's sister's husband got run over by his truck when he was working on it and didn't put a chock under the wheel. He got pinned down by the arm and his head curled up onto his chest and Tammy heared him shouting and jumped in the truck to get her foot on the brakes and thought she was going to scream herself hoarse before anybody got there and she just **laid** on that horn and no one came for the longest time. Her parents heard them but thought it was next door. A neighbor down fishing in the creek dropped his hook and came running. She was so upset she couldn't get the truck started and it's a good thing she didn't because she probably would have tore his arm off tearing up the hill. Her brother-in-law, Sissy's husband, just happened to stop by and he pushed on that truck with his truck and there was so much strain on his truck that you could smell it burning for a long time after that.

The body becomes a *sign* in which dense metonymic associations link physical, mental, emotional, and social states.

> MADIE CLEMENTS: I told you about this boy having these **knots** took off his head didn't I?
> Well, the way she **talked** I thought it was just like four but she said it was twenty—said his head looked like a **patchwork quilt.**
> I figure it was **cancer**, she didn't **say** that but now she was **talkin'** about somebody else had somethin' like that and **he died** and I said well what did he **die** of and she said **cancer.**
> So I figure that maybe that's what he's **had.**
> She thought that maybe it had affected his **mind**—'cause she's never heard him talk like that before—he said he was goin' to sell his car and be like the **common man.**
> He just went in and had it done and then went back to classes two days later so I reckon he just didn't have time enough to **rest** and that maybe it didn't affect his **mind.**
> **Well,** now he **took off** and she went looking for him in Las Vegas. I'm kindly worried about her 'cause she left out of here and didn't know where she was **goin'.**
> I figure she'll have called Sammy today or she'll call me, **one.**

The self-as-body is constituted relationally in a series of loose metonymic associations of self and world enacted in a poetics of bodily effects. People *take to* some foods and not others, some people and not others, some *places* and not others; shows of affection are described as giving and getting *sugar.* Events and images aggravate people to action; they take spells—kids take spells of climbing, adults take spells of running their mouths. Sugar, tobacco, alcohol, coffee, and cigarettes dramatize the effects of things on the self as body and mark the relation of self and world as a movement of desire. Birthmarks on a baby are taken to be the direct effects of the pregnant mother's unfulfilled desire, so a woman who craves beets or hamburgers will have a baby born with the *mark* of a beet or a hamburger on it. The idea of using discriminating judgment for good nutrition is viewed with suspicion.

> You know they say there's all this **salt** in things, I went and looked on the cans and it doesn't even **say salt**, it says "**sodium**" and if you didn't know to **look for it** you'd never **know.**
> So why do they put "**sodium**" on the can?

I don't see how it'll make no **difference** not eatin' **salt.**
If somebody **wants** something they ought to just go on and **eat it,** no sense makin' a federal **case** out of it.
And kids want **pop.**
They'll just get it theirselves anyway or they'll just want it all the time where they cain't **have it, you know.**

Rather than encode the body in a medicalized discourse of good and bad influences, they embed it in a poetics of daily pains, eccentric markings, and monumental peculiarities that open onto the space of a social imaginary. The body is not incorporated into the self as inert substance or bodily "self image" but retains an affecting agency of its own.

They describe the body itself as an "Other" that can be seen, felt, and encountered. The body, like the hills, becomes a collection of *places* that *remember* events, haunt people, and take on a life of their own. Medical discourse pales in comparison to the drama of encountered effects.

DWIGHT LILLY: That place in my back grabbed a **holt** a me and pulled me down on the **floor.**
I thought I'd like to **never** got **back up.**

DREAMA BLEVINS: Well, I had that **leg** there to give me some **trouble.**
I cain't do nothin' **with** it.

BUD HALSEY: I got me this **place** right inside here, hit's been a **workin'** on me and hit just won't **quit, buddy.**
Well, I went down to the doctor and she give me some **pills** for the blood.
I said honey it ain't the **blood** that's aggravatin' me, it's this **place.**
So she said take them **pills.**
I said well, all right, and I took one, and it didn't do nothin' **for** me.
So I **quit** it.
But now that place **works** on me 'til I cain't **sleep** and I cain't **eat,**
buddy I mean I cain' even git out 'n **fish.**
You **know** I got trouble when I cain't git out an' **fish.**

JUSTICE ACRES: I had me a **big** ole knot in this here **leg** an' hit would come on in the **night.**
I'd git in the **bed,** and git ready to go to **sleep,** and that **place,**
hit'd **start up** sure as I **laid down.**
Well, I git up and **work it out,**
sometimes it might take me half the **night.**
And then I git in the bed and the **rooster** starts in.
Next night, buddy, hit's the **same thang.**
Well, hit's just like it sleeps all day and **sets in workin'** of a night.
Hit's the aggravatinest thang ever **was.**

LACY WOODS: Well doc gimme some **pills** for that there **place** in my chest
where I tuk the **cold.**
It's what they call "**erythromycin**"
and I tuk it but it didn't do me no **good.**
And that **nurse** she's got down **there,**
b'lieve it's the one they call **Sue,**
she called me up on the **telephone,**
said, "Are you a **takin' that pill?**"
I said, "**Yeah, I took** that **pill,** but it didn't **do nothin'.**"
She said, "**Well,** are you still **takin'** it?"
I said, "No, I **quit** it."
She said, "Well you've got to keep on **takin'** it."
I said, "Well, all right, honey," and I kep' on with them pills 'til they was gone
and by that time that place had done **quit.**
So that nurse, she called me back **up again.**
She says, "Well, did you **take** 'm like I **told** you?"
I said, "**Yes mam, I sure did.**"
"**Well,**" she said, "**did they work?**"
I said, "Well, I don't **know.**"
She said, "What do you **mean,**" and she asked me was I **still sick?**
I told her, "**No mam,** I feel **fine** and that **place** does too."
But you cain't say if its the pills worked on the **place** or the place worked on the
pills, that's the way I look at it.
Might be the **place** just kindly worked itself **out.**
But I said, "I thank you for **askin'.**"
I thought that was **awful** nice of her to call what with them so **busy** an' all.

The body takes on a life of its own in the drama of an encounter with
it. Riley Meadows has always pulled his teeth out himself. Whenever one
would hurt him twice he'd pull it out. Some he pulled out himself, some
he used a string. And no, it didn't hurt. You just do it and go on. He still
has quite a few of his teeth in his head. You set your mind to it and stick
to it. Don't feel sorry for yourself, wantin' to be babied. Miss Henson
says her son Jack, who is confined to his bed, has a place on his belly
where it ruptured when he was born, it ain't like you and me. One time
he had sores all over his chest. She took and used an old remedy her
mother used on them when she was a kid because they never ran to no
doctors and didn't take stuff like they do now. They went barefoot and
they'd get sores all over their feet. And they'd wrap them in old bedsheets
but clean—that was the time when things were clean. And they put a salve
with sulphur—it come in a box. She took some of that sulphur and mixed
it with a pound of lard and spread it all over Bill's chest and told him
don't tell me it smells because I'm leavin' it on you. She put it on and left

it for a few days and those sores were gone, you might not believe me but they were. Noxious-smelling salves made with garlic and vinegar can be used to draw out an infection, like attracting like. "Heart leaves" can be chewed to soften the heart; "shame weed" or "sensitive plant" will shame a hardheaded fool. The poison of tobacco can kill poison in the system. A fever should be "drawn out" with heat compresses; putting something cold on a burn or a fever will only force the heat in. They say when a limb is severed you can bury the limb deep in the ground to stop the stump from aching. Of course most people say all that is just superstition but yet, they say, that's not to say there's not a truth in it.

It is as if the felt friction of bodily events could enact the conflictual nature of desire itself. Desires and social conflicts are written onto the body and can be read out again as *signs* of a force encountered. Debbie still shudders at the thought of her first husband's dirty hands when he got home from his work as a mechanic—"him pawin' at me." Then she says she got worms and went after him to see how he liked it. Bud says he just took a notion to quit tobacco one day and he put it down on the table right here and never did touch it again. "It set there for the longest time right here on this table and I never did thank about it, never wanted it again. That was it." Ruby says she was always too backward to go to the dentist so she lost all her teeth. And this moves into talk about the day she went to the beach with her daughters and grandchildren and rolled up her pants because it was such a pretty day at the lake and it just felt so good. And you should've **seen** them girls at the lake with nothin' on but them little skimpy bathing suits, well not hardly **nothin'** at all. And she sat there the whole afternoon and it was cool on the lake. And she got home and started itching and she put on stockings and went to church and by the time it was over she just couldn't stand the burning anymore, up all night, went to the doctor next day and she told her she had third-degree burns. She gave her salve and right after that was when the trouble (endometriosis) started in and it's been months. The doctor did things to her (a physical exam and a Pap smear)—"Oh! I liked to **died! I hate** that. I just absolutely cain't **stand** it."

When the body becomes a site of a social imaginary, it exceeds the image of a bounded, closed unit and takes on the imagery that Bakhtin (1968) identified as grotesque realism. There is a fascination with the transgressed boundaries of things "inner" and "outer." People who are ugly on the outside might be beautiful within. Ecstatic states perform inner transformation through outer *signs*. They say people acting shameless are just showin' theirself. Schisms, feuds, and church revivals are all imaged as a bursting out that results from overcrowding, people being "too close" or a *confusion* of elements. Illnesses work their way out. Parents threaten to "beat the fire out of" disobedient children. The blue-black scars on miners' faces are said to be from where the coal has penetrated the body and is working its way back out. Bud remembers a time when he was so sick that throwing up went past throwing up anything to where he started to throw hisself up—that lava that people have inside them come up. Patty's palms are still red from that time when she got shocked touching that stove.

Seemingly discrete objects and the worlds of thought, action, and body merge in a mess of unified effects. Kinship lines are seen as a *mess* of interrelations, and cooking centers on the pleasures of mixing up a *mess* of greens, a *mess* of beans, a *mess* of fried chicken and biscuits. Grease or gravy serves as a general medium that smothers boundaries to make a whole; biscuits and eggs are covered in it, favored dishes of chicken-and-dumplings and berry cobbler are made by dropping uncooked biscuit dough in a soup of shredded chicken or berries; salad is made by pouring hot grease over lettuce to wilt it. The pleasure of cooking centers on the excitement of mixed concoctions: upside-down cakes, cakes made by filling hollowed centers with sweet liquids, friendship cakes made by adding cans of mixed fruits into a souring mash every few days for six weeks and then saving some of the mash back from the cake to pass it on to friends.

In the doubly occupied place of the hills, then, the body does not easily lend itself to the internalized discipline of the order of things but stands as complex *sign* and site of encounter. Far from being a map easily read, or inert matter that can be easily incorporated into a totalizing schema of rigidly bounded "subjects" and "objects," it asserts a space of encounter with things that are "Other" yet emerge from within, graphically visible yet mysterious, inescapably felt yet transient, stultifying yet drifting in the slippage of a gap between sign and meaning.

Hollie Smith's Encounter

One day I took Hollie Smith—a member of the worst *trash* family up Devil's Fork holler—to the county Occupational Rehabilitation Center "to see about gettin' a job." When I picked him up he didn't want to go, although he was dressed up for it in black pants, white shirt, and borrowed black shoes with pointed toes that he had shined to a fine gloss. On the ride in he was tense and quiet, and when we got there he paced up and down the tiny waiting room until a counselor called him into his office. In a few minutes the counselor asked me to come in too. I could see Hollie standing in there, staring down at the shiny pointed tips of his shoes. So

I went in and stood next to him, leaving the two clients' chairs vacant in front of us while the counselor went back to his desk.

The counselor asked me how much schooling Hollie had had, whether he could read and write, whether he had a car, whether there was anything wrong with him that prevented him from working, and whether he had tried to find work. Hollie acted as if he didn't understand the questions—he said he couldn't "hear" the man—and he would turn to me to discuss what the answer might be, in-filling the space of interrogation with a sense of the ongoing encounter of discourses and ways. Well, he said, he could read some, but not so you'd say he could read; he had a car and drove because he put it together and that was what he wanted a job at—fixing cars—but he didn't have an *operator's* (i.e., a driver's license) for the hardtop because he took fits. He described his spreading graveyard of junked trucks and offered a graphically grotesque account of a fit he had had when he was driving his mother to the hospital "where she was all swole up black." When the fit hit, he was swerving all over the road, biting his tongue, flapping his arms, blood everywhere.

The interview went on and on, excruciatingly. The counselor—a very nice man—was trying to figure out a way to help Hollie in his Real Circumstances. But his direct, instrumental questions enclosed Hollie in a finished symbolic order of personal and cultural deficiencies that read like a textbook on "Appalachian culture"—he lacked schooling, he lacked money, he lacked skill, and in the end he lacked the will (see, for instance, Ball 1968; Gazaway 1969; Looff 1971; Weller 1965).

The counselor suggested Hollie go to a live-in occupational training center about an hour and a half away so that he could be certified to be an auto mechanic. In response Hollie shifted his discourse into two precise local modes that might fit the situation at hand—the discourse of demanding help from more powerful others and the common performative discourse of men's trading, or making a deal. He said he was willing to "go along" with the man if he would help him, and then he began to haggle over the details of what he would have to do. Finally, when it became clear that Hollie would have to stay at the training center, at least during the week, for a few months, Hollie withdrew from the deal saying he thanked the man for his help but he could not be away from the holler like that, away from his mommy and daddy. It was time to go.

The counselor did not understand and suggested several other occupational placements that were closer, though they were not for auto mechanics. Hollie discussed them with him, again haggling over the details and literally trying to "figure out" the problem of getting from one *place* to the other. One of the training centers was in a nearby town where a man Hollie knew worked. Maybe he could hitch a ride with him. He knew someone who worked at another place the counselor suggested—a work shelter for the disabled. He liked this guy all right. Finally Hollie just said, "**Well**, maybe someday I might get to come back and see if you have anything **for** me," and we left.

Looking back, I can see how as the interview progressed, the two interpretive spaces had divided and drawn further apart. The counselor's language had become more instrumental and problem-solving—more removed from the logic of encounter itself—while Hollie's mired itself in the encounter, became more entrenched in the localizing strategies of encystment, immanence, encounter, and excess. Like Forest, Hollie had "become" his Otherness in the course of the encounter with the professional, embodying his "white trash" status with his own words and manners—he was "backward," refusing to leave the holler and his mommy and daddy, he was illiterate, he took fits, he told graphic, grotesque stories, refusing to stick to the simple questions at hand. Far from incorporating Hollie into the center, the counselor's instrumentalism had only further encysted him in his local, marginalized ways.

When it was all over, the counselor's interpretation of the encounter was enclosed in systematic, analytical, universalized principles—why didn't Hollie want to better himself? why doesn't he listen to reason? In the psychological jargon, he embodied the infamous Appalachian "separation anxiety" (Looff 1971). But Hollie's interpretation of the encounter took an "Other" direction. He drifted into the philosophical, the figurative, the grotesquely graphic. The counselor became something like a mythological figure and the encounter itself haunted him as a figured event. He set about re-membering it. He repeated fragments of it, salvaging images to study on and make something **of**.

The ride home in the car was passed in a brooding silence broken only by Hollie's occasional lyrical ruminations on fragments of the encounter itself:

I guess that **place** he's talkin' 'bout would have to
be way up **yonder** beyond **Charleston**, wouldn't you? . . .

and

Man says you got to have **papers** to fix a car. I ain't never heared that b'fore.

and

And that man, he had one **good** eye and one **glass**, a pale **blue** eye. . . . [I hadn't noticed anything different about the man's eyes.]

When we got back to the holler, Hollie climbed out of the car, thanking me "kindly" for my "trouble," and disappeared into the vast graveyard of dismembered trucks and cars and other trash that surrounds the family's cluster of shacks. Later I saw him still sitting on a chair out in the middle of it.

Like Forest, then, Hollie turned the "routine examination" into a heightened experience—a performance of encounter. Like Nimrod, Sissy, and Forest, he reopened the space of encounter by tracking through remembered events for their faults and fissures. Like the others, he read the encounter in a way that did not discover a direct referent, or a meaning, but if anything made it harder to read through things by stretching the length of perception into a caesura in which to study on thangs. He embodied his position relative to the professional with graphic images of his attachment to the holler, his unruly body, his collection of trashed machines. Like the others, he tried to make something of the encounter and this meant decomposing the finished texts of an encompassing other—the texts of the company with the big machinery, the shameless man with the lawn that nobody can walk on, the shameless judge, the examining counselor—into mythic figures and allegories on which the mind can stare itself out. It meant creating gaps and fashioning them into room to maneuver. It meant fragmenting the picture-perfect and piling up fragments as a graphic surround and a contingent position from which to speak. It meant unsettling consciousness and sending it backward and forward through cultural forms and remnants, probing for signs of life.

This took some vigilance—some care to *place* people and to *re-member* things and a proliferation of cultural ways. Like the others, Hollie used culturally precise discourses to *place* himself: Sissy used the complex discourses of neighborliness, shamelessness, and back talk embodied in the graphics of tended lawns covered with cement and boundaries disrupted by an uncontained sociality; Nimrod used a fatherly "teaching" discourse and an activist political rhetoric embodied in the graphic figures of a father with a son on his knee and the machinery of the corporation thrown into the middle of the sea; Forest used the old men's lying discourse, trickery, and joking parody embodied in a parodic, self-signifying body; Hollie used a subordinate's demand for patronage, trading discourse, and the dissociative graphic images of *talk* from way up the holler embodied in a self incapable of assimilation and at home in a world of dismembered things.

All of this, we could say, is talk that inspires the production of fragments and holds open a sense of uncontained meaningfulness or a space of excess and desire. We could say that it bespeaks the position of a subjected subject caught on the side of the road and readied for encounters with a world that surrounds. We could say that it creates a symbolic lacuna which permits a space for poetic reconstruction and expands out beyond the boundaries of hegemonic enclosures. We could say that through the logic of encounter such talk becomes an aperture into an "Other" more local and contingent realm that fashions identities fixed by power relations into a struggle of forces filled with moments of emergence, proliferation, and reversal.

Afterthought

I was reminded of Hollie's inability to "hear" the counselor a couple of years later in the middle of a tense phone call with a man I had known to talk to on the street when I was doing fieldwork. I had called him to ask whether he knew whom I might talk to about something I was wondering about. He, like Hollie, was very nervous, hesitating to speak at all. He kept saying he couldn't *place* me and he finally went to turn off the television, saying he couldn't "hear." When he came back I told him what kind of car I drove, and with that he went into a fast flood of talk—"**Oh, yeah,** I know **you,** you had that little rusty **brown car** that Smith boy tried to paint for you. I heared about that time you **let it git away from you** down at the **'Migo post office** an' chased it **clear across the road,** half in and half out. Like to **killed yourself** . . ." He went on like this for a while with several other parodic stories that objectified me as the owner of a strange little brown car which always seemed to be trying to get away from me. Then he apologized for not knowing me. "I thought you was one a them **agencies.**"

6

The Space of the Sign

IMAGINE SOCIALITY in the camps and hollers as an act of giving and reading *signs*. Picture how neighbors literally look out for one another, how one neighbor's act is another's story, how what one does will be seen and what one sees is not just what meets the eye but a story enacted, how everything is noticed but don't nobody say nothin' **to** 'm. How local ways of talkin' and ways of doin' people emerge in the gaps of a gaping sociality that catches every act and word in a web of half-read signs of shifting connections and disconnections.

> DOVIE WALKER: Never a dull moment 'round this place, worse than a **soap opera, honey.**
> I could write a **book** about it.

Picture a sociality fashioned out of a gap between event and representation, an act and a sight overseen, an intention and a voice overheard. How, in the order of signs, "reality" is left always already mediated by the socially contingent, and the "self" is always already located in the textual roles of narrator, audience, and object of narration. How social, aesthetic, and ideological concerns can be culled into a sight or a sound, a momentary presence or absence, how a sight read as a *sign* can be culled into a lyric image that overwhelms and haunts or fashioned into an accusation left unvoiced but gathering force at every new sign of trouble.

Imagine how everything depends on talk that is nothin' but just talk is all, and yet it makes things happen, sets things in motion, pushes people together and apart, catches them up in one situation and then another. Imagine how, in such a space, signs are not just reflective but productive, not just transparent mirrors of an extraverbal "real" but acts and situations that are themselves in-filled with the density of a "written" and read sociality (Volosinov 1976, 1986). Imagine what happens when discourse is socially constructed and the social itself is discursively constructed and read as a *sign*.

Picture the social weight of such signs and the complex social logic of their meaning. Picture how they undo the nominative function of language, displacing the illusion of a true or fixed referent in the dense fabulation of social slights and desires. Picture, for instance, the time that a Graham girl was bitten by a dog while she was playing in the Meadowses' yard. The Grahams talked about suing the Meadowses even though it wasn't their dog, and this set the others to talking: why would the Grahams want to sue? Sissy said Linda had always been awful nice to talk to but then there was the time when she had blamed Buddy for what her son Shawn had done. Lendo Polk couldn't understand it because he had always thought that Bobby Graham was awful neighborly like the time he had helped Fred Wall make his truck payment when he was going to lose it. There was a consensus that "people's got sue crazy anymore," and everyone stopped letting other kids play in their yards out of fear that they too would be sued—"You cain't tell what might happen." But this only created more trouble in the camp as signs of broken sociality proliferated in angry reactions to people's keeping the kids out of their yards.

Finally Lacy Forest announced that he had heard that "by law" if you had a NO TRESPASSING sign on your porch you couldn't be sued. So everyone went to the store in Beckley to get the official kind of sign. Neighbors brought back multiple copies and put them up for those too old or sick or poor to get out and get their own. Then everyone called everyone else to explain that the sign did not mean them. In the end, every porch and fence (except for those of the isolated shameless who don't care) had a bright NO TRESPASSING, KEEP OFF sign, and people visited together, sitting underneath the NO TRESPASSING signs, looking out.

Here sociality lies caught in the exchange of signs and truth lies emergent in the contingency of retellings. My own account, too, mimics the logic of retelling. I heard of the event, which happened shortly after I left the field, from Betsy, who told me the stories that she had heard as they unfolded over the course of several weeks. I know only what I heard through what she heard. The local retellings begin in the particulars of who said what to whom, gather to accusations, and disperse again in the flurry of countervailing signs of sociality. Mine gathers to the ironic sensibility of NO TRESPASSING signs folded into social uses. The story of signs is, for me, a story about the complex conjunctions and disjunctions of signs and their meanings. The process of "reading" such signs, then, depends not on the picture-perfect fusion of sign and referent in the humanist symbol but on a close tracking of what signs do and how they come into play.

The Social Semiotics of Signs

Picture how, in the gaping sociality of signs, even the process of naming things does not so much fix a sign to a referent but marks the space of a gap between a *real name* and *what we call it*. Names trace the social

26. House with NO TRESPASSING sign, Amigo. Photograph © Harriette Hartigan, Artemis.

densities of naming itself as an act caught in local ways of seeing, acting, and talk, and mark the space of the mediation of a cultural real in social and aesthetic forms.

Amigo, Red Jacket, Ruin, Helen, Odd, Viper, Black Eagle, Iroquois, Hard Shell, Winding Gulf, War, East Gulf, Coal City, Decoy, Prosperity, Cook Town, Corinne, Lillybrook, Josephine, Paw Paw, Red Star, Twilight, Quicksand. Picture how the names of the camps and places stand as signs of a written landscape and a doubly occupied place. Some, they say, were named after mines (Amigo, East Gulf) and coal operators' wives (Helen, Corinne, Josephine). Others remember the old family places (Walkertown Mountain, Lilly Mountain, Tommy Creek) or refer iconically to shapes and qualities of the landscape and its inhabitants (Winding Gulf, Beard's Branch, Soak Creek, Lick Branch, Devil's Fork holler). Others bear religious referent (Ruin, Viper, Hard Shell, Egeria, Beulah Flats). Others are whimsical, eccentric, and othering (Amigo, Iroquois, Red Jacket, Black Eagle) or make social comment (War, Quicksand).

The *real name* of "Cook Town" is "Ury" and some people call it "Division." Why the three different names? "I don't have no ideal. They just started in callin' it by Division, but most people always called it by Cook Town. But now its real name is Ury." In the marked slippage between a real name and what we call it, names become just names just as talk becomes just talk, and they are subject to the same foolin' with things. Once, for instance, I heard that Odd got its name in the sixties when the U.S. Postal Service required that every place with a post office have a name. They say a handful of people got together to think up a name, and finally one man, they say, said it was an "odd" place like an odd sock or an odd-sized foot that fit no shoe. And so, they say, they just started in calling it Odd and the post office bears a sign—ODD, WEST VIRGINIA. Another place is just called Nameless.

Even people's real names refer to a moment of inventiveness or poetic license. In the older generation, siblings of the same two parents sometimes have two or three different surnames that may or may not match either of the parents' surnames. They claim only a vague sense of the origin at best: "Well, they just give me the name Johnson, I b'lieve that might a been mommy's **maw maw's** [grandmother's] name, but now I **don't know**" or "Well, I'm a Graham, it's just what they called me is all. But now **Sissy's** a **Lilly** and **Dwayne's** a **Lilly** and all the rest of 'm are **Hensons** like daddy. But they call me a Graham." Picture how women's names mark the poetic license of association with flowers, songs, famous country singers, months, days of the week, jewels, and places: Rose, Pansy, Violet, Daisy, Flossie, Opal, Ruby, Jewel, Pearl, Ivory, Dreama, Crystal (after Crystal Gayle), Tammy (after Tammy Wynette), Tanya (after Tanya Tucker), Reba (after Reba McEntire), Tuesday, Wednesday, Thursday, April, May, June, Stella, Dovie, Dallas, Dixie, Georgia, Easter, Beulah, Melody. Picture how men's names mimic character traits or refer to the odd-sounding and eccentric: Justice, Creed, Clownie, Forest, Lacy, Hersie, Dewey, Jasper, Otis, Curnal, Carlee, Harley, Garland, Arlie, Dewayne, Shelby, Arnette, Arbutus, Troy, Romie, Elmo, Vergie, Cleo, Erskell, Lendo, Okey.

Nicknames proliferate in the face of odd sights and slips of the tongue: Peanut, Cricket, Buckethead, Sonny, Bear, Bubba, Fruitbat, Tomato Cup, Shortbread, Catfish, Dusty, Dixie, Jinx.

> ME: Why do you call him **Bear?**
> FLOSSIE ANDERSON: Honey, I don't **know.**
> ME: Is it because he **looks** like a **bear** or **acts** like one?
> FLOSSIE: **Oh no!** It's just what we **call** him is all.

People pressed for an explanation of a name *remember* the event of the naming itself.

> ME: How did he get to be called Jackrabbit?
> VERGIE GILLESPIE: Well, they say when he was a **boy,** and one day they had a fire at old **Miss Gaskill's,** they say he went into the burnin' house and the flames and they thought sure he was **lost.** But after a while he come **out.**
> And Carlee Adkins, he was standin' out th' alley watchin', you know, and when he seen him come out, hit **come** to him to call him **Jackrabbit.**
> ME: Why was that? Was that because he **looked** like a Jackrabbit, or . . .
> VERGIE: I don't have no **ideal,** honey, hit just **come** to him is all I reckon . . . well, people just picked it up and that's what we've always **called** him. They're awful **bad** to **do** that.

Picture, then, how names just happen, just as *thangs happen,* or how they emerge with a slip of the tongue that sticks, how the link between a name and an event or between one thing and another is left open or forgotten entirely so that a name becomes the site of a shifting commentary. Picture how names pick up associations so that the local becomes visible in the gap of naming. How everyone knows that the "dogwood" tree has a "real" (scientific) name and that "dogwood" is just what we call it, and how they also call it "sarvice" because it is the first thing to flower in the spring: "It's where used to the preachers would come at the first thaw to bury the dead and that was the first service of the year."

Picture the proliferation of unspecified associations when people read things as signs of fleeting, half-visible associations that dwell in the corners of the mind, or rest in the underbellies of thoughts only to show themselves as if by accident when things happen. Imagine, on the one hand, a practice that insists that elements hidden in objects and scenes come forth as mysterious *signs* that can be read. And, on the other hand, picture a reading based on mimetic resemblances in a semantic mirage of accidental collisions that set off strange correspondences and analogies in the space of the gap. Picture how things seem to work on each other and how associations that somehow show themselves remain mysterious and uncanny as the social act of interpretation burrows into the cryptic language of half-known signs. Remember how a baby is born with the *sign* of a beet or a hamburger because his or her mother craved it in pregnancy. How a man's truck shows the signs of accidents and the act of foolin' with things in the look of scrapes and dents and the sound of moving parts. How Miss Banks's canned goods have that special quality because she's special and Jewel Birdsong's cabbage always sours because the woman is sour.

Strange things happen in gardens where people plant and harvest by the *signs*. Two neighbors using the same seeds produce one very good and one very bad crop of beets. One person's potatoes come up well but his broccoli does poorly while someone else has the best broccoli ever but her potato mounds, when she goes to dig them up, are empty. Lou Acres had a four-foot zucchini; one whole row of my yellow squash came up as a half-breed squash-gourd, and the neighbors all came over to see for themselves (one claimed that when he cooked one in safflower oil and bacon fat it filled and turned soft and tasted like butter beans). Planting by the signs adds an uncanny, associative dimension to the bare facts of soil, seed, and weather and the vagaries of chance. Some say plants that grow down (potatoes, beets, carrots) should be planted on the dark side of the moon (when the moon is on the wane) and when the stars are in the feet.[1] Some say seeds planted when the stars are in the bowels will rot and vegetables sown next to flowers will "bloom theirselves to death."

Yet planting by the signs is not a matter of belief in the direct effects of things written in the stars but a matter of reading cryptic traces of patterns and parallels discovered in experimental activities. Miss Cox says she plants in the head for a good head of lettuce and don't prune back on your apple trees in the full moon because it will draw the sap right out of them. Miss McKinney never plants her potatoes when the signs are in the feet because when she did one year her potatoes came out covered with toes. Bud Halsey always prunes his orchard in the middle of a moonless night in October. Miss Cox has it from her mother, who has "seen it," that only men can transplant rambling roses (because men are wont to ramble) and a menstruating woman should be careful not to step over weak or newly transplanted plants—it might kill them, you don't know.

The *signs*, then, are not an explanatory order but a way of reading likenesses, frictions, and antipathies. They point to an otherness in the everyday, a gap in which strange associations remain possible. The logic of *signs*—whether social, astrological, or mystical—opens the question of signification to include not only the symbolic aspect of the sign with its reference to culturally conventional meaning but also the indexical and iconic aspects of the sign that, like sheer markers of signification itself, give signs the power to mimic or point to an association regardless of their message or their meaning in a cultural order of things (Peirce 1974; Feld 1988; Urban 1988). Icons and indexes take on a power of their own as *signs* waiting to happen or vibrant half-associations waiting for completion. Some people, they say, are just superstitious. Because death always seems to come in threes, one death can be taken as a *sign* of two more to come. Because graves are often dug under a pine tree, a pine tree without a grave can be taken as a *sign* that someone will die; to plant a pine tree in your yard is to invite the death of a family member.

Some people will claim to have had an omen at a friend's death—the vision of his car driving up the road by itself and three days later they found out he had died at just that moment, the vision of an old friend's face at the window trying to say something and come to find out she had just died. Others try to keep a check on loose tongues that express a dangerous *feeling*. When the Blevinses were driving back from a visit with relations in Ohio, Dreama said she had a feeling that the truck would break down. Bud told her, "Hush up Dreama," but it was too late, they already had a flat tire. Sissy's sister Julie was spotting in the third month of her pregnancy. Sissy wanted to tell her to go to bed for the rest of the pregnancy because she, too, had spotted in her third month and finally miscarried. But she was afraid to say anything for fear that something might happen. When Cassie Graham was giving birth to her first child, she cursed repeatedly—"OH GOD, OH GOD"—and her husband, flinching with each curse, kept shouting, "Cassie don't **say** that, you'll hurt that **baby**," but nothing happened.

Located always in the space of a gap, *signs* can suggest association but they can also deflect the dream of certainty. Names lodged as signs follow the logic of association and its diffusion. If kinship names can stand as a *sign* of traits inherited in the blood and festering through close association, nicknames can be used to diffuse stultifying identifications into shifting associations with things that happen. If nicknames themselves "stick," they can be displaced with new nicknames or their origins can be disremembered or disclaimed with a reference to the arbitrary order of naming itself—hit's just what we call it is all. The lines of association grow loose and uncanny, half-known and lingering as a *feeling*, and yet that is their power.

In the end, both real names and nicknames can be displaced by generalized modes of address signaling kinship, humor, and respect; all the women are called "Sissy" or "granny" or "Miss" or "Mam" and all the men are called "Bud" or "Sonny" or "Cuz" so that the only way to figure which "Bud" or "Sissy" someone is talking about is to scan for contextualizing social signs. Talk is peppered with hyperfamiliar generalized modes of address like "honey" and "buddy."

VERLEY EPPS: **Honey,** I'll tell you, I come down that there **hill** fast as anyone, beast or man, has ever done an' I'll a tell ya **one** thang, **buddy,** I ain't a **never** goin' back up hit, **honey.**

At times, people will claim they cannot remember names at all. Al Maxwell, an African-American retired miner, lived in an all-black holler tucked way out in the hills around the remains of a worked-out mine. He and his five brothers were all big men with a reputation for standing up for themselves and for helping others. He and his wife Dovie had both been active in Community Action and various miners' movements, and they used their living room as a gathering place for people from over the hills.

AL MAXWELL: **Well,** a name don't **mean** nothin', not no more than the color of a man's **skin** or what he had for **breakfast.**

Al just calls everyone "shorty" or "curly" or "slim," and anyone who shows up at his door will be met with a rush of rhetorical informality.

AL: Well, **hello there, shorty,** how you **doin'** today. I don't know your **name** but I seen your **face.**
DOVIE: **Girl,** don't you **take** them **shoes** off, we don't **do** that here, just **come on in** if you're a **comin'.**

Signs of Sociality

Picture, then, how people notice everything in the mode of not watching. How windows are kept veiled by thin white curtains through which the "half language of appearances" (Berger 1982) can be overseen or noticed out of the corner of the eye.

Picture how people scan appearances for signs of God knows what. How, at the first sight of each other in the morning they search for signs of things that happened in the night. Dark circles under the eyes stand as a sign of troubled sleep but the others don't say nothin' to 'm. Aches or tired muscles may refer back to dreams of having been chased or to a fight in the night. Bud and Sissy's argument at 2 A.M. will have been overheard

27. Alfred Guerrant in his living room, Winding Gulf.
Photograph © Em Herzstein.

but don't say nothin' to 'm. Miss Cadle had her kitchen light on at 2 A.M. where she couldn't sleep and sat up with a pot of coffee and a pack of cigarettes; the young women whose husbands are on hoot owl were up visiting or cleaning house all hours of the night; Bud Henson fell asleep on the couch again with the blue lights of the TV flickering through the windows where the sound helps him sleep.

Idioms of "acting," "seeing," and "talk" intertwine in the mutual self-constitution of the one who acts and the other who sees and remembers and makes something of thangs in a fluid space of continuous engagement and encounter. First thing in the morning people stick their heads out to show theirself, sit on the stoops to drink their coffee, go to the post office to get their mail, and stop to speak to those they meet. Those who fail to show will be noticed and those who fail to speak to people will be marked as *no account*. The men stop to talk in their trucks on their way out to work, and the women sweep the dirt out the kitchen door or hang their newly washed rugs to dry on the line to show that they're starting the day off right. The morning is a flurry of phone calls and short visits to borrow or return things or just to see about someone: "Let me get your screwdriver while I'm **thankin'** about it." . . . "Mommy needs an egg because she's making a cake." . . . "Mommy says thank you for the egg and she hates to bother you but can you give her half a cup sugar." . . . "Mommy says give you this egg where she got one from Sissy [her sister]."

Picture the fundamental sociality of a self constituted in the act of giving and reading *signs*. A visit begins and ends in a ritual display of signs of social accountability. Entering the kitchen, the visitor will stand on the mat or try to take off her shoes, claiming to be covered with mud, while the host begins a loud banter.

> ROSE BLEVINS: **Hey, girl! Don't** you take them thangs off! **Who** do you **thank** you **are?** This place is a **mess.**
>
> ZINNY MASON: **Well,** I smelled somethin' **cookin'** over here, said **well** looks like Sissy finally decided to try and **feed** somebody, said **well,** I'll just go on over and **git** me some.
>
> ROSE: Well **whatsa**matter with you, don't that old man **feed** you none?
>
> ZINNY: Oh, **yeah,** he's a **real** big help, now if he could find the **stove** he'd be doin' all right. [Laughing.]
>
> ROSE: **Well,** set yourself **down** if you can find a **place** in this **mess.** Will you take some **coffee?**
>
> ZINNY: Well, don't **care** if I **do,** Sissy.

If the visit is a long one, it will settle into a rhythm between the slow heavy talk of worries and tragedies and the light banter of *just talk*. But at the end of the visit talk will rise again to a quick recital of signs even between people who visit every day.

HOST: Well, where you runnin' off to s' soon?

[The visitor mumbles something about things to do and people who are "countin' on me."]

HOST: Well, come and stay all night with me.

VISITOR: Well, I just might do that, you're not careful.

HOST: Well, y'all come back now, hear? Don't be a stranger.

Picture how, in the countervailing responsibilities to notice and remember without sticking your nose in, to signify people without fixing them in a finished identity, noticing grows automatic and embeds itself in intermeshed ways of acting, seeing, and talk. November 3, 1981. Second visit to see Tammy Blevins. The living room was dark, curtains drawn, and the television loud (a soap opera). Tammy and her sister Rose were sitting on the couch talking; kids tugged at them and dogs ran in and out barking. The visit floated in a rhythm of continuous action (getting coffee, smoking cigarettes, answering the phone, passing around photographs, checking the fire, watching the beans), noticing (the kids, the TV, passing cars), and talk (stories of recent tragedies and odd behavior, yelling threats of a beating to the kids). At a lull in the talk they turned to a detailed discussion of an ad for a gospel sing that had come over the radio in the kitchen while they were talking of other things. I had not even noticed that the radio was on, but they had caught the time and place and were arguing over the name of one of the singing groups that would be there. Rose remembered a story she had heard about a young girl who followed a Christian band from place to place to her eventual ruin. Christian or sinner, you would think a girl would know better than that. Then, standing at the door, I noticed a familiar truck go by. Assuming that Tammy and Rose could not have seen it from where they were sitting, I asked them if they knew who had a red Chevy with a beat-up fender. Looking blank and uncomfortable, they said they had no *ideal*. I said I just wondered because I had just seen it go by.

TAMMY: Oh that's Tommy Shrewsbury. I thought you meant somebody else, I couldn't thank who else has a truck like 'at.

Well . . . let's see now, there's Bud Hall, he's got one looks a little bit like that one a Tommy's and Riley Meadows is got one, ain't he Tammy?

ROSE: Ah hah. . . . b'lieve Cline's got one ain't he?

TAMMY: No. Now he got rid a that one he had.

ROSE: He did.

TAMMY: B'lieve he did . . . But now Tommy, he's brothers with Jethro, b'lieve you might know him. [I said I did.]

Yeah, because I seen y'all a talkin' out front your house one time.

But you know Miss Woods don't you? [No.]

Oh Lord, she's the sweetest **thang** ever **was**.
That was her little old **blue** car went out little ways back, you oughtta go **see**
her. She just loves to have comp'ny in and now she's got a **way** with words.

Tammy and Rose figured it must have been Miss Woods's nephew,
Sammy, driving her.

Miss Woods likes to get out and see her sister down Fireco but now it's been a
right smart while.
She always wears that little ol' blue coat with the wood buttons all up the front
of it.
They say it was her **mommy's**—she never got over her, you know. But I always
liked that coat.
    ROSE: Did she have it **on**?
    TAMMY: She **sure did, bless** her little **heart**!

Born in the mediated space of read signs, sociality walks a fine line
between the obligation to make somethin' of thangs and the excesses of
hyperbole, obsession, loose tongues, misplaced or shameless action, and
imaginations run wild. People will run their mouths or brag that they
know something for certain and there's no telling what they might do. So
neighbors literally watch out for each other across the expanse of veiled
windows and the exchange of signs, walking the line. Those who "have"
help the old and sick, visit those who can't get out, and *carry* those who
don't have a car. But a visitor will call first or sit out in the truck and honk
the horn to wait for someone to stick their head out. Someone being carried to the store or the doctor's office will be allowed to pay for gas as a
sign that they are of account. Neighbors will carry a plate of food to
someone who lives alone or is sick or has been working long hours. But
the gift will be tempered by elaborate signs to lighten the load of pre-
sumption and leave room to maneuver: "Well, it ain't much. I just acci-
dentally made too much and I'd just have to th'ow it away so I thought
you might could maybe use it where I seen you come in s' late and maybe
you ain't had **time** to cook. Looks like they're workin' you to **death** over
there **ain't** they?"
    Those who fail to visit and get out and go might get squirrelly and get
a little off; they might go t' studyin' on thangs and worry theirself to
death; they might get *lazy*, or *turn* and get *backward*. They might go
mean, go to carryin' on and showin' theirselves. They say children are
naturally mean and carry on; they have to be taught both to respect people and to stand up and speak for theirself. But adults who carry on, show
theirselves, and act no account will be called shameless. In the hands of
the shameless, shifting relational identities can turn in on themselves and
stultify into demanding egos or permanent backwardness; social, read-

able signs can become internalized traits. The shameless, then, can endanger the mediated order of sociality itself; disengagement signals social collapse; someone who fails to fashion talk and action into signs endangers whole families and whole camps.

They said Mrs. Cooper was just showin' herself when she sent her kids over to borrow cigarettes from Sissy every hour for two days when everyone **knew** that she had plenty of money and could as easily send her kids to the stand where everyone else bought their cigarettes. But Sissy "didn't say nothin' **to** her, you know." Mr. Cooper showed hisself when he bragged.

> JOHNNY WALKER: Well, he brags he's a preacher and he says he goes out walkin' of a night like don't nobody know no better.
> Says he goes walkin' for his heart trouble.
> Well, I guess hit **is** too but he ain't just walkin' for his health.
> Miss Lilly had to take out that phone down there [i.e., a pay phone at the stand] where he 'bout wore it out callin' that woman at his church where her old man works **hoot owl.**
> He aggravated her [i.e., Miss Lilly] to where she had to have it tuk out and she **did** too.
> Now that man is **shameless.**
> **Well,** he woke us up at two in the mornin' sneakin' down the back alley where his lights flash in our window.
> And he tells her he's out **walkin'** all hours for his **heart.**
> Well, she **knows,** she'd **have** to, but she don't say nothin' **to** him.
> **Oh** and he brags on coon huntin' and ain't never **oncet been,** or ain't nobody never **seen** him, **one.**
> Well you cain't tell what that man'll say next.
> Well, just last week he was out here braggin' that old truck a his couldn't be fixed and that **Milan** boy, he fooled with it—well he weren't out there thirty minutes, because I was standin' right here the whole time talkin' to **Bud** and that thang runs like new.

People used to *talk* about Cooper because he *talked* so much himself— braggin' on things he claimed he'd done and preachin' at people when everybody **knew** he was the biggest sinner of them all. Still, Lacy thought it was terrible when Dreama told Cooper one day when he'd been going on and on to her about his religious beliefs and what was wrong with all the other churches that if she wanted to hear him preach she'd just go on down to his church. Just don't say nothin' **to** 'm, don't get into it with them. But on the other hand people shouldn't take nothin' **from** people either.

Kenny Macken *remembers* the time Cooper messed up a borrowed car real bad and had to leave the state for a month until things cooled down because the police were after him to spend twenty-four hours in jail. And he *remembers* how the whole family had lived off her mother when she was alive.

> I've seen it with my own eyes. When Miss **Guerrant** was still alive they'd be **laughin'** at her out there.
> She'd be so tired some days when she was down sick that I've seen her have to crawl up them stairs and them a **laughin'** at her to crawl. You've seen it, haven't you, Bud?
> BUD: **Oh, yeees.**
> KENNY: **Oh** she had to **take** it **from** 'm, they done her **awful bad.**
> But now Patty thinks they're **quietin' down** here lately, I said they must be **wearin' out.** [Laughing.]

And one day while I was living in Amigo the men in the alley finally got around to filling in the huge sinkhole from the broken water main that trucks had been falling into all winter. Mr. Cooper refused to help, but then he stood around overseeing while he leaned on a shovel and yelled out to people passing that the whole thing was his idea.

> KENNY MILLER: I could a beat the **fire** out a **him**, just a **showin'** hisself is all. **Mean** as a snake.
> But we didn't say nothin' **to** him.
> Just go on and don't take nothin' **from** him is all.

The shameless don't care. No account, mean, hateful, and lazy, they brag, carry on, and show theirself, or they refuse to speak for theirself, hole up, and turn backward. Cut off from the daily traffic in signs, they grow helplessly self-conscious or fester in a coldhearted pride. Turned around, they can turn on you. They can be possessed by alcohol or demons or shame. They can take things to heart, brood, and get down. Or they can grow bigheaded and hard-hearted and speak and act without thinking. They can grow clannish, inbred, melancholy, and bitter. A living specter of a world got down, people say their hearts are turned to stone. They say there's no tellin' what they might do.

There is no shame in poverty or kin line per se; the Birdsongs are poor and saddled with bad blood and hard luck, but people say Bobbie Jean and Jack Wesley, at least, do the best they can.

> Bobbie lost **one** baby where her shoelace got stuck on the bridge and tumbled her down in the creek and she was gone 'fore they even **knew** it.
> And she lost another one got bit by a dog and they say she must of died of the rabies. They never knew what was ailin' her 'til she was gone, pore thangs.
> **Jack Wesley,** he never has been the same since Buddie, that's their oldest, got hisself kilt in **Vietnam.**

Well, he used to be a preacher up here at the fork, worked in the **mines**. But he never did preach another word and he never did step foot back in the mines after that day. **Tuk** to his bed and never got up again. They say he has **visions**. But then, both their families is **bad** and that ain't a lot to come from.

Bobbie Jean's sister, Jesse Mae Bowens, is an ideal because "she does the best she can and then some." Her house has a cardboard door with electrical tape for hinges, and dogs and cats and grandchildren wander in and out and stand in the corners staring. Her husband and sons are "taken to the nerves and the drank. But Jesse, she keeps that family together." She raises grandchildren when their mothers turn bad and take off, remembers checkups at the doctor's office, always finds somebody to carry her to the store. "She's got a heart big as all the rest of 'm put together." And every morning she walks the two miles down the holler to the post office and back, stopping to talk to whoever she meets—"Ain't nothin' backward about **that** one."

In constant disclaimers throughout the day a local moral and social hierarchy asserts itself against the bare outlines of the hegemonic value of class: she may be poor but she visits her neighbors every day; he may drink but he's good to his kids and he takes care of his mommy and daddy; he may be slow but he's good to talk to and just as sweet as he can be; she may be crazy but she's **real** good to talk to. Local ways of talkin' and ways of doin' people reassert value in dramatic encounters with a world got down.

But in the hands of the shameless, impersonal givens of social place—kin line, poverty (or wealth), illiteracy (or education)—stultify into fixed attributes of the self. Old man Henson is shameless in his pretentious brick house with the well-kept lawn and his high and mighty ways. Stiff and forbidding, he never tells stories and he brags of what he has: "He's s' hateful even his daughter don't come around him no more." Cora Lee and Verlie Birdsong are shameless where they stay into it. They run moonshine, lay out of a night, and "have all kinds of people up there." The county police are always up there about something. "Now they just don't care. Ain't nothin wrong with them two but meanness."

KITTY WALKER: That Cora Lee, she always was a little off in the **face**.
It was like it was kindly caved in on itself, you know.
And so when she was small and she went to school out here on the school bus, they made fun of her. Kids can be mean as snakes. And that's how they done pore little **Cor'Lee**.
Well, they kep' up and kep' up and she never **did** say nothin' **to** 'm and that right there is what it **was**.
She always was **backwards, awful** bad **shy,**

come down from way up the holler and hadda mix with them from the camp.
Well, she just slowly **turned** and she never would stand **up** for herself atall.
Now she's got just as hateful as can be, now she still won't **speak** to nobody but
her own. And I mean not **nobody**.
She won't talk **to you** but now she'll talk **about you**.
People's tried to do somethin' with her but she's like a **treed coon, buddy**.
Well . . . People don't take much to her but really you cain't **blame** 'm.

In the hands of the shameless, things can get down to where the others
say they just cain't see it: "You have to **do** somethin' is all, don't stop and
thank about it."

TAMMY YOUNG: Well, I went down the library
and they was a pore little old thang in there a lookin' for a book and she was
about **blind**.
And they got that one **mean** one workin' down there and she **ask** her, said, can
you he'p me where I cain't see too good and that woman was s' **hateful**! Said,
"**Well** if you cain't **see** too good how you thank you gonna **read**? Can you tell
me **that**?" Said, "No mam, I'm sorry, I **cain't**." And she just hung her **head**
down and went **on**!
Well I was fit to be **tied**!
Said, "**Well, now** don't you have some a them books they got in the big letters
for the old people?" And said, "And **don't** you have none a them what they call
them **braille** books?"
Well that just made me **mad** her a doin' her that a way, now I just cain't **see**
that, can **you**?
Pore old thang, she's probly lonely and don't have nobody to **talk** to, said
b'lieve I'll go **see about** her.

The sociality of talk and action demands a vigilant watching for *signs*.
In the face of shameless ignorance the others are moved to fill in the gap
with loud back talk and a dramatic, heroic form of acting without stopping to think. One day I was sitting on Sissy Miller's porch with her and
the other women in the alley. Anna Mae announced that her daughter
was going to a Beckley hospital for tests and that she might have to have
an operation on her "female parts." It had already been rumored that it
might be cancer, but everyone heard the news politely as if for the first
time. Anna Mae never mentioned cancer and the others did not ask but
moved closer in around her so that bodies touched. They said it was good
she was going to that particular hospital. Then they started in with a
series of horror and injustice stories about "the other one."
Sissy had taken Johnny to the emergency room of the other hospital
when he was a baby and in a high fever. She had to beg all night for

attention for him. She felt bad too because there was an old woman lying there all night who had had a heart attack.

Drugged her up and left her a layin' in that hall the whole night.
Didn't nobody even look at her and I mean she's a **callin' out,** buddy: "**Ohh,** somebody **help** me, **help** me **PLEASE.**"
They'd tell her, "Now just be quiet and the doctor, he'll be here in a few minutes."
And do you know that doctor never **did** come?
And her a layin' out there all night in that **white** hall and her with a heart attack and all.
Well I just couldn't **stand** it, I told 'm, "You git somebody **down** here to **help** that woman 'fore she dies and it's on **your** head." But nobody never **did** come.

    TAMMY: Well, I've been there **one time** and honey I'd **die** b'fore I went back to that place.
They got **one** nurse down there, she's the **meanest** thang, ever'body knows about her.
Well, I felt so sorry for this pore old man they had down there and she was a yellin' at him, hurry up and git out of her way and he practicly fell over hisself a **tryin'**, buddy. I said, "**Don't** you **do** him that way, cain't you see he's an old man and ain't **got** nobody?"
Well, then she let in on **me.**
And I wished that old man would of just tuk his **cane** and **beat her up side th' head** with it.
You know, the old people, they're s' **sweet** they don't **know** no better. They thank be nice and people will be nice back, they just cain't understand it.
Pore old thang, he just stood there, started to **cry.**
Buddy, I was a **seein'** red.
Because now that there, that's a **shame.** Now I cain't **see** it.

    KITTY: Well, I don't see how they can **do** people that way, really I don't. They don't **care,** because I **seen** 'm all the time I worked up there. I mean there good ones and there bad ones, some a them aides down there, they really **care** and they try and do their best by people and buddy some**times** it ain't **easy.** People's got sa **hateful, buddy** I could tell you some **stories.**
But now some a them down there is just **evil** and they abuse the **old** people, I don't know where they git the **ideal.**
And them others don't know to do what's right and **they** ain't no **better.**
This **one woman** she was eight months pregnant and fell in the bathtub and they called the doctor and he said don't bother me unless she's a **bleedin'.**
And that woman was in **awful bad pain** all the day long and them nurses, they wouldn't call that doctor back and tell him git his self down there and **see** about her b'cause she wasn't **bleedin'**!

Don't that just **beat all**! She could a been in there a **dyin'** but didn't nobody care
if she weren't come out with no **blood**. Well that made me **mad**.
So I told her and I did, I said, "Just tell 'm you're a **bleedin'** down there," and
I took me some blood from the blood lab and put it down there on the sheet for
her.
And she told 'm and they called him and he come down and tuk her to the
emergency surgery and do you know that baby was just about dead when they
got to him? And her all **a bleedin' inside**, hit just hadn't made its way **out** is all.
And the doctor said, "Well why didn't you **call** me?"
Well that just about made me **sick**.
But I guess about the worst was the time I seen one a them nurses kilt a baby
gettin' borned. She kilt that baby and I said anybody ever ask me **ah'm** a tell 'm
way it **was**.
Course she didn't do it on purpose, now, but now one a them other nurses tried
to show her, but **nooooo**, she screamed at her and **I mean screamed**: "Well, just
who do you thank is the **supervisor** around **here** and **you** do what **I** tell you."
And she kilt that baby.

The vigilant scanning for *signs*, then, arises in the face of a claim that
things have got down. Local ways—performances of seeing, acting, and
speaking—are reasserted as *signs* in themselves in dramatic encounters
with shamelessness and injustice. A claim to *ideals* emerges in a space of
desire for missing standards and checks and embeds itself in the gaping
sociality of the sign.

The Space of the Gap

When sociality hovers on the brink of the gap between event and representation, person and signifying talk and action, the act of not noticing
things or the failure to respond appropriately can be taken as a *sign* in
itself. Then the rhythm of seeing, acting, and talking can fall into the gap
in a sudden faint, leaving things open to the unchecked *signs* of mysteries,
tragedies, and fates. Dwayne Priddy walked right by his aunt May—
didn't even recognize her—and that set people to talking about what
might be wrong with him. After his wife left him, Bobby Mason was
turned around; when he came over to visit his friends Jimmy and Tammy,
he walked right into the living room wall where they had moved the doorway months before. Kenny Miller was furious with his mother and so
ashamed that he had to leave a family dinner when he realized that the
man he had been talking to all evening was not his sister's new boyfriend
but a cousin he grew up with and had not seen for twenty years. Days
later he was still going over it in his mind: although he had spoken nicely

to the man and at length, he had not spoken as he would have to a "close" cousin and he felt bad about it. He was not speaking to his mother because she had schemed to keep him in the dark for a joke and made him look like a fool. The cousin had gone back to his place out of state, and there was nothing he could do to set things right.

Dwelling in the space of the gap, things haunt people and in-fill the space of seeing and acting with a stultifying hesitation. Opal Lilly still worries on a bowl she saw at the swap meet in Beckley last year. It was an old glass bowl with blue flowers painted on it and she wanted it but she didn't know how much the man would want for it and she hesitated to ask. All afternoon she circled back around to peer at the bowl while Arlee and I waited at the car. But she never asked and now she still thinks about that bowl.

Without the light, continuous engagement of noticing things and acting without stopping to think, things turn back on themselves and take on the weight of a hypersignificance. Not noticing things can leave you vulnerable to unseen forces; noticing without acting can leave you caught in the endless replay of desire in the space on the side of the road.

May 5, 1982. Miss Lela Lavender came out of the doctor's office and opened her eyes wide, startled:

> Why it's done **rained**!
> And me settin' in there and didn' even notice!
> **Lord have mercy.** I told him when I got up from the bed, I said, "They's somethin' in this day," said, "somethin' **funny** here."
> Here now, it done **rained**.
> That's how **lazy** I am today.
> I'm a git me on **back** 'fore somethin' **happens**.
> Where **is** that man [scanning the parking lot for her husband's car although he is walking toward us in clear sight].
> Mmmm **hmm**. Honey, I'm **too** lazy today.

As if to enfold her back into the social, Miss Miller, who was also waiting in the parking lot for her old man to pick her up, took Miss Lavender by the arm and put her in her car.

> Well, Miss Lavender, you just go on **home** if you want to, hit's just accordin' to what you want to **do** is all.

But as she was being driven away, Miss Lavender rolled down the window and called out in a foreboding voice:

> Y'all be **careful** now, better git on **home** 'fore somethin' **happens**.

Action that is *of account* arises to fill in the gap of not noticing. Icy Martin was all turned around when she realized that she had been enrolled in a new health care plan for the past three months and didn't even know it. The whole thing was a bureaucratic mistake; she had gone to them to try to enroll, but they told her she wasn't eligible because she was too old and sick so she went home. Three months later they sent her a bill for coverage received. Rather than call them up and straighten it out, she insisted on paying the bill before she quit the program because they thought she was enrolled and she didn't feel right in her own self. She had to raise chickens and sell the eggs to pay for it on a payment plan and she didn't feel right until she had burned the last "bill paid" notice.

In the claim that things have got down, action grows heroic and takes on the weight of a value in itself. Kitty Walker tells the story about the time an old man did not pay a $51 light bill. The bill never made it to him—lost somewhere in the mail, or more likely the light company kept it from him—so the old man went on innocently, unsuspecting. Why should you have to pay for lights anyway when the lines are already there and it comes, on its own, into the house? The man only found out about the bill seven years later when the company claimed his house. But Kitty herself keeps up with the light company. One time Johnny was out on strike and they had no money, but they paid what they could each month. Then suddenly the bills were huge and growing all the time—$140 and the next month $165! Each time she called to try and straighten things out, the woman on the phone was hateful, trying to make her feel ashamed for not paying. She said the company was always right and could not make mistakes. She called Kitty ignorant. They refused to come down to the camp to fix the meter and see for themselves. But they sure came down to cut off the lights quick as she didn't pay the bill. But by then Kitty had "took all I was gonna take." She chased them off with a shotgun and took up her ax and cut down their pole. "**That** got their attention."

The Space of Performance

April 30, 1982. Dovie says she believes she's seen everything now. Her sister-in-law Ivory came over and told her to come see the "new neighbors." So she went to see and what she saw haunted her so bad she couldn't sleep at night. Al said, "Dovie, go to sleep," but she could **not** get it out of her head.

> Well, we went down the holler and I said, "What in the world you talkin' 'bout? There ain't nobody stays down there!"
> She says, "Well, you jes look **here**."

And here is this **white woman**, and her **retarded** boy, he's about **fourteen**, and
they are a livin' out **in the field**.
Honey, I mean **out of doors**! **Girl**, I mean to **tell you**.
And here she is, got her a **refrigerator** and a **stove** and she's got her **bed**,
oh, she's just set up just like she's settin' in the couch readin' the **damn paper**!
Shiiit! the lamp ain't got no **lights**!
I said, "**Girl, somebody** got **you** turned around." Said, "**What** are you a **doin'**
out here like this, you cain't **stay** like this."
She's talkin' at me about the **mosquitoes** botherin' her.
"**Mosquitoes!**" I said, said. "**What** are you a **talkin'** 'bout mosquitoes? Honey
you won't have to worry 'bout **them** long, because the **snakes** gonna come get
you in **your bed!**"
Well, she says she cain't **he'p** it.
Says her old man come after her with a **gun**, said, "You can take some furniture
but git out."
And they loaded her stuff up on the pickup and dumped her off side th' road.
Hah! I said, "Say what? You **cain't** let no old man run you off like **'at!**"
He's got a **gun**! Huh! Buddy I'd get **my** gun and shoot **his** damn **head** off. I told
her, "**Honey** you need to git yourself somebody **he'p** you."
Run her off!
I said **Lord have mercy**, I'm a **tellin' you**.
Well, I went on **home** but I cain't **sleep** with all that **goin' on** up there.

Haunted by the image, Dovie told and retold the story as the pathos
gathered intensity. She saw "that po' little ol' mental boy" go past with
his radio, and a few hours later he passed again carrying a little bag of
groceries and no radio. "He sold his radio—the only thing he had in the
world—for a little bitty sack of food." Still the woman in the snaky field
did nothing. Short of shooting her old man's damn head off and moving
back home, she could have back talked her situation by figuring herself as
"a woman dumped on the side of the road in a snaky field by a no-good
man" or by fashioning the image of a family put out of doors to resonate
with the image of the strikers who were put out of their company houses
in the twenties and sat outside in the alley "like they was in their own
living room and the snow comin' down." Instead there was only the flat,
empty reality of her helpless presence. Finally Dovie and Ive were fit to be
tied with all that goin' on down there, so they went and told her she could
move into the deserted shack that had been Dovie's mother's place and
Ive got some windows for it and made the men put them in, and Dovie
took the woman to town to get on welfare and had a fight with the welfare worker:

She looked at me like I'm **crazy** or somethin' and I said, "Honey, this ain't **my**
problem, I'm just tellin' you what it is and **here** it is."

I said, "Go on now, tell her what that man done to you, tell her your **own** damn self, **you** got a tongue like anybody **else**."

In dramatic back talk and heroic action people reassert a social order of signs in which the "self" is not a fixed object but the subject, agent, and interpreter of storied action. The self enacts itself as a creative interpretive space of unknown possibilities and unintended consequences—a space of desire in which anything can happen. In the process things become in-filled with unforeseen possibilities, and what looks like laziness or back-wardness might be a sign of a wilder potential in people to go "off."

> ROSE McGRAW: You know he makes me mad.
> He tells me I'm **lazy** where I like t' set out here and read a book of an evening. Well, **really** I cain't see where it's no more lazy than settin' in there a watchin' TV, now **do you**? It ain't like they're **talkin'**, you know, and I cain't **stand** that TV. I just absolutely **hate** it. Well, it's all right but I don't **like** it. That's just how I **am**.
> I don't care **what** he says, he ain't nothin' but **jealous**.
> Only time I ever see any quiet.
> But you know I don't even **have** to read. I can just set in the dark and **go off**.
> Well, really I don't **need** no TV, I got my own built-in drive-in **movie theater** right up **here** [patting her head, laughing]. I told him, said, "You keep on **talkin' buddy** and some day I might go 'off' and not **never** come back."
> Hah. Call me lazy![2]

Assertive back talk turns a flat reading of signs into a performative space of claims and counterclaims, mutual misreadings, and momentary excesses that push things to the limit of the "ordinary" and draw atten-tion to a space of unseen forces. In banter and rhetorical claim the "self" comes always already mediated by forms of talk. Set social roles and fixed identities twist and turn in the shifting double entendres of claims that someone is lazy, crazy, mean, ornery, ignorant, or backward, and local ways reemerge as nothing but just talk.

One day Betsy went to visit Justice Priddy and asked him how he had been. He said he'd started in to whittlin' that morning and got lazy and disremembered th' post office. He showed her his carving of a knife han-dle and then turned on her, said he figured she must have been down there stickin' her nose in because he'd never known a day when she wasn't. Said (smirking) he figured she must be waitin' on somethin' **special**, she must have got **herself** a friend. But he'd got **lazy** and plum forgot to go. Then he went "off," claiming that someday he might just forget to get up of a morning, or forget to put his clothes on and give them old women somethin' t' **talk** about. Then he said he knew all about those books she had in there and he watched her when she'd go scurrying in to scribble things down. Then, when she tried to leave, he wanted to know if she'd brought him his mail, and she said no, she didn't know he'd **missed** it and anyway she knew he wouldn't want anybody to touch his mail where he was so mean. He feigned shock that no one had even thought to send on his mail to him and complained that he could be dead in there and didn't nobody stop and **see** about him. "Y'all 're lazier than me this mornin'." Betsy said something about how he was too mean to die, mean as a snake, and he told her she didn't know nothin', probly never even seen a snake and she wasn't even **from** here and she said something about how she'd have to go home and write all this down in her book in there and he said, "Now don't you go gittin' me in **trouble**. You don't know the **half** of it and you better watch yourself, **you** ain't above trouble."

Banter turns meanness and laziness into a form of expression and catches up the meaning of signs in the gap of juncture and disjuncture where words and actions are things to be performed and read and meaning is a thing asserted and disputed and then finally displaced in favor of the social excesses of making something **of** things real and imagined. In the gaping order of things social and fabulated, things happen.

A Visit(ation)

In a world in which things happen and people scan things for *signs*, the uncanny can lie gathered in the ordinary, the sacred can penetrate the profane, and a visit can become a visitation.

One day Sissy was over visiting and we were talking about meditation. Her voice shaking in fear, she told us of a strange visitation. The others had claimed it was just a dream. But we—the ethnographers with the books to scribble in—were all ears, listening in order to retell.

> But this weren't no **dream**.
> It was too **terrible** to be no **dream**, it was **real**.
> And I had it proof **positive** three, four months after that when I took out a book
> from the library and I took it home with me and I opened it **up**.
> And **right there**, on page **three hundred and three**.
> I turned that **page**,
> **three hundred and three**,
> and **there** he **was** a starin' right into me.
> And it was **the Beast** [i.e., the Beast of Revelation].
> Because I didn't know what it was and I hadn't never seen him, you know, like
> to **drop** me down dead.
> I said **Jesus he'p me** and the hair was a standin' right **up** on the back of my **neck**.

Oooh, I hate to thank about it even now and it's been back maybe five or six years back, I don't know.

Well, I closed that **book** and I got in the **car** with it and I didn't **rest** until I had it back to that **library** and **gone** from me.

Well, for the longest time after that I wouldn't get near that library and, tell you the truth, I **still** don't like to go in there but now I **do**.

It might be silly but now that's the way I felt because this weren't no **dream**, I don't care what **nobody** thanks.

Well, it was just after **nine of a mornin'** and I was in the **bed**.

I was feelin' just kindly **down**, you know, and I had **Johnny** with me in the bed. He weren't but a **baby** at the **time**.

And I heared them **big ol' heavy boots** come up on the porch and stand there stampin' that nasty **coal** mud

and he come on **in**.

And I said, "Well, what's Kenny doin' in, this hour?"

But I didn't think nothin' **of** it at the **time**, I just figgered he **forgot somethin'**, you know.

An' I kep' on a **layin'** there, I just couldn't seem to **git up** that mornin'.

And I could hear him walkin' **around** out there like he's **lookin'** for somethin' and he didn't never say a **word**.

So I **ask** him, said, "Well, **Kenny, what** are you **a doin'** here?"

And no answer.

And then, honey, my blood run **cold**

an' I knew he was **a standin'** in the door

and his eyes a **bor**in' into me

and I knew who it **was**.

It was like I could see a **picture** of him in my **mind** and I knew "don't open your eyes and don't look **into** 'm because you'll be **lost**."

Well, I never seen him **b'fore**, and I pray Jesus don't **never** let me see him **again**. He was heavy **ever'**where, and he had muscles all over his back and on his chest.

Oh, it was just a terrible sight.

Them heavy boots stompin' and I could feel them muscles jest a **ripp**lin' **buddy** and him just a **star**in' into me.

Well, I **tuk** to prayin'.

And it's a wonder I didn't smother pore little Johnny to death because honey I had a holt on him and I was a **holdin' on**.

And I prayed for Jesus to **help** me, please help me, prayin' just as loud as I could.

Kep' on, **kep'** on.

And then I felt him just kindly **slip away**, he just slowly left, first he was **there** and then little by little he was **gone**.

He didn't leave like he come in, it wa'n' **like** 'at, but there come a time and I knew he was gone.

And I come up out a that **bed**, buddy, and I run and locked me all the doors and windows.

I'm a tellin' **you**, I ain't never felt the fear **before or since**. And it was **The Beast** is what it was, same as I saw in the **picture**.

You know, there's demons all **around**. That's why they say you shouldn't meditate all the way, don't **open your mind** all the way like 'at.

But when I asked her if she was afraid to walk home alone, the question confused her.

Oh no, you cain't let 'm **worry** you. I was **raised** here, or **just about**. I don't pay 'm no **mind**. **Nobody** does 'cept for old **Opal** over there and **she's** skeered of her own **shadow**.

7

The Accident

JULY 1981. After the accident that killed Hollie, Bud sat in his overstuffed chair in the living room for three days straight drinking beer, staring out at the creek, and playing old country songs over and over—maybe thirty or forty times at a stretch before he would get up and change the record. Dreama said, "He's feelin' a *big meanin'*." She herself was so haunted by her brother's death that she had not been able to rest for fear of what might come to her if she lay down and closed her eyes.

It had been a terrible car crash that killed five children as it was just getting dark on the straight stretch outside Helen. I was pulling off the road to visit a friend when I saw that the road up ahead was jammed with traffic and clusters of people huddled together. When I tried to walk up to the scene, a group of men warned me that there was blood everywhere. "You don't want to see it."

> A MAN: Hit's Jackie and Fred **Walls** and all the young'ns and that **retarded** boy, from up 'Miga holler, you know who I mean.
>
> ME: **What**, you mean **Hollie Cox**?
>
> THE MAN: Yeah, Hollie Cox. They said they're **all dead**—the kids and that **Hollie** boy.

I went on to Julie's. (Now, years later, Julie begins her story with my face suddenly appearing at her door—"and she was as white as a ghost.") Over the course of the next hour in her trailer five or six different people stopped by with a strange assortment of details, and by the end of the night we had a story that featured villains and victims, righteous and demonic forces, fate, prophecy, and the search for revelations.

The drivers of the three cars involved were all members of the terrible Walls family from "way back in" Devil's Fork holler. Two cousins, Jackie and Fred, had spent the afternoon drinking and drag racing the straight stretch in cars filled with a frightful *confusion* of women and children. Fred had Jackie's wife Cor Jane in the car with him (they said the two of them had been carryin' on for years), and Jackie had Cor Jane's fifteen-year-old cousin Mae with him (said to run around with men some) and two of his and Cor Jane's kids, one of Fred's kids, and Hollie Cox who had begged to go along and Jackie said he didn't care. Fred's car was racing along on the wrong side of the road when it hit head on with a

third car driven by his cousin and Jackie's brother, Leslie, who was coming back from town. Jackie's car, with all the children, was somehow
"sandwiched" between the other two cars and then flung against a boulder, killing everyone but the drunk driver. People said "somethin' bound
to happen."

> **Well**
> they been a **carryin' on** up 'Miga holler for a **right smart while**, livin' all piled
> up in a mess,
> somethin' bound ta **happen**, you just cain't **do** that a way.

Leslie, the driver of the third car, was coming back from town after his
first day back to work in years. They said Leslie was the only one of them
Walls of any account and it was ironic that he should be the one who hit
them, that he should be driving just that stretch of the road at just the
wrong moment, on his way back from his first day back working and his
last chance for a new start where he had just quit drinking and fixed up
a truck and overcome the notorious Walls backwardness to venture out
into the world.

Theories of an ironic and tragic fate spiraled out like a wave from the
central arresting image of the wrecked car still spinning in the road with
the kids trapped inside, their blood running out of the cracks to form a
pool in the middle of the road. It was ironic that the accident happened
just as they were about to quit racing—on the last run of the day, on the
last curve of the road, at the only boulder on the road—the same boulder
that had killed Bud Henson three days before . . .

> ONE MAN: They said it was a foggy night
> but no ice
> and said hit looked like from the tracks like his jeep went right into that rock
> for no reason.
> ANOTHER MAN: Well, is that the place they call the **spider's web**?
> A THIRD MAN: No, that ain't **spider's web**, that's on **this side** by **Rhodell**
> where that man kilt his **brother** with a knife.

They say death comes in threes and it's always the drunks that walk
away and the innocent ones git kilt. That's how it works. They said there
had been a prophecy made "six months ago to the day" by a visiting
preacher at the Amigo Holler Free Will Baptist Church that there would
be a terrible tragedy "if this holler don't straighten up and fly right."

In a story that quickly reached mythic proportions, victims and villains
figured sheer principles of the situated and the shameless, the contingent
and reckless agency gone wild. The victims—children of *confused* unions
and the "retarded" boy along for the ride and in the wrong place at the
wrong time—lay trapped in the spinning car, their bodies dismembered

to become a mess of impacted parts. This was the unforgettable, haunting image that people spent the next weeks studying on. We could say that it stood as a graphic, literalized metaphor of the sheer impact of events on lives caught, through no fault of their own, in a local space of contingency in which things happen.

The villains, on the other hand, figured the sheer principle of shameless, reckless no-account action. They were carryin' on, they were drinking and literally runnin' the roads, and after the accident they were markedly unresponsive and, unlike the victims, unstoppable. They said Jackie, Fred, and Cor Jane had vanished from the scene even before the car had stopped spinning. It was rumored that Fred had actually backed up and run over one of the kids as she lay dying on the road. Someone said Jackie had had the top of his head cut off and somehow he had dragged himself along the railroad tracks all the way to his aunt's porch in Helen. They found a pool of blood on the porch in the morning but by then he had been sighted "out of state . . . in Ohia" where he repeatedly escaped arrest over the next few weeks. It "came out" that Jackie was not really "from here" at all but had moved back and forth between West Virginia and Cincinnati all his life. There were people in Helen who had grown up and gone to school with him, but the newspapers reported that he was born in Columbus and had been arrested on several counts of car theft there in the past ten years and even served time in an Ohio penitentiary.

In the face of unspeakable events and unforgettable impacts, narrative plot fragments into lyric images and principles culled into stark oppositions of impact and escape, ignorant action and big meanings, drifting exile and the sudden, forceful realization of the inescapable relatedness of things. A man cannot really get out of a crushed and spinning car in front of dozens of spectators without being seen, a mother cannot really leave her dying child, a man cannot really drag himself hundreds of yards with the top of his head cut off. But in the fictional space of the free, unplaced action of the outlaw, people go too far and elude arrest, and in the fictional space of victims left behind, fate hunkers in to catch people up in its arresting, enveloping maw.

Notions of fate rise to address the order in disorder, and the weight of immanent meaningfulness surrounds the narrative recounting of events. At such moments it becomes clear that narrative is not just a plot which follows a sequence of events from beginning to end but a thread of thought that traces the precise moment when there is a "turn of events" in which the possible becomes probable and the immanent or emergent is finally instantiated in the actual. In the face of such narrative moments everything that happens stands as evidence of encompassing forces that lurk behind the choices of the ordinary and the everyday. At such moments "action" becomes more than mere acts in the world, and stories refer not just to a sequence of events but to a struggle of *ideals* and ways. Narrative becomes a form of perception that traces lines of force with a life of their own into the space of big meanings that leave people reeling.

The night of the accident Dreama and her kin sat in her living room, the heavy silence broken only by fragmented images of the scene on the road and the story of following the ambulance over the mountains to the hospital in Beckley only to have the doctor pronounce them all dead on arrival. A litany of unspeakable questions arose around the specter of last thoughts: did they suffer, did they call out for their mommy and daddy, were they saved, did they have a *sign* that death was coming, were they ready to go, were they afraid, did they call to Jesus to come into their hearts?

> Hollie, he never had a **chance.**
> Well, he **warshiped** Jackie, and he **did**, too,
> and he'd follow him **ever'**where he went if he **could**, you know.
> **Jackie**, he didn't **care**, tol' him he'd take him **fishin'**.
> He thought he was gonna get t' go **fishin'**.
> They said he still had his fishin' pole in his hand when they found 'm and they had to **break** it in **two** just to git him out. He was just a **holdin'** on.

In the days that followed, people traced the moves of the survivors. They said poor Leslie was "all tore up over it and his nerves is gone." They said when he tried to pull his nephew out of the car, his arm come right off in Leslie's hand. The next day he was spotted going into the local health clinic "said he looked like he hadn't slept at all and he had *places* all over his face. Said he had something wrong with his leg, they said his leg was like wood." They said he was "back drankin'."

People from all over the area were tore up and turned around. They had bad dreams, they forgot things, they turned and got mean, they took spells of the nerves, they forgot to pick up the kids from school, they passed friends without saying a word. Hundreds went to the wake and saw dismemberment, claiming that a head or limb looked like it sat askew where it must have been sewed back on. Cor Jane, the mother who had left the scene as two of her children lay trapped and dying in the other car, came back for the wake but "they say she's like wood"; she sat surrounded by the five small caskets, unmoving and without a word to say. Afterward people gathered outside, leaning with their backs against buildings in a long line that stretched for blocks, and the talk came only intermittently in overpowering fragmented images of the little girl, Susie, walking down the road with a blue ribbon in her hair, and Hollie shoveling Miss Shutt's coal for her every morning and the baby staring out at the cars from his bed on the porch.

At such moments the ordinary world appears as a pale front and people find themselves caught in an endless search through the traces of *re-membered* sights for *signs*. In the intensity of a reading that cannot stay on the surface, a force field gathers itself into a spatial representation where the difference of the visual-literal and the spiritual-metaphorical collapses onto a single overarching plane (Ricoeur 1984:29). Fragmented images fashioned into lyrical *signs* cull the weight of narrative desire into a nonnarratable excess that points to a world in which "accidents happen" with a force that can overcome the fragile hierarchy of "system" over "accident," culture over nature, order over disorder, reality over fiction. The lyric fashions a space on the side of the road in which the meaning/feeling of "gap" can be dwelt in and on and the search for meaning begins with an impact suffered.

In the weeks that followed "the accident," as everyone came to call it, Dreama waited for Jesus to give her a *sign* because she just couldn't see it. Then one afternoon as she was lying on her back in the upstairs bedroom trying to rest, she had a vision. The rafters of the roof opened up and a massive cloud filled the sky and then moved down toward her, growing bright as it drew closer. Then the sky was a beautiful blue and the cloud was a rainbow. A figure emerged from it, walking toward her. It looked like Jesus but as he came closer she realized it was Hollie. He paused and "looked into" her, smiling. And then he deliberately turned and walked away. She knew that Hollie was happy in heaven "where he just turned and walked away," and with that she could let him go, although she still missed him. Later, Dreama's four-year-old son Gary Lee told me that he had seen Hollie sitting in the overstuffed chair on the porch.

The relief felt from *signs* comes not from a reconstructed unity with the lost loved one; Hollie is kept gone and at a distance, under a cloud, a resident of another realm subject to other laws of order. Nor is the relief from a thematic coherence; the "idea" or "meaning" is ambiguous, blurred, evasive. But what is given form and rendered clear is the structure of desire itself—the sense of an absent presence that leaves behind its traces and an uncontained surplus of meaning. *Signs* like these instantiate the power of desire itself in a world got down—the ability to read the "really real" out of the contingent, the accidental, and the senseless.

A Visit(ation)

February 1985—a visit back. Dreama sat in the living room with picture albums, coffee, cigarettes, and ashtrays spread around her. The TV was on, the beans were on the cookstove, there was a cake in the oven, her rugs were soaking in the ringer washer, she had just washed the floor, and she was on the phone with her sister. There was an awkwardness between

28. "Gary Lee" with his chair and stuffed dog on the porch, Amigo.
Photograph © Em Herzstein.

us—a space made by my long absence and our inability to *just talk* about neighbors and the camp. She asked if I was still in Michigan and if I liked it there. She said she herself could never leave West Virginia and never would. Then we began with talk about bodies: Opal was eight now and still weighed only forty-two pounds. Gary Lee and Opal got glasses but they broke them right away; it was almost a year before they got them fixed and now the eye doctor said Gary would have to wear them for years instead of for just six months if he had worn them when he first needed them. Dreama had had a hysterectomy after years of hemorrhaging and her organs hanging out down there. Then the endometriosis got so bad that she finally consented to another operation. But they "still didn't git all of it," and now the pain was getting bad again and her stomach was distended again as if she were pregnant.

> But I won't have another one, I figure they tried **twicet** and they didn't get it.
> Bud's doctor says he'll be dead in a year if he don't quit **drankin'**. There ain't
> nothin' wrong with his **liver** but they say the **likker**, hit's poisonin' his system.
> Ever' day when I come home I look for him to be **dead**.

The statement is surrounded by smaller statements about livers and modes of death and the places Dreama is coming back from when she "looks for" him to be dead and how "good he is with the kids and don't take nothin' **from** us for his likker" and how

> he never has been **mean** but for the one time when I was big with Sissy and he
> got **into** it with me and tuk off with that **Birdsong** woman.
> But he **come back**.
> They fuss at me to throw him out where he **dranks s' bad** but I couldn't never
> leave him now, not and leave him all alone.
> We get along good. He says he don't **wanta die** but he says he cain't **he'p** hisself.
> And you can see how his belly's got. That ain't fat on him, he don't **weigh** but
> a hundred twenty pounds. He don't **eat** nothin'. It's bloat where he's poisoned
> hisself and he cain't **he'p** it.

Then the talk moved to people leaving the area to find work—talk of displacement and opportunities and broken hearts and broken homes and broken links of communication.

> **Ricky** and **Ellen, they** went **off**, and they went down North C'raliny I b'lieve
> they went to work and they weren't down there **no** time and she **found** herself
> somebody and **Ricky**, he come on **home**.
> I seen him go up the road yesterday but they say he tuk it **awful** hard.
> But she **found** herself **somebody** and **Ricky**, he come on **home**.
> They say **Buster Reed**, from up over Graham's store, he's kin to Miss **Reed** and
> them, he went down North C'raliny.

Had him a job waitin' for him when he got **down** there.

And he went to work for that R. J. Reynolds company they got down there.

But he come back when he got him a job on one a them **tree** farms.

Now **he** had him a job set up for him to come **back** to.

I seen him goin' up the **road** little while back.

Then them **Lacy** boys and **Grahams, they** been goin' **in and out**. But they's just **boys**, you know, they hitchhike down and back all the time but I ain't heared if they ever found **work** yet. Seen some of 'm yesterday runnin' up and down the road.

Then there was one a Miss **Taylor's** daughters, left out for North C'raliny, tuk the **kids** and **all**.

But I ain't heared nothin' 'bout her.

Miss Taylor closed up the **stand**, said nobody wasn't comin' **in** no more and she had to give it up for a while and I hate to see it **go**.

Well, way it is, you got to go all the way down the **Dairy Queen** to git your cigarettes.

Buddy, I'm lookin' for the stand to git back **up**.

In between stories there was the continuous action of noticing the dogs, the beans, the washing, the creek, and the constant phone calls back and forth tracking people's whereabouts—"Has Bud got up there to take mommy?" . . . "**Well**. Ewolt said he seen him down Iroquois while back . . ."

> DREAMA: **Mickey Heath** from down at **Wyco**, he went out to some place in Ohia.
>
> They said the rent's **$350 a month** and that's just **rent**.
>
> Then you got your **lights**, and you know that's gotta be high in the city, and you got your **cookin' gas**.
>
> **All right**. Then there's your **phone**, there's your **cable**.
>
> And nothin' left for **groceries** I don't **guess**.
>
> **Mickey** and them, **they** come on **back**.
>
> But they already done **sold** their house, **now** they ain't **got** no place.

Her nephew Wes called to give Dreama the plot of the "story" (soap opera) she missed seeing yesterday.

> I didn't git to **see** it where Bud was a layin' **home** and he tuk to wantin' to watch the **cartoons**.
>
> Oh! I was s' **mad**!
>
> Well, it's been up over a year and a half he's out a work this time and he's got s' bad to lay home and I can't get none a my **work** done where he tries to get me to set and **talk**, you know.
>
> . . . **Well, all right.**

29. Riley Meadows's kitchen in Amigo, chairs left facing out the window where he and his wife used to sit and eat before her death. Photograph © John Hartigan.

Dreama's sister called to say Bud got there and left to take their mother to the doctor's.

Mom's been down **awful** bad, well, she never did get over **Hollie.**

Bud came in with stories of the parking lot at the doctor's office: " . . . an' I seen Miss Lavender down at the **tracks.** Somebody oughtta go **see about** her." Dreama's nephew Dewayne and Bud sat at the kitchen table drinking beer and staring at me out of the corner of their eyes. From time to time one of them would quietly add something to the talk.

I told them some stories I had heard the day before. One was of a woman who went to Ohio and had to take an apartment that had no bathroom (even in the city they have places without bathrooms) and they had to "rig up somethin'" in the kitchen. Another was of a woman who had been gone for years and came back to show off her big fancy car and diamond rings. Then I remembered Jerry Graham's story of how thangs had got down in Iroquois and the people were being shipped by bus to the tobacco fields in No'th C'raliny and how those people out there wouldn't even give them water to drink and how the wind came and blew away their trailers and all their stuff and how they lost everything and had to come home and were livin' all piled up like cats and dogs.

Dreama repeated the images after me, and then, after a silence, she launched into a litany of her dead whose pictures hung on the walls— some in coffins, some in uniforms, the ancestors in ancient photographs that she had had colorized. Some were mounted on small wooden shrines. She pointed them out one by one where they hung amid her collection of vibrant, heartrending things—the letters from her people in Michigan and Ohio who had "left **out** of here," the Sacred Heart of Jesus, pierced and dripping blood. I said how beautiful his eyes were. She said she just loved hearts.

I don't know **why,** I just always have **tuk to** 'm.
That there is **Liam,** he got kilt in the **war.**
Then **Peanut,** he **drank** hisself to **death.**
He was up **Cook Town** one day, wasn't even drunk they said
and they said he just **laid** his **head** down,
well, they didn't even know he was **dead,** just thought he kindly seemed to go
to **sleep,** you know.
Peanut just put his **head** down and **died.**
Then **Sissy,** that's the one that hurts the **most** 'cause she was **special, buddy.**
She'd **stand up** for us, you know, **talk up** for us if somethin' **happened.**
She left her inspiration on ever'thang she come near.
Well, **Lenny,** that's her **husband,** he'd go cut down **trees,** you know, and sell the wood where he was outta **work.**

This time she begged him, "Lenny, don't you **do** it" where it was **Sunday**.
Sissy told **mommy**, she said she had a bad **feelin'** like somethin' was gonna
happen, you know.
But he went and he made her to come **with** him, he made 'm **all** to go.
Well, first tree he **cut**, and it started to come down on Sissy's **baby** where she
was a **playin'** and Sissy jumped to push the baby free and the **tree**
hit come right down **on** her
bust her head all to **pieces** on the ground.
They said they had to cut her out from **under** it.
I just **never could** get over that. . . .
Course you **know** 'bout **Hollie**,
He was the **sweetest thang** there ever **was** and never did hurt nobody.
Thought he was gonna get to go **fishin'** and Jesus tuk him **on**.

Bud and Dewayne went out and sat in the truck. The room was nearly
dark and the air was heavy with heat and smoke. The next time the phone
rang Dreama told Ellen,

Bud and Dewayne are back **drankin'**.

We could hear them playing Waylon Jennings in the driveway.
   The kids came in from school and climbed up on us. Dreama said the
house was haunted. Bud saw a beautiful woman standing in the doorway
staring at him ("like ta **skeered** him to **death**") and once the lid to the
washing machine lifted itself all the way up and then slowly lowered itself
down.

We **all** seen it.

Several times they heard people moving around in the rooms upstairs,
and there was often a tapping on the back window up there.

Not like they was tryna **git in** or **git out**
but just **tappin'**, fast.
I ain't seen nothin' since I got **saved** again
but **Bud, he** sees thangs.

Opal whimpered: "Mommy, you **skeered** me, you **skeered** me bad."
Dreama explained:

She means **that night**.
I was a layin' in the bed and I seen Sissy [her dead sister] kindly **slide** around the
corner of the **stairs** like she'd just come down from up**stairs**,
I could see her like a shadow out the corner of my eye, and she come and **stood**
right **there** at the foot of the bed and beckoned me to **come on, come on**, just
like that.

30. "Gary Lee" and "Opal" with dog, Amigo. Photograph © Em Herzstein.

Honey, that like to **skeered** me near to **death** an' I set up in that **bed** and screamed and **I mean screamed.**

I thought she meant come on **right then** out of this **world**, you know.

So I made 'm to turn on all the lights and we had t' sleep with all the lights on for the **longest time** after that happened.

Well, I'd been a **dreamin'** on her ever' night when she **come to** me like that. But this **here**, this weren't no **dream** b'cause it **skeered** me too **bad** to be no **dream.** But what skeers me **worst** is **people.**

Anymore, it's got to where you don't know **what** they might try and that **glass** out in the **door**, well, anybody could just reach in and git the handle and come on **in** on us.

And the **bridge** worries me **awful** bad.

Last week 'nother one a them **ties** come out and went in the creek an' Opal says **she's** skeered to try and make it **acrost**, small as **she** is, if we lose another one. **Lenny, he** won't fix it.

After **Sissy**, he married **Corlee**, that's **Liam's** widda, and they bought **this** place. Somethin' happen to that **bridge,**

and we'd be here with no way to git the **truck** out.

But I just **love** it out here and I wouldn't **never** want to leave.

Well, this place is **home** to **me.**

A Postcard

Three years later I got a postcard from my old neighbor Sissy Miller that read simply: "Just a word to let you hear from me. Your house burned down in a terrible fire and three babies burned up. It's all gone now." On my next visit I heard the shocking stories of how they never wanted to rent to those people to begin with but they begged them. They had all been in the bed together and the father just saved himself, somehow squeezing himself through the tiny half-window, and left the children inside. You'd think he would have passed the children out first but seems like he just didn't care. You could hear one of the babies crying at the door and the men tried to break in the door but they couldn't get to them in time and all the father cared about was his stereo and when they finally let him get back inside he carried that melted thing out like it was the crown jewels or somethin'. Nobody knows how the mother ever got out but she never was "right" and someone saw her walkin' around stark naked like she didn't know nothin' about it. After all that happened they just tore the house right down to nothin'; Jimmy uses the old shed to store his tools but he don't even like to go **over** there.

31. Bridge, Black Eagle. Photograph © Harriette Hartigan, Artemis.

8

The Place of Ideals

PICTURE WHAT HAPPENS when meanings do not rush to conflate sign and referent but grow "big" in the space of the gap and lie nascent in mediating forms. Ideas, pronounced, significantly, as *ideals*, are launched from within a narrative world and its intrinsic sociality. They become not the mirror of, or model for, an absolute Real World but the means of creating and tracking a cultural real in which there is room to maneuver (Chambers 1991). They become both the subject of *talk* and notions subject to the moves of *talk*. They follow the logic of signifying forms themselves—a logic of mimesis, retellings, and immanence.

> MISS LAVENDER: Honey, don't put that down in that book, that ain't nothin'
> but just talk is all. These people like to hear theirself talk . . .
> Well, I could tell you a thang or two but I'll tell you one thang, there ain't
> nothin'
> 'round here
> but just talk.
> This place is all talk.

The Space of Mediation

Picture how in the narrativized space of the camps people say everything is just talk and they don't have no ideal what things "mean"; everything is ways with words, nothing but meanness, lyin', braggin', and people runnin' their mouths. Yet they also say that stories and images just come in the mode of things that just happen. Talk follows along in the wake of events, searching for the noticeable and the signifying; what begins as an automatic chronicling of "things that happen" ends arrested by accidents that have the force of fate behind them.

Remember, then, the tense rhythm of restless action and scanning followed by moments of just settin' to make somethin' of thangs. How people out roaming the hills come across places that remember. How big meanings culled out of the proliferation of stories, monuments, memories, and litanies come to be written through with the texture of words overheard and sights overseen and are in-filled with the density of rhythms, intonations, and partial, accidental associations. Picture the

32. Pete and Clemmy Acres, Odd. Photograph © Em Herzstein.

sense of "something more" emergent in talk and culled, at moments, into ideals of a mysterious, encompassing order. Picture, in short, how the rhetorical drift of *just talk* can end, as if by accident, in the space of *ideals*, and how ideas take on both the overwhelming authority of things that just come and the moves of tricky, polemical, or playful talk.

In the inescapably mediated space of a narrated world it is as if the tension between talk and idea calls attention to itself, and the gap between word and world becomes an object of fascination, signaling mysterious effects and unforeseen possibilities. Events grow texted as narrative performance fashions utterances into coherent, effective, and memorable signs (Bauman and Briggs 1990:73; Hanks 1989). "Things that happen" are imbued both with the expectation of anomaly or chance occurrence and with the quality of revealed distinctions, overarching laws, and moral-mythic orders (White 1981). The gap between sign and world grows fecund and is written through with the countervailing metaphorics of event/idea, history/stasis, seeing/knowing, inside/outside, partiality/transcendence (S. Stewart 1984). The world seems to speak itself and to speak itself as a story written through with narrative coherence and moved by the force of desire. Yet everything remains *just talk*.

In the accusation that everything is just talk—a matter of rhetoric and style—the referential "truth value" of talk is undermined and "the act of speaking is put on display, objectified . . . [made] communicatively accountable" (Bauman and Sherzer 1974:xix; Bauman 1977; Hymes 1975). Yet the very claim that everything is *just talk* highlights the poetic function of talk—the order of effects linked to the message itself and not to an "external" referent (Jakobson 1960)—and promotes "the palpability of signs, deepens the fundamental dichotomy of signs and objects" (Jakobson 1960:356). In the very process of attending to the relation of language to reality, then, talk of *ideals* turns back on itself, tracing an order of poetic effects that has the power not just to reflect the real but to give it form. It reveals the constructed effects of forms and draws attention to the force of textuality itself—the "quality of coherence or connectivity" in a storied cultural real (Hanks 1989:96).

In the fundamental mediation of events, identities, and social orders in narrative form, the question is not how narrative rearranges preexisting subjects and objects but how things are written into the "ideology of form"; how the aesthetic act draws the density and texture of sociality, history, and cultural politics into itself and carries their weight as an immanent subtext—a "political unconscious" (Jameson 1981); how images cull the power of mediating form into a felt, socially shared object in the world—heavily voiced and embodied and filled with tropic patterns and resemblances (Urban 1991); how forms index a "something more" beyond particularity and the everyday yet lodged within it. Talk is at once

33. Bedroom with matching patterns. Photograph © Harriette Hartigan, Artemis.

denaturalized (Culler 1975) and given renewed force. On the one hand, it carries a reminder of the irreducible sociality of meaning and the inability of any discourse to "dictate" its meanings absolutely (Chambers 1991). On the other hand, it carries the weight of desire for an intimate, mimetic union of word and thing, image and meaning (Genette 1979; S. Stewart 1984), a union of the "real" world and the imaginary space of desire "on the side of the road" where meaning grows incarnate in things, voices emerge from the woods, and the traces of hidden meanings show themselves as if of their own accord.

The very accusation that everything is *just talk*, then, motivates a search for things that just come. There is both a sense that "nothing is sacred," that things are not what they seem and there's no telling what people might do, and an encompassing sacralization of every act and word and every piece of wrecked material so that the traces of things that happen haunt the "ordinary world" with the absent presence of what could be despite everything, and what should be if only, and what "must be" indexed in signs gathered out of the traces of contingent effects.

Claims and Counterclaims

Kenny Miller is not a religious man yet he was outraged when his teacher in a college history course "put down" the Bible, bragging that the Truth lay in evolutionary science, not creationism, as if he knew for sure.[1]

> Took his Bible and put it down.
> Now that's just **ignorant**, any fool can see **that**.
> Well, look at the creatures—big and small, male and female, and ever' one of 'm has a **place**. You don't see a coon and a fox fightin' over their places, do you?
> No sir, that's where you know it's a **God**.

In the quality of coherence of a texted world it is "as if" there is a God. Yet just as Kenny's *ideal* emerges as back talk to his history teacher's bragging claim, his own claim, too, remains open to the accusation that it is *just talk*. What happens, then, when people venture to *talk* of *ideals*? This is talk that perches precariously on the ephemeral, shifting boundary between claim and truth. It scans things for signs like a hungry scavenger feeding on lurking presences and then returns to its perch with nothing but bloodied claws and the graphic memory of its flight. In one moment it catches hold of a claim that there is an order of places in the difference between neighbor and kin, Christian and sinner, black and white, male and female, a McKinney, a Graham, and a Bowens. But in the next it finds itself caught in counterclaims and disclaimers.

Take the "orders" of race or gender, for instance. There are black and white sections of a camp, black and white hollers, and black and white churches. Camps with a reputation for too much mixing elicit fear and repulsion in an apocalyptic language of the End Times. Blacks and whites can be close lifelong friends as neighbors but the thought of interracial sex makes people sick to their stomachs ("I don't know why. It's nothin' against 'm, hit's just the way we was raised up is all"). The women have their houses and the men have their trucks and the burned-out cinderblock bars for heavy drinking. A woman walking the roads is just looking for sex; a man who is not kin does not step foot in a woman's house without arousing suspicions of illicit sexuality; a woman who walks into a bar or a stand where men are gathered to talk will stop talk in midsentence, and the men will turn and stare until she states her business and gets out.

Yet, as if caught in the act of making claims, the order of places and ideals elicits the counterclaim that people are people, that Christians who claim to be better than other people are worse than the worst sinners, that everyone is black underground in the mines, that there is nothing so ridiculous as a man so babyfied he can't cook a meal for himself or a woman so feminine she can't chop a pile of wood or shoot off the head of a thief who comes in the night, that ever'body 'round here's related to ever'body else, is all—hit's a mess is what it is, don't ask **me**, I don't have no *ideal*, go ask so and so, come back and tell me what she says, I'd like to **hear that.**

It is not as if *ideals* were like fixed norms set in a heaven of ideas above the daily poetics of agency, encounter, and conflict in the camps. Rather, they emerge in a social semiotics as *signs* to be deployed and read, and they themselves become the subjects of talk. Deployed in a contest of claim and counterclaim, they give rise to a social imaginary that grows dense with the tension of a cultural real.

There is the elderly African-American man in Rhodell who lives in such fear of racist attack that he still keeps his windows blacked and sits at night in a dark corner at the back of the house listening. There is the elderly black woman at war with her white neighbor who drops hints of her powers in witchcraft. Al Maxwell lived in an isolated black holler and used his living room as a stage for his stories about his family of six brothers, all over six feet and all over two hundred pounds, who took on injustice in wild rages and rampages and nobody could touch them; his stories about the bad motherfuckers in Wyoming County (a predominantly black county to the south); his stories of how he and his buddy would find a dark corner in the mines and lie down and go to sleep and nobody could see them because they were black; his stories about the crazy black miner who one day cut off his finger just to collect workmen's compensation and got a pink Cadillac out of it and then did it again and again until he hadn't but two fingers left—the thumb on his left hand and the pinky on his right—and that guy was crazy rich. There were the African-American kids in Rhodell who would march down the middle of the road six or seven abreast blasting a boom box and dancing. There was the hoodoo talk about big old sores that came up all over a woman's legs and the hoodoo doctor from North Carolina gave her a salve for them and she put it on and then threw the tube of salve over her shoulder into the creek without looking back and the sores came out worms and dropped off her legs and were gone, or the hoodoo talk about talking coins that you were supposed to boil in some water in a little pot on the stove and the coins would sing. There was the white man who lived way out and one day came upon three or four white men who had a black man tied spread-eagle and naked to the hood of a car and were getting ready to do something to him and the man ran home and got his shotgun and ran them off and the black man escaped into the woods miles and miles from his home in a black camp where they said he had gotten a white girl pregnant. There are the young white men from way up the holler who decorate their trucks with the Confederate flag. And there is Eva Mae— poor, black, and crazy—who walks the road between Rhodell and Amigo all day, waving an ax or a butcher knife at people who stop to give her a ride and the women get a kick out of her because she doesn't take anything from people and she's good to talk to.

They say women and men may have their places but anyone fool enough to take anything from a spouse will draw disapproving comment.

> EASTER LILLY: Way she **takes it,** she acts like she's an animal, or a robot or somethin'.
> Like that movie, *Stepford Wives,* you cain't **blame** them women for what they did [i.e., for killing the men and blowing up the town after the men tried to turn them all into robots] 'cause **that's** aggravatin', now it **is.**
> Well, you gotta turn it **back** on 'm.

Sissy Miller got mad when her husband Buddy suggested that she could be more sexual and she "turned it **back** on 'm."

> Because I don't have to **take** that from him.
> So I said, "**OK** honey, if you **say** so," and me and Joyce got to **talkin'**
> and we went down **Hoover's** and got us a bucket a red paint
> —the **bright** red—
> and we painted that bedroom red from the floor to the ceilin' and we didn't spare no **paint,** buddy.

Well, we like to **died** laughin'.
An' he come **in** and I told him, "**Honey**, come **in** here a minute."
An' his eyes come up out of his head like a big ol' fat **fish** or somethin'. **Hah!**
An' said, "Well, what's wrong, **ho-ooney?** You want me to act like a **whore,**
now I got me a nice red **room** for it."
Well, we like to **died**.

They say men work in the mines and women keep house and have
children, but the very ideal/idea of gendered places and roles is articulated
only in the course of stories of negations and reversals that end in representations of sheer agency or spirit. Speaking as a woman (or a man) is a
matter of "speaking for yourself." A notion of "natural" differences gives
way to the mediation of gendered *ways* of talking and acting. In a gendered discourse, women do not assume that they are "naturally" good
mothers or housekeepers, but every woman claims that she, for one, is
"not the type" and fashions her own passage into and through a female
sphere as a drama of encounter and desire. They say marriage makes
women "spread and get fat," and they launch radical diets in a battle with
the body and with jealous husbands who would just as soon keep them
fat so they can't "do nothin'" (with another man). Housework is a battle
with *the nasty* that can one day send a woman to the bed smothering with
the dizzy and the next day propel her into a fit of cleaning and tossing
things out at an incredible pace. Childbirth is recounted as a dangerous
and bloody accident in the truck racing over the hills to get to the hospital. They brag that their children are mean (i.e., independent, back-talking, clever, self-assertive), complain that they hang on them, and threaten
to "whup the fire out of 'm." They liken their men to the men's trucks—
all wrecked and broken down with their parts hangin' out—and picture
them as babies with their (liquor) bottles: "They aren't **like** babies, they
are babies." They talk among themselves daily—talk that grows bawdy
(R. Green 1984), grotesque, and hilarious—and their friendships are tight
and lifelong. They claim to be *crazy*—no tellin' **what** they might do; they
disappear, if they can, into a magazine or a novel; they have visions; they
long for the perfect man or a big house or union with Jesus; they weep
inconsolably at the deaths of their mothers, their siblings, and their children and long to be reunited with them in heaven; they hold to their
memory with shrines and mounted photographs and little bits of things.
    Men are not naturally good husbands or providers but "by nature"
given to drinking and fighting and running the roads. They get turned
around in middle age in sudden Christian conversion—"I put that bottle
down and I never touched it again. Never wanted to"—and their testimony dwells on their wild days, performing a poetics in which, they say,
people have to "get all the way down" before they can "see."

ARBUTUS ANDERSON: Oh, I was a sinner. I'd do just **anythang** atall.
I'd get **drunk** and **lay out** all night on my **wife**, **gamble**, **rob** people, oh, just anythang, I didn't **care**.
Me and some of my buddies, we'd go lookin' somebody to **beat up**.
And this **one** boy, we got him down to where he couldn't git up no more and I kicked him in the mouth and the blood a comin'.
That's **right**! That's how I **done** people! And I jess stood there and laughed a watchin' that blood come and havin' me a **good ol'** time.
But **praise Jesus, He saved me.**

Mining, they say, gets in the blood and, though passed on from father to son, is not "natural" work but a dramatic encounter with danger. Some come out of the mines and take to their beds—"Never did go back into the mines anymore after that." Others claim it is the fear itself that kills—"You have to put all that out of your mind." I remember visiting Jack Wesley Birdsong with the doctor who gave him shots for the vitamin D deficiency that came of his years in bed in the middle of the family's shack with the sheets pulled up over his head. He would talk of visions he had had while his *crazy* wife yelled about how her sons had kicked in the door in a drunken rage and the flood had taken their kitchen (you could see the water rushing underneath).

The men, like the women, talk among themselves, weaving fantasies of revenge and escape, talking dirty about women, and keeping up with who did what. They claim women cackle like hens, they disappear on hunting and fishing trips to the Smoky Mountains, they drink until they see the devil or study on the Bible until they see Jesus crying outside their windows at night. They teach their children how to do things and how to take care of themselves just as their daddies taught them. They sit together in the cab of a truck in the alley in the dark, hardly talking at all.

Talk of *ideals* raises the problem of tracking how cultural forms simultaneously produce both naturalizing claims to order and identity and denaturalizing critiques and dissimulations. As with any claim to "truth" they can be asserted only through the positing of a "law," yet every law also produces a loophole and raises the specter of lawlessness (Lyotard 1984). A code asserted creates, in that very assertion and at the same moment, an "Other" space perched "in the interstices of the codes that it undoes and displaces" (de Certeau 1984:78). Ideas do not emerge spontaneously but "come up" in the course of countervailing tensions or alternative possibilities. In a notion, yet another notion is always already at work; an *ideal*/idea emerges only in the enactment of the extremes that delimit its own internal dialectic; it depends on the graphic depiction of its negation as the very condition of its existence (Žižek 1991:68).

The problem of *ideals*, then, is not that of a simple tension between a notion and its always incomplete realization, or between the ideal and the real, but a split born within the dialectical structure of the notion itself. The internal split, or gap, in *ideals* creates the possibility, if not the necessity, for complex appropriations, resistances, and excesses. It posits not just the possibility of different voices or points of view but a wound in the very notion of the natural, the necessary, or the good in the social order. It introduces an "Other" order of mysterious discontinuities and continuities, strange reversals, surprising revelations, and unexpected eruptions of agency.

In the dizzying spin of naturalized and denaturalized meanings, *ideals* (ideas) are read out of acts and appearances as if they were *signs* that could reveal something more. They show themselves and retreat again, at once submerged in and emergent in an immanent subtext that reads events in the mode of "as if." *Ideals*, then, take on the weight of the very dialectic of centripetal and centrifugal forces (Bakhtin 1981) itself—the sheer chronicling of "things that happen" in a dialectic with a sense of something more and underlying, the revelation of a hidden meaning discovered in the accidental contingencies of the everyday, the gathering of the accidents of birth and circumstance to the momentary clarity of ideas of fate and social *place*, the dismantling of the seemingly natural in the face of critique and surprise reversal. The space of a fluid and shifting boundary between naturalized "ordinary" speech and poetically marked speech-that-turns-back-on-itself gives rise to both affirmative, reproductive, hegemonic forces in culture and critical, innovative, counterhegemonic impulses (Bauman and Briggs 1990). Both are formed together in *ideals* as a form of semiotic praxis that is itself a social act. Like all language taken as a form of social praxis, they are deviations from the reductions of the "ordinary" and "standard" and proliferations out of the bare bones of the Really Real (S. Stewart 1984; Thibault 1991; Volosinov 1986).

Ideals/ideas, then, hold open an interpretive space in which everyday events are taken as a test of principles, and yet their "meanings" are asserted not in the certainty of an indicative mode that claims to re-present fully present objects but in the indeterminacy of the subjunctive mode—the mode of "as if." In "Social Dramas and Stories about Them," Victor Turner (1981) suggests that a subjunctive mode centered in the indeterminacy of "that which is not yet settled, concluded and known" (153) arises as an orientation in moments of breach or crisis that may ultimately function to restore the indicative mode of a known social order. Here I am suggesting that the subjunctive mode and what I have more generally called a "space of desire" may be seen as an effect of the "crisis" of signification itself once signification is taken as a social praxis always already

in-filled with social conflicts and cultural poetics and politics. The social
order is itself mediated by forms and so subject to doubt and room for
maneuver (Chambers 1991).

Ideals in the Space of Desire

Ideals stand as material signs not of positive objects and finished facts but
of latent possibilities. They track the sudden eruption of agency out of
nature, or fate out of accident, the sudden clarity of desire in the face of
a world got down, sudden reversals of identity or order, the sense of a
latent meaningfulness that is always already lost or waiting ahead just
beyond reach.

Take the *ideal*/idea of neighborliness. The story inevitably begins with
the disclaimer that a neighbor is not just someone who lives next door but
an idea enacted.

> LACY REED: A man, he might live right up next to you in the same alley, and
> he'll steal ever'thang that ain't nailed to the ground and them **too** if he can find
> some way to pry 'm **loose**.
> That man, he ain't my **neighbor**, he don't care nothin' 'bout me.
> I might be a layin' on th' side a th' road a **dyin**' an' a callin' somebody come
> **he'p** me, **he'p** me **please** and **that man, he'll** pass me by, and never think twicet.
> But **another man**, he might be a **stranger** to me, maybe he ain't never seen me
> in his life, but now he'll stop.
> He'll breathe his own last breath into you and never think twicet.
> **That man**, he's a **neighbor**.
> And he'll go out of his way to help you just any way he can.

The ideals of kinship begin in naturalized idioms of blood ties but bog
down in a logic of exceptions, transgressions, and eccentricities. Kin are
your people; they're just people you have; with kin you can be yourself.
The difference between a Mills and a Graham is instantiated in a mysterious affinity of blood: the Millses are lazy, the Grahams always did run
their mouths, the Bowenses take fits of fightin' and layin' out of a night.
Bud Lilly is stubborn because he's a Lilly; Sissy Walker has a green thumb
because she's a Walker. Kinship is as natural as the air you breathe
(Erikson 1976) and forms an all-pervasive web of associations that *just
come*. It is impossible to think of someone without also thinking of their
kin. When Joyce sees Patty out walking alone she says, "There goes Patty
an' them out now"; when Patty asks after Miss Lavender she says, "Have
you seen Miss Lavender and them," even though Miss Lavender lives
alone; Bud Halsey says he knew "Buddy and them back in high school"

34. House with crosses and "Jesus Is Coming," Black Eagle. Photograph © Harriette Hartigan, Artemis.

even though Buddy is the only one of the Meadowses he has ever met. People assumed that Betsy and I must be "kin" where we were so close and looked alike—the *signs* were there; they were constantly calling me "Betsy" and calling Betsy "Katie"—"I don't know why I **do** that, honey. When I look at you, I **know** it's you but I just thank of **Betsy** because she's not **here**."

Yet it is not as if the idea of kinship refers to an objective order of bloodlines. Kinship is evidenced in affinities of blood that seem to *just come*, but people will back off the task of delineating precise genealogies with the disclaimer "I don't have no *ideal*." Genealogical reckoning is a speech genre (Bakhtin 1986) in itself and its mode is far from orderly or objective; it becomes a kind of rhetorical game (S. Foster 1988) in which people spin off names and associations in a faster and faster litany until the effort is derailed by knots or confusions of double and triple relations, inexplicable multiple surnames in a family of blood relations, obvious elisions or outright disrememberings of particular kin, or claims that an objectively close kin tie is only a distant relation (Bryant 1983:46). Then reckoning opens into the digressions of stories of tragic deaths and crazy ancestors who didn't care: grandfathers who went to the pen for running shine; moonshining great-uncles who gave the *revenuers* a run for their money racing down the hollers and over the ridges they knew so well, putting nails in the road for the revenuers' cars, and standing to stare them down down the barrel of a double-gauge sawed-off shotgun; drunken brothers who cut each other with knives, splitting the family lines with their blood; strange families who took religion and bit off the heads of chickens and drank their blood; outlaws living way up the hollers—"so far in they ain't never comin' out." The talk leads not to a sense of a codified order but to dramatizations of agency and accident, fate and excess. In the end, dramatic, devil-may-care incidents and characters point to the sheer force or spirit of a bloodline, and prolific, twisting, unmappable ties give kinship the quality of an uncontained and uncategorized *mess* like a mess of greens: "Ever'body 'round here's related to ever'body else, is **all**. Hit's a **mess** is what it is."[2]

Kinship may be as natural as the air you breathe; however, it refers not to codes and norms and objective ties but to the texting of the everyday and contingent as an order of signs to be read. It remains an idea—a texted sign that signals the radically mediated nature of things. Fashioned in the subjunctive mode of "as if," it reads between the lines of codes and objective orders in a logic of strange and unexpected associations—a logic of excess, revelation, reversal, negation. It is as if affinal blood carried a mysterious affinity; it is as if a woman's family surrounds her by association when you see her driving out the alley alone; it is as if the strangely ordered lexicon of *places* that stretches from "the animal kingdom" to the order of social *places* signals an underlying agency. Most fundamentally, the practice of reading ideas out of the world marks the space of interpretation itself and is written through with all of the anxieties, contradictions, and mysteries of a mediated world.

We could say that it is this "social fact" of a mediated world—this sense of something more beyond behavior and the look of things—that people defend in the ideas of kinship, neighborliness, and Christianity. These are ideas that remain open to maneuver and subject to doubt and contradiction. Sissy Miller came back from the annual McKinney family reunion mad at a man who was there.

> Havin' hisself a **good** old **time,** just as friendly as could be and come to find out he wasn't nobody but a boarder at Aunt May's!
> **Well, all right.**
> Half of 'm there don't know each other, they're just there to have a good time and find out who they **don't know.**
> But now when he started in a **takin' pictures,** that made me so mad I had a mind to **say** somethin' **to** him.
> Goin' around takin' pictures and we don't mean a **thing to 'm!**
> Well, I don't hold to "family right or wrong," I don't hold to these mothers, and I know I'm one, think their kid can do no **wrong,** but buddy **that** guy made me **mad.**

Julie Walker was irate when two women from the next alley showed up with bags of used clothes and curtains as charity.

> Do they think I don't have **kin?**
> Now I don't hold with them what won't he'p nobody but their own, you should he'p anybody **needs** he'p but now **them** two ain't nothin' but **hypocrites.**
> Won't even **talk** to me on the street but they'll **haul** their old **stuff** over here like they're **better'n us.**
> I told 'm, "**Leave it outside,** I got **washin'** to do."

There is a difference between a stranger and a neighbor, a neighbor and kin, a Christian and a sinner, but the difference depends on the ability to enact ideas that are themselves written in the subjunctive mode of "that which is not yet settled, concluded and known" (V. Turner 1981:153)— the mode of "as if." We could say that it is this very indeterminacy that gives claims of ideals their force. The kin at the McKinney family reunion may not even know each other but they know better than to act as if they were kin when they're not. And still yet it is not as if Sissy means to say that the *ideal* of loyalty to kin has the status of a fixed law writ large on the Real.

Well, I don't hold to "family right or wrong," I don't hold to these mothers, and I know I'm one, think their kid can do no **wrong**.

Neighbors should help each other and get out and visit, but it is not as if Julie Walker doesn't have kin or can't tell the difference between a neighbor and a hypocrite. And still yet again it is not as if people shouldn't help neighbors.

Now I don't hold with them what won't he'p nobody but their own.
You should he'p anybody **needs** he'p.

Kenny Miller may not be a Christian but he is not about to talk as if there is no God. Yet it is not as if he is religious.

In the religious discourse, a *sinner* might be the sweetest person in the world and never did a thing to hurt nobody in their whole life and everybody loves them but it is not as if they were saved. Preacher Acres, preaching at a Free Will Baptist Church:[3]

Maybe you never hurt nobody
and you try and he'p people because it **looks good**.
Or maybe you really want to be a good **neighbor**, you know.
And you holt your head up **high**, brother Lacy.
But buddy you're a goin' straight to **hell** if you ain't a **borned again**.
The Lord said, "**You must be borned again**."
He said you **must** be borned again,
He didn't say maybe you **might want to** if you git a **chance**, or it would be a **good ideal**.
He said you **must** be **borned again** if you would be with **me** in **heaven**.

Christians are people changed by a sudden conversion experience that turns them around—a flash of white light, a nervous shock, a sudden insight that marks the world with meaning and makes colors brighter and details more distinct so that they find themselves staring at a pile of leaves, fascinated by intricate patterns and every vein and crumpled edge. They have opened their stony hearts to Jesus and entered an "Other" realm of seeing and interpretation. Everything hinges on the dramatized experience of conversion—a stepping over the line from the ordinary into a space of desire. It is a dangerous passage filled with excess and a sudden surge of sheer energy. People come under conviction and are torn apart and turned around until they give themselves up to be washed in the blood; then they stand waist high in the muddy river for baptism while the others taunt them with threats of snakes hidden under the surface and preachers who hold people under too long. They come up out of the water gasping for breath with their heads flung back and their eyes flung open.

In the Realm of Negations

In the mode of *ideals*/ideas things get turned around and identities do not hold. Against the claim of a straight and narrow path stands the seductions of the broad highway to hell. The ideals of Christianity, kinship, and neighborliness come to light only in the face of their abject negation. What seems high may become low; the heroic may emerge out of a demonized realm or vice versa. They say you know you're saved when the devil is working on you. Christians say you have to choose; there are no two ways about it: "You cain't drive a car two ways. You might want to but you just cain't. No. You go forward or you go backward, one." Yet Christians can be borned again in one moment and backslide in the next. *Ideals*/ideas reemerge as a vigilance. Brother Lacy Woods, testifying in a Free Will Baptist Church:

> The problem is **brangin' thangs in**—a little a **this**, a little a **that** and perty soon you're all **turned around**.
> You have to judge your **own self**.
> Sin is like a **cancer**.
> Once hit's got **started**, why, **buddy**, hit **spreads all over**.
> **First thang**, you might thank you'd just like to have you a **cigarette**.
> **Well**, you say, there ain't nothin' wrong with that.
> Lord knows I ain't pointin' the finger, I smoke myself, but it ain't the **cigarette**.
> That old **cigarette** cain't hurt, there ain't no **devil** in it.
> Cain't nothin' hurt you but your **own self**, **buddy**,
> you're your **own** worst enemy and that's the **truth** right there.
> **(Amen)**[4]
> (That's **right, Brother Lacy**)
> (**Bless him**, Lord)
> (**Thank you, Jesus**)
> **OK now**, maybe when you smoke that makes you wanna have yourself a little ol' **drank**.
> People say there ain't nothin' wrong with **Bingo** in the churches and maybe there **ain't**.
> But now, with **sin**, hit's like with **cancer**, you got to get **straight** and put yourself under **conviction**.

A code for conduct slams into place in the face of graphic transgression and people say they "get a blessing" from *hard preaching*, praising a preacher for a moving performance. Yet a preacher who takes it upon himself to "point the finger" runs an immediate risk of a counterattack. Julie McVey back talked the preacher at the Black Eagle Church of God for preaching that women shouldn't wear jewelry or pants.

Now I know it says in the Bible that it is abomination for the woman to take on the signs of the man but I ain't givin' up **my pants** for nobody I don't care who he is.

I don't believe it's **wrong**, now I **don't**.

A lot a them women was sayin' God **convicted** 'm over it.

Well, **all right**.

If it puts you under **conviction**, that's **one** thang.

But God ain't never convicted **me** over it and I don't care **what** they say.

They oughta **mind** their own **business**.

Like Miss Smith [her mother-in-law] a tellin' me quit **smokin'** where she had her a dream the bed caught on fire.

Now that might a been a conviction on her, you know, I b'lieve it might a **been** but now I didn't **have** no dream and this preacher **down here**, now ah b'lieve he's **crazy**.

He tells 'm, "You cain't wear your weddin' rings," and all this and he walked right down and pointed the finger at pore Rosie Cadle. Now that ain't **right**.

He ain't nothin but a ol' **hypocrite**, probly lays out all night with half the women in the church.

And I'm a gonna tell him, he gits after me, said, "This here's my **marriage** sign, **buddy**, and I ain't **about t'** take it off."

Now I'll wear a **dress** to church b'cause I b'lieve that's **right**.

But I'll tell y' **one thang, buddy**, ain't **nobody** gonna tell me I cain't wear pants in my own **house** and I don't care **who** he is.

Ideals remain lodged in dense spaces of interpretation and sociality. To have the force of conviction they must enact the tension that the Christians call "coming under conviction" and they must follow a logic of redemption—a reading of *signs* of something "more" or "Other" in a world got down. They arise from the state of being in between where the poles of an idea are evident and pressing and then push into a space in which *signs just come*. Preachers assert their authority to speak by raising the specter of those "Other," hypocritical preachers who lie, steal, and run around with the women in church or preach only what people want to hear to keep the dollars coming in. They claim that, for them, the words *just come*, divinely inspired. Testimonies from the congregation begin with disclaimers of person and status—"I ain't had a education and I ain't no good at talkin' but I had to stand up for the Lord this mornin' and tell Him I love Him because I do" ("Bless her, Lord," "Amen, sister Polk"). Johnnie Milan does not know why he is "preaching" in the middle of his Sunday school lesson—"I don't know no better than to stand up and praise the Lord." Naomi Graham does not know why she came to church this morning (she had company in but something told her to come on anyway); Helen Mills reads the Bible every night and loses track of time—just reads and reads. Ultimately the "truth" of things, and the authority to speak, lies in the immanence of felt signs. People say to get saved all you have to do is just stand up and take one step and Jesus will carry you to the altar—"I didn't know what was gonna happen or what I should do. I just started cryin' and I laid down at the altar."[5]

The very *ideal* of kinship emerges only in the presentation of the tension between this idea and the equally potent script of anti-kin in a world got down. There are stories of siblings who treat aging parents like dogs or take them in only so they can steal their checks and then feed them scraps and make them sleep on the floor. There are stories of shameless brothers, caught under the spell of a conniving greedy wife, who offer their starving relatives a "great business opportunity" only to bilk them for every last cent they had. There are no-good sons who sponge off their frail, poverty-stricken, pious mothers and beat them in drunken rages and bring home women for loud sex in the living room just to shame them. There is the mother who left her children to die in the road and then turned to wood. There is the mother—a drunk—who let her son roam the hills until he was electrocuted on an old mining wire and hung suspended while the meat of his heel blew out and fell to the ground. You never know what people will do, yet it is in the very face of that uncertainty that texted *ideals* rise to the surface as a mode of questioning the forms of the world.

The very ideal of neighborliness arises in the face of negations in which a neighbor turns out to be worse than a stranger or a stranger turns out to be true neighbor against all odds and despite all evidence of foolishness and orneriness. The logic of ideals follows a narrative logic of tracking along in the wake of events, discerning sense out of the look of things, fashioning agency out of the accidental and contingent, redeeming signs out of the constant spin of confusions, reversals, and betrayals.

One morning I met Amos Shrewsbury on the street and he said he'd been up all night—hadn't I heard about it?

Well, it was 'bout a quarter after eleven, come on the CB.
An' hit was a little **girl**, couldna been but five or six year old. First you couldn't hardly **hear** it, but then she come just as **plain** as me standin' here next to you talkin'.
Snow was a comin' down **real** bad an' **little baby girl** cryin' somebody come he'p her.
And I mean **hit** was enough to **tear** you **up**.
Seem like they'd went off th' road, her and her daddy, and she's a **callin'** him, like he ain't **movin'**—"**Wake up, daddy, wake up.**"
And then somethin' 'bout a **church**—like she could maybe see one—and then **nothin'**.
Never did hear nothin' more **from** her.

And I come out and got **Tommy** [his brother] and we **started out**.

Well, we tried out **Tommy's Ridge** at that ol' broke down **church** buildin' they got up there and we tried all up **Devil's Fork** and out **Steve'son Road** and all crost **Rhinehart Mountain** and up them lumber roads past the **Reeds'** and oh, just **all over**.

Lord, I guess I been places last night that I ain't **never** been b'fore.

And we had a **time** of it, too.

But they was all **kinds** a folks out a **lookin'**.

I guess we seen **fifty** people and they was trucks off the road all over, just a slippin' and a slidin' **buddy**.

Well, we pulled **several** of 'm out of a ditch, we was **out in it** all night.

But nobody never did **find** 'm and I guess they **ain't out there** or **froze up** by now, **one**.

But, now, **buddy**, I'll **tell** y' **somethin'**. I don't **b'lieve** she's ever **out** there.

Well, we'd a **heared** on the radio b'now and there ain't been not near'y a **word**. Just a **cryin'** wolf.

Now, buddy, **that's** how they'll **do** y'.

But I'll tell y' somethin' **else**, now they keep **on** that a **way** and there's gonna come a day when ain't nobody gonna **care**.

Because people's just **about fed up** with it, and, **really**, you cain't **blame** 'm, it's where people's got s' **mean** anymore.

They're just tryna git people **riled** up is all, lookin' to **start somethin'**.

Then Amos went on to relate horror stories he'd read about where a killer raped a little girl in a parking lot "just like the one we're a standin' in right now" and a babysitter boiled a baby.

Them people, they're nothin' but **animals**.

It might be awful to say, but they oughtta just **kill** 'm.

Because if you **thank** about, what would make somebody **do** a thang like 'at? There ain't nothin' in **this** world would make **you or me** do a thang like that **there**.

Ideals twist and spin in a logic of negation and redemption. Kenny Miller likes to tell of the night some of the Wallses tried to steal his cement mixer "right out from out front of the house."

Way we are around here, we don't miss much.

So this **one time**, I reckon them boys wanted money **pretty bad** and they forgot about the **neighbors**.

Well, don't ask me how she **done** it, but Jesse, she seen 'm out there from **way** down **her place** and they was **at it**.

And she called up here to **Joe**—that's her **daddy**—and **he** called **me** up.

Buddy, here I come out the back a my place
and **here come Joe** out back a his place.

And them **boys**, they got that big ol' thang right out **in** the creek, and they's tryna push it **upstream**, just a **sweatin'** and I mean **fallin' down pushin'**, **hit** was a **sight**.

Well, I didn't care about that old cement mixer, hit don't even **work**, but **they** thought they **had** t' **have** it, **you** know.

Well, I guess they thought they'd git **rich** and go off and live like the **Rockefellers** and them, **you know**.

Well, **me and Joe**, we come a **runnin'** like we's fit to kill.

And them boys, they tuk out a there and jumped in them bushes on Andrew's side th' creek, like couldn't nobody see 'm, and we went over there and hauled 'm **out**.

Andrew, he was a watchin' from the porch and just a **studyin' on it** like he'd never git it **straight** and his face all kindly pushed in.

Well, we told them boys, said, "Whad you wanna do **that** for, **that** old thang ain't **worth nothin'**."

And them boys went on **home**.

We left the cement mixer in the creek out from Andrew's place.

Well, come on back to the **house** and find out **she** called the **law**!

Oh, I was fit to be **tied**. I told her, said, "Whad you wanna go and do **that** for?" Said, "**Git** on that **phone**," said, "and tell 'm **forgit** it," said, "and don't come **down** here." We don't want the **law** down here. **Lord**!

Well, she don't **care**, she's mad where them Walls come and git people's **stuff**. Oh Lord! So the law was already on the way and we had to wait on 'm.

And buddy the law don't **like** to come down '**Migo**.

Well, they **got here** all right and we hadda **time** of it **too**.

We told 'm, "We don' know **nothin'** 'bout it," and they was **mad, buddy**.

And we had ourselves a **time** of it.

But **them boys**, they just live right up the **holler**, we don't want no **trouble**, y' know.

Be **differn'** if they wa'n't from **around** here.

The *ideal* of neighborliness gathers dramatic signs of connection and disconnection into an idiom of automatic noticing and helping out. Yet neighbors who steal are worse than strangers. Yet again, in the end the principle of a local order of "people from around here" asserts itself against the unimaginable imposition of policing force and the abstract order of the state's laws of property. The idea of kinship gathers twisting relations and the scripts of monstrosity and heroics into an idiom of blood. Still yet strangers can be like kin. Christianity gathers class and ethnic subordination, the fear of death, the suffering of disease, and the failure of the will into an otherworldly order of paths through ecstasy and despair, freedom and bondage. In heaven you won't even remember all your lost kin, and all the troubles of this world drop away in the *ideal* of heaven as a final resting point where Christians will be at home with Jesus at last. Still yet, the final resting point is effected only through the violent reversal of the End Times that turns everything on its head.

BROTHER JOHNNY LILLY: Glad to be here this mornin'.
It's good to see so many here this mornin' in the Lord's house.
Because you know, you never know.
You might come here next week and this place ain't gonna be here.
It will be rubble.
No seats and the windows broke out.
This ain't nothin' but a buildin'.
Jesus said he's a comin' back!
You know, Brother Lacy, we like to put things off to tomorrow, don't we.
(OH YES)
But you cain't put off salvation til tomorrow, b'cause there might not be a tomorrow!
You might leave out from here right now today and git in your car and have a wreck.
You don't know when you're goin' on.
And you don't know when Jesus is comin' back.
And when the time comes, honey,
you cain't run and hide in no buildin'
and not under no rock,
And the rivers will run as one blood
and the heavens will open and spill out
and the sinners will run for cover.
Ohhhhh! They might run deep in the mines where it's cool and dark but there ain't no place to hide, Brother Lacy.
(Bless him, Jesus)
(Come on)
And the day is a comin' when you're a gonna wake up
and it might be the middle of the night.
Aha
and you just woke up
and you don't know why
and you go downstairs to the kitchen for a drank of water, Brother Johnny, you're thirstin'.
But it's dark
Aha
and you cain't see
and you raise the water to your lips
and the water is running as blood
and you drank of the blood
and the water is thick with blood
and you know the time is come and the time is run out.

35. Church, Josephine-Lilly road. Photograph © Harriette Hartigan, Artemis.

In the end the logic of ideals of sociality gathers itself into an immanence through the moves of negation and reversal and the search for
signs. In the end it is Halloween, not Christmas, that becomes the public
ritual of community. People's places are transformed into elaborate gory
scenarios—bloody heads hanging off fence posts, bloody signs threatening violence to trespassers, entire household scenes set up in front yards
where the father sits in a stuffed chair reading the newspaper while his
head rests in his lap and the children sit "eating" at the kitchen table with
their heads resting grotesquely on the edge of their plates. On Devil's
Night young men roam the hills and the hollers seeking illicit sexual adventure, pushing over outhouses, felling trees to block the roads, and
frightening old women living alone on isolated hills. The next day angry
neighbors clear the roads and fix old people's outhouses, grumbling
about how no one else will do it. And on Halloween night ghosts roam
aimlessly up and down the unlit alleys without speaking to those they
meet.

Placing People

Ideals emerge as ideas in the course of daily rituals of sociality like the
constant effort to *place* people. In a sociality based on indeterminate
ideals/ideas and the constant possibility of transgression, misinterpreta-
tion, and betrayal, the everyday has grown in-filled with *signs* and *ways*.
They say people should get out and visit and they should speak to whoever they meet. But there are *ways* of approaching someone's place that
signal participation in an order of signs. A stranger who emerges un-
announced from the woods will be met with hostile stares and a shotgun
poised at the ready until he states his business or retreats. One day when
I was walking up Devil's Fork holler some young men threw rocks at me
when I tried to pass their place. I retreated back down the holler, crossed
the creek, and passed their place under cover of the woods, careful not to
tread too loudly on a branch. Yet they cast piercing stares in my direction
as if they knew I was there, and when one of them shouted I crouched in
fear that they would hunt me down like an animal.

People who meet must *place* each other (Kingsolver 1992), sifting
through signs of identity that drift off into drama and mysterious connection in the narrative logic of contingency, engagement, encounter, and
revelation. Social place becomes a sign not of a fixed social order but of
the social imaginary immanent in *ways*. One day Miss Cline and Sam
McKinney met in the waiting room of the local health clinic and immediately began to *place* each other, drawing a sense of social and natural
orders in around the bare outlines of names and bodies.

MISS CLINE: You know my **maw maw** was a McKinney.

SAM: Well, what McKinney **was** she?

MISS CLINE: Her daddy was **Justice** McKinney. It was them that stayed out Odd and there's some down Besoco, they're some kin.

SAM: Well . . . My **daddy's** people's from out **Basin Mountain**. I don't reckon we're any **kin**.

MISS CLINE: No.

Might be **your daddy** and my **maw maw** was **cousins**.

SAM: Might **be** now, I don't **know**.

MISS CLINE: Well, didn't he have a big ol' **place** on his **arm** like a **walnut**?

SAM: A **walnut**. No, I don't **b'lieve** he had a **walnut**. But now, he got a place where he got hurt in the mines.

Then Sam told the story of an explosion in the mines that killed his father's work buddy and left its mark on the grieving man's arm.

. . . lost his only friend in the world.

MISS CLINE: **Well** . . . them places can be aggravatin'.

SAM: **Oh yeah**. They sure **can be**.

Then Miss Cline, picking up the association of *places* on the body, told a story about how she fell out of a tree when she was a child visiting her grandmother at the old family place.

An' hit come a place big as a **baseball bat**.

Hit's a big ol' place still **yet** [and she showed it].

Another time Keyford Johnson and Miss Woods tried to figure how they knew each other. But again, the reading of relations quickly shifted from a process of trying to figure out lines of connection to a process of figuration itself.

KEYFORD: **I know I know** you but I can't **place** you.

MISS WOODS: **Oh yeah**, you **know** me, I'm a **Johnson**. My **daddy** worked with **your** daddy up at **East Gulf**.

KEYFORD: That right? . . . well, is that **Lendo** Johnson or would that be **Vergie** and them?

The conversation moved on, circling in on which Johnsons, where they lived, at what "time" the two men had worked together, and the way of life of that time.

MISS WOODS: Well, I went to school with Bobby **Meadows** and them and didn't they live out next to your **brother**—can't thank of his name.

KEYFORD: **Who**? You mean **Buddie**?

MISS WOODS: No, now hit's not **Buddie** 'cause **I know him**. The one stays out **Cool Ridge**.

KEYFORD: Cool Ridge . . .

Well, **now** I've got **several** brothers out that way . . .

There's **Buddie**. He's in that trailer **side th' road** where it turns up what they call **Hick holler**.

MISS WOODS: **No**, it ain't **Buddie**.

KEYFORD: **All right**, then there's **Dewayne**, he's got a **place** down b'low th' stand with all the Chevies out front.

MISS WOODS: **No**, it ain't him. This here I'm talkin' 'bout, it was a **white** house a way up on a **hill**, whole **graveyard** a **trucks** around it.

KEYFORD: Graveyard a trucks . . .

No . . . don't b'lieve that's no relation to **me** . . .

'less you're thankin' 'bout my baby brother **George**.

He used to have a place up there, b'lieve that's who you're thankin' 'bout, but now he left out a here—oh **Lord**, hit's been **years** ago . . .

Well his **wife**, one a them Reeds **kilt** her in a **car wreck**.

She was **no good**.

Drankin' and a **carryin' on, awful** bad to drank.

But now it was a **shame**. They said they went off the four-lane right there at **Beaver Dam**.

Said the car sunk down like a stone.

There was a man **saw** it and they said he tried to **he'p** 'm but he couldn't get **to** 'm. They had to get one a them big dredge shovels, come **dredge 'm up** from the river.

They said they was **scratch marks** on the winda where she tried t' get out.

Left all them **kids**.

George, he went up **Ohia** and the kids, they went **with him**. They all went up there to stay. Never did come back no more after that.

She was awful bad to carry on but it was a shame.

MISS WOODS: Well . . . I didn't know he'd left out.

KEYFORD: **Oh yeah**, been years now . . . I didn't know you knew him.

MISS WOODS: **Oh yeah**.

The ritual of "placing people," then, like other rituals of talk in the everyday, produces a narrative proliferation and a web of mysterious associations. *Ideals*/ideas lie embedded in it as *signs* of the force, density, and texture of cultural production itself. Culture lies present in traces and catches itself up in a space on the side of the road where a gap in meaning is a *sign* of forces at work, and voices embody both the coherence of a texted world and the inevitable indeterminacy of "meaning" and desire.

36. Truck. Photograph © Harriette Hartigan, Artemis.

9

A Space on the Side of the Road

THE LAST CHAPTER ended with a beginning—the ritual of "placing people" that stands as a pretext and condition for *talk* that turns to story. It is then, and at countless like moments, that the space of story in a doubly occupied place grows dense with signs once again: signs of suffered impacts *remembered* in *places* in the hills and on the body, signs of sociality read out of a willingness to talk and lodged in the intense particularity of local forms. Such moments signal a fundamentally mimetic mode of cultural production and critique in which meaning grows immanent in narrated and re-membered things. They both insist on the situated and contingent and demand an interpretive space in which people can make something of things through mimesis, remembrance, and desire. This is because they are fundamentally a re-telling that carries the weight of all the previous re-tellings and begins again.

The space they delimit—a space ultimately intensified and graphically re-presented as "a space on the side of the road"—is a space grown more, not less, prolific in the face of modernity and postmodernity. Caught in a cultural order of things and yet still ex-centric and vulnerable, it depends on the claim that things are not what they seem. It slips discontinuous local effects into the space of "America" and fashions out of them a room to maneuver (Chambers 1991). It embeds the mythic in the ordinary and gathers the past and future into the present. It elicits a logic of encounter and a dream of redemption and return. It grows dense in the gap between word and world or sign and meaning where ideals are discovered in their negations, laws take the form of hearsay, "truths" are lodged in ways of telling and multiple, shifting retellings, and culture itself becomes an anticipation, a mode of questioning (E. Taylor 1992a), a fecund indeterminacy (Taussig 1987).

At once concrete and ephemeral, tactile and uncanny, restive and caught in a deadly calm, it exceeds the space allotted to it by its own history. It replaces bourgeois notions of order with its own more lyrical order (Gates 1988), interrupting the hierarchy of system over accident or reality over fiction long enough to imagine something more or "Other." It draws attention to differences and borders and to moments of boundary/passage between inside/outside, wildness/civilization, animal/human, life/death, revival/decay. Then it catches itself up in its own nervous trajectory through a minefield of forces. It becomes fascinated with accidents

and derailments, watching to see what happens when things collide or
de-compose. It encounters things, takes to things, piles things up, smothers, and has to get out and go. It digs itself in and grows vigilant. It claims
a place for itself only through the constant experimental activity of foolin'
with thangs, and so it finds itself vulnerable to things frightening and
sublime, uncanny and disastrous.

It grows overcrowded and squirrelly in the constant proliferation of
back talk and mimetic excess, in the nervous oscillation of truth and lie,
the flights of fancy, the restless coming and going, all the runnin' the
roads and people runnin' their mouths, the sights noticed out of the corner of the eye. It culls meanings into heightened performances—scripted,
mediated re-presentations that give pause to imagine a cultural real. It
culls the density, texture, and force of things into overwhelming lyric images and grows ruminative and melancholic.

Following a scripted narrative logic into the twists and turns of things
that happen, it takes anecdotes as graphic theoretical models. It spectacu-
larizes. It bends plot to *ideal*, culls disparate effects into *signs* that haunt,
and fashions structures of transformation into moments of dramatic conversion. It spreads contagiously and amasses itself in things. It digresses,
drifts off into retellings and versions. When it reaches the end it begins
again, slipping and sliding through partial recognitions, juxtapositions,
delays, and the indeterminate trajectories in which it sees itself as "action" itself. From a narrative perspective caught up in the movement of
unfolding events and the remembrance of impacted bodies and objects,
there is literally "no telling" what might happen or what people might do,
yet there is also, in the very moment of the aporia, the desire to watch out
for things, to chronicle, and to make something of things.

Now that the fieldwork is long over, I am reminded of "a space on the
side of the road" through other intensely mediated forms—the field notes,
the visits to West Virginia, the phone calls, postcards, and letters, or the
bits and pieces of things I read in the news about this and other such
places, or the things glimpsed out of the corner of the eye or overheard on
the streets of Austin, Texas, where I now live. Like the pieced-together
house on the creek that I pass every day on my routine route back and
forth to the office through South Austin. Or brief encounters like the one
a few weeks ago as I was standing in a photo lab dropping off pictures for
this book. An African-American man pushed open the door and stuck his
head partway in, motioning me to come closer.

> THE MAN: [Quiet, hesitant, mumbling.] Can you help me?
> ME: [Irritated, in a hurry to get out of there and beat the rush hour traffic
> home.] **What?**

THE MAN: I was, I been walkin' up and down that . . . is that Nay, Nagray, **Nnay-Chay**, I been up and down over there, walkin' up and down for a looong time, I'm lookin' 1900 block **Nay-Chay, Nay** . . . Is that . . . there's spoze t' be bus stop on **Nay** . . .

ME: [Confused.] **What?**

THE MAN: [Embarrassed, looking down, points to a street sign across a busy street.] **Nay** . . . there's no 1900. I went up one side and there's all these big houses like fraternities or somethin' in the 1500s and 1700s and up the other side and there's a office buildin', but I cain't see if—is there a bus goes up there?

ME: [Peering across the street at the street sign.] **OH**, that's **Nueces**, is that what you're **lookin' for?**

THE MAN: [Looking at me, uncertain.]

ME: **Ah,** let's see, this should be the 1900 block right about here, ah, **yeah,** see that sign right there over there—that's Nueces too, it jogs around here and goes down here [pointing].

THE MAN: [Following my finger, looking nervous.]

ME: **This** should be the **1900 block** right down **here** because this is **Martin Luther King** and that's **19th Street, isn't it?**

THE MAN: Martin Luther King? Is there a **bus stop?**

ME: I don't **know.** But that's **Nueces,** 1900 block. Go right down there and **look.**

THE MAN: Right here?

ME: Yeah, go **down there.**

When he left, a man who had come in in the middle of all this turned to me and said, "I think he's illiterate—he can't read the **sign,**" and I said, **"Oh my God,** I guess **so."** A few minutes later I ran across Nueces to pick up fajitas at Taco Cabana, and I saw the man standing with some other people at the bus stop, looking nervous and talking.

The news from West Virginia is always cryptic and intense like the postcard about "my house" burning down or Denny Graham's story about his daughter's suicide after he got down with the unemployment and wouldn't **go** and didn't **do** nothin' and I guess she just couldn't **take** it no more, or Ollie Lilly's story about the man who took a used stamp off a letter he got and stuck it back in the mail on a bill as if nobody would notice, or Stella Smith's visions of the fat man who lives under a rock in the woods, or Orlie Hogan's story about years ago when he was sixteen and he got bad drunk—first time he ever got drunk—and he used to go down there to the teen town in 'Migo and this guy he didn't know beat him up and he had blood from head to foot—worst beating he ever took and he didn't even know it—too drunk.

I called Miss Hansford when they were having trouble with their son-in-law where he was on drugs and alcohol and Valium and he hit rock

bottom and then he finally got saved. Her daughter kept all this from
them and when they found out they couldn't say anything because you
can't interfere with a marriage. They forbade the boy to come to their
house when he was drinking and using profane language and then they
had to go get their daughter because he was going to hurt her. He came
for her too, said he wanted his money so Mr. Hansford went to the door
and gave him the money and he threw it over the back wall. He didn't
want the money, he wanted her. They couldn't tell if he had a gun or
what—turned out to be a hatchet—and they found out he'd gone to the
neighbors' and asked to borrow a pistol. They had no choice but to get a
warrant for him. She feels sorry for the young ones but it's the older ones
who don't even use the stuff themselves that's pushin' it. Her son-in-law
finally gave it up without any help—all they need is willpower. And a
little help from the Lord. Used to you could leave your door open no
matter where you went, now you can't go nowheres without lockin' it.
She doesn't like the idea of having to use a gun on somebody but she
doesn't believe the Lord would mean for you to have them break into
your home.

Sylvie Hess writes me letters that always begin "Just a few words to
let you hear from me" and continue, without punctuation, "I been
down sick all winter You know the winter is hard on me I can't hardly
get out to feed my chickens where the ice is bad and its been awful
bad to snow Dovie Bowens comes over to stay the night with me I
don't know what I'd do without her It gets awful lonely with Riley
and mommy gone and nobody to talk to I got out to church this mornin'
and had a good time and we have a new pastor . . . Well I sure hope
you get to come in an' stay for a while this summer if you get all your
work done You know I love you and y'all be good and write to me real
soon."

Sanie Walker says she feels bad where she has enough and other people
don't. She thinks about it a lot, she really does. She has these renters who
can't pay their rent. He was working on the WIN program and then he
didn't get hired and they were getting checks and then they got cut off
those and he started work at Charlie's (a gas station) but he only gets
thirty-five dollars a week—that's a job for a young, single man, not for a
married man. And the wife cries but Sanie's not gonna do a thing about
it, she'd be the last one to do a thing about it. She's got the nerves
somethin' bad, she gets so out of breath after workin' for ten minutes she
can't even say hello to you. She goes to bed at night and she can't sleep at
all and she just screams. Screeeams. The room spins around with the
dizzy and everything gets just as black as coal. She sent away some card
to get some Valium in Williamson, Kentucky. She lost the prescription

Dr. Ross gave her. Why doesn't she get another one? **Oh no**, Dr. Ross would kill her.

Betty Ranson had a terrible spell of the nerves when her sister called and wanted to take her to Florida where their brother was getting operated on for cancer and it wouldn't cost her a cent, they'd pay for her food and stay in a hotel—take three days. But she couldn't go because she didn't have everything ready. Fred says, "Well you ain't got the kids' clothes laid out for school" (she's still got two in school). Her daughter says Florida's a long way off—"You might not make it back where it's too long and you'll get the nerves or somethin' might **happen** to your brother and you might be too **upset** to make it back." Betty says she'd have **went** if she had time to get **ready**. Next time she gets an opportunity to take a trip, she's **gone**. Only time she's ever been anywhere is when they had to take Fred up to the hospital in Morgantown and another time when her brother died in Ohio—you know, on the other side of Washington. Ohio's a long way. They left at seven o'clock that night and got there at four in the morning. Then they stayed all day and stayed in a **motel** and come on back. Her daughter said, "You think Ohio's a long way, **Florida's** a whole lot longer'n 'at." She don't care, she likes to **see things**. Her daughter's going up to Williamsburg to see the museums and all. Betty's got some tops and some new jeans laid away for her at the Dollar Store in Mullens. She has to get down there the first of the week to get them out so she can bring them back and have her to try them on. That way she can bring them back if they don't fit. She has the hardest time getting clothes for her—she's so fleshy and only fourteen. She's wantin' to get up to the Salvation Army and get some more stuff for her. She needs a suitcase. Well she **has** a suitcase but it's not very **nice**. She'd like to get her a suitcase. She and her daughter both got their hair cut short for her daughter's trip.

Easter Lilly got on a plane to go visit her daughter in South Carolina when she had twins. She was terrified—just a country girl tryna git on that big ol' thang and go and she was just a holdin' on and just about screamin' the whole way. But she just had to see them grandbabies and Bud had to stay and work. Well, she got out there all right and they had the biggest ice storm they'd ever had come all over the south—a foot thick all over everything. I heard a lyrical description of it on National Public Radio with people telling stories about the spectacles they'd seen, and you could hear the trees snapping in the background. I called Easter and Bud, and Easter had just got back—she just absolutely refused to get back on that plane and Bud had to drive all the way down there and get her and bring her back. Well, she took a bus halfway and he went and found her and brought her back. But the strangest thing happened when she left.

They had these ducks in the pond out yonder and the mamma duck died
one day about a week before Easter left—just walked out in the woods
and died. And that papa duck mourned her just like he was lost without
her. Well. That day Easter left Bud walked out on the porch and there was
the duck come up from the pond and just a standin' there at the door. Bud
thought he was sick and brought him in to look him over and that duck
crawled right up in Bud's lap—now this is a wild duck—and he just set
there and kept him company all week long until Easter come back and
then he went on back to the pond. Bud says animals know about these
things. I asked them about the ice storm and they said **oh yeah**, never seen
nothin' **like** it. One minute it was just as **still** and nothin' movin' and the
next minute it started in a **crackin', buddy.** Sounded like a war zone, fast
crackin' one after another. Whole **limbs** come down, whole **trees** split
down the middle, the whole **place** was a crackin'. I imagined that I could
still barely hear the cracking in the background.

Such story fragments and lyric images are not easily captured by transcendent theories of culture but flood the very effort with voices and forces of
their own and an "Other" epistemology. To re-present them is to retell
them in another context that must itself grow nervous in the wake of its
own partial understandings and dense under the weight of its own political unconscious. It, too, must admit the space of the gap in signification
and make something of it. Here, too, there is inevitably an ideology of
form, and form cannot be separated from content; there is no way to
retell the story except by re-forming it (Trinh 1991:162). "The story does
not express a practice. It does not limit itself to telling about a movement.
It *makes* it. One understands it, then, if one enters into this movement
itself. . . . The storyteller falls in step with the lively pace of his fables. He
follows them in all their turns and detours, thus exercising an art of thinking" (de Certeau 1984:81).

    Culture, as it is seen through its productive forms and means of media-
tion, is not, then, reducible to a fixed body of social value and belief or
a direct precipitant of lived experience in the world but grows into a
space on the side of the road where stories weighted with sociality take
on a life of their own. We "see" it, as Agee (1941) insisted, only by building up multilayered narratives of the poetic in the everyday life of things.
We represent it only by roaming from one texted genre to another—
romantic, realist, historical, fantastic, sociological, surreal. There is no
final textual solution, no way of resolving the dialogic of the interpreter/
interpreted or subject/object through efforts to "place" ourselves in the
text, or to represent "the fieldwork experience," or to gather up the voices
of the other as if they could speak for themselves. When people in the
camps and hollers say, "I don't have no ideal," they are speaking the

truth; culture isn't something that can be gotten right. At best it is a point of entry, like talk itself. Truth claims emerge in the performative spaces where signs (talk) and meanings (ideals/ideas) collide—the space on the side of the road. But this is the very motive for telling the story and its point in the end.

Notes

Chapter 1
The Space of Culture

1. Thirty percent of the people in the counties of southwestern West Virginia live in trailers since 80 percent of the land is still owned by coal, oil, and gas companies.

2. In *The Origin of German Tragic Drama* (1977) Walter Benjamin articulates a theory of allegorical thought as a process in which the mind stares itself out on luminous images. In *Mimesis and Alterity* (1993) Michael Taussig traces the politics of this phenomenon in "primitive" mimesis and "magical thought" and its resurgence in contemporary life.

3. The term *stand* derives from the farming days when local merchants would establish stockades or "stands" alongside the road where the animals being driven to or from market could be fed and watered and the travelers could stay the night. They developed into local trade centers where farmers traded corn and other products for retail goods (Eller 1982:14) and finally became the local version of the urban corner store and the suburban convenience store.

4. The powerful leader of the United Mine Workers of America in its heyday.

5. John F. Kennedy visited West Virginia in 1960, focusing national attention on the problems of Appalachia as a "depressed area."

6. On invented traditions and imagined communities see Anderson 1983; Batteau 1990; E. Bruner and Gorfain 1984; Cantwell 1993; Dorst 1989; Frykman and Löfgren 1987; Handler and Linnekin 1984; Hanson 1989; Herzfeld 1982; Hobsbaum and Ringer 1983; Newcombe 1979–1980; Roberts 1989; Shapiro 1978; S. Stewart 1991; Thornton 1988; Wagner 1981; Whisnant 1983; Wilson 1973.

7. See Abu-Lughod 1991, 1993; J. Atkinson 1990; Behar 1993; Butler 1987, 1990; de Lauretis 1984, 1987; di Leonardo 1991; Ginsburg and Tsing 1990; Gordon 1988; Haraway 1985, 1989; Hooks 1989; Kahn 1973; Kondo 1986, 1990; Kristeva 1976, 1980, 1982; Lavie 1990; MacCormack and Strathern 1980; Martin 1987; Ortner and Whitehead 1981; Rapp 1979; Reiter 1975; M. Rosaldo 1974, 1980; M. Rosaldo and Lamphere 1974; Scott 1988; Steedly 1993; Stoler 1989a; Strathern 1987a, 1992; Trinh 1991; Tsing 1994; Visweswaran 1988, 1994; Weiner 1976; Yanagisako and Collier 1987.

8. See Appadurai 1988, 1990, 1991; Asad 1973; Bhabha 1990, 1994; Fabian 1983; Feldman 1991; Fischer 1984; Gates 1988; Ghosh 1992; Gilroy 1990; Glassie 1982; Heath 1983; Hooks 1989, 1994; Hurston 1935; Limon 1991, 1994; Pratt 1992; Roberts 1989; Said 1978, 1983, 1986; Scheper-Hughes 1993; Spivak 1988, 1990; Stallybrass and White 1986; Steedly 1993; Stoler 1989b, 1992; Taussig 1987, 1989, 1992, 1993; M. Taylor 1990; Terdiman 1985; Trinh 1991.

9. See, for instance, Babcock 1977; Bakhtin 1981, 1986; Barthes 1957, 1974;

Basso 1984; Bauman 1977, 1986; Bauman and Briggs 1990; Bauman and Sherzer 1974; Brenneis 1984, 1988; Briggs 1990; Briggs and Bauman 1992; Caton 1990; Chock 1986; Clifford 1983a; Crapanzano 1992; Favret-Saada 1980; Feld 1982, 1984, 1988; Finnegan 1967, 1977; Foucault 1970, 1972, 1977, 1978, 1979a, 1979b, 1980; Genette 1979, 1980; Halliday 1978; Hanks 1989; Harding 1987, 1990; Heath 1983; Herzfeld 1985; J. Hill 1985, 1986, 1990; Hymes 1975, 1981, 1985; Jakobson 1960; Johnstone 1990; Kristeva 1976, 1980; Lacan 1977; Mannheim 1991; Pratt 1977; Preston 1982; Rabinow 1986; Ramanujan 1989; Sherzer 1983, 1987; Sherzer and Woodbury 1987; K. Stewart 1988, 1990, 1991; S. Stewart 1983; E. Taylor 1992a, 1992b; D. Tedlock 1972, 1983; Thibault 1991; Titon 1988; Tompkins 1980; Urban 1985, 1988, 1991; Volosinov 1976, 1986; White 1973.

10. See, for instance, Abrahams 1985; Bauman 1977, 1986; Bauman and Briggs 1990; Ben Amos and Goldstein 1975; Brenneis 1988; Briggs 1990; K. Brown 1991; Cantwell 1984, 1993; Cosentino 1982; Dorst 1983; Favret-Saada 1980; Finnegan 1967, 1977; Glassie 1982; Heath 1983; Herzfeld 1981; Hymes 1975, 1985; Jackson 1982; Johnstone 1990; Keeler 1987; Kirshenblatt-Gimblett 1975; Limon 1994; Lord 1960; Maclean 1988; Narayan 1989; Peacock 1968; Peacock and Tyson 1989; Ramanujan 1989; Schiefflin 1985; Smith 1981; Steedly 1993; J. Stewart 1989; Taussig 1987; B. Tedlock 1992; D. Tedlock 1972, 1983; Titon 1988; V. Turner 1979, 1981.

11. See Appadurai 1988, 1991; P. Atkinson 1990; Bakhtin 1981, 1984; Barthes 1986a, 1986b; Batteau 1980, 1990; Bauman and Briggs 1990; Behar 1993; Berger 1973, 1980, 1982; Boon 1982; Bruner and Gorfain 1984; Cantwell 1993; Clifford 1983a, 1983b, 1986a, 1986b, 1988; Clifford and Marcus 1986; Cottom 1989; Crapanzano 1977, 1980, 1992; de Certeau 1984; Deleuze and Guattari 1983, 1986, 1990; Derrida 1970, 1974, 1978, 1981; Dorst 1983, 1989; Dumont 1978, 1986, 1988; Dwyer 1977, 1982; Favret-Saada 1980; Feld 1987; Fischer 1986; H. Foster 1983, 1985; Geertz 1988; Ghosh 1992; Ginsburg and Tsing 1990; Hanks 1989; Hebdige 1988; Herzfeld 1987; Karp and Lavine 1991; Lavie 1990; Limon 1994; Marcus and Fischer 1986; McGrane 1989; Mercer 1991; Pratt 1986, 1992; Rabinow 1977, 1985, 1986; Rabinow and Sullivan 1979; R. Rosaldo 1989; Scheper-Hughes 1993; Scholte 1973; K. Stewart 1988, 1990, 1991; S. Stewart 1984, 1991; Stocking 1983, 1989; Strathern 1987b, 1991; Taussig 1987, 1991, 1992; Thornton 1988; Todorov 1981; Tyler 1984, 1986; Ulmer 1983, 1985; Van Maanen 1988; Volosinov 1986; Webster 1982, 1983, 1986; Williams 1973, 1977; Willis 1981.

Chapter 2
Mimetic Excess in an Occupied Place

1. An earlier version of this story and its discussion were first published in K. Stewart 1990.

2. An earlier version of this story and its discussion were first published in K. Stewart 1990.

3. This resonates with, and may be derived from, a Johnny Cash song, "One Piece at a Time" (1976), which describes the building of a Cadillac over years and

years in the fifties and sixties as the parts are stolen, one by one, from the car factory where the narrator works the line.

Chapter 3
Unforgetting: The Anecdotal and the Accidental

1. See Ulmer's (1985) discussion of Derrida's concept of the "gramme"—the graphic trace—as a symptom of the end of the metaphysical era.

2. An earlier version of parts of this section and the next were first published in 1991 in *Social Research* in an article entitled "On the Politics of Cultural Theory: A Case for 'Contaminated' Critique."

Chapter 4
Chronotopes

1. Amigo was once a collection of four camps stretching up the holler—'Migo 1, 'Migo 2, 'Migo 3, and "the colored camp."

2. Historically sensitive ethnographies of an "Appalachia" undergoing change and reacting to it include Batteau 1983; Beaver and Purrington 1984; Fetterman 1967; Fisher 1993; Fisher and Foster 1979; S. Foster 1988; Gaventa 1980; Hicks 1976; Kaplan 1971; H. Lewis, Johnson, and Askins 1978; J. Puckett 1989; Schwartweller, Brown, and Mangalam 1971; Stephenson 1968; Walls 1972; Whisnant 1980.

3. For discussions of Appalachian migrants in the cities in the seventies and eighties, see Ardery 1983; Coles 1971; Gitlin and Hollander 1970; Howell 1973; Obermiller and Philliber 1987; and Philliber and McCoy 1981.

Chapter 5
Encounters

1. See also Berman 1982; Frykman and Löfgren 1987; Lowe 1982.

2. See Couto (1975, 1989) for a discussion of poverty and health and the political economy of health in Appalachia.

Chapter 6
The Space of the Sign

1. In the *Farmer's Almanac*, the astrological signs are charted to parallel regions of the body.

2. An earlier version of this story and its discussion were first published in K. Stewart 1990.

Chapter 8
The Place of Ideals

1. An earlier version of some of the stories and discussion of gender in this section was first published in K. Stewart 1990.

2. For extended discussions of kinship in Appalachia, see also Batteau 1980, 1982; Beaver 1986; Bryant 1983; Erikson 1976; Fetterman 1967; S. Foster 1988; Halperin 1990; Hicks 1976; Mathews 1965; Pearsall 1959; Stephenson 1968; E. Taylor 1992a, 1992b; Waller 1988.

3. There are churches on every holler and in every camp. All are ecstatic fundamentalist. Denominations vary in their rules about acceptable *signs* but all denominations, including the predominant Free Will Baptists, the Pentecostal Holiness, Assembly of God, Jesus Only churches, and the myriad Community churches, stress "the spirit" in opposition to "the church." Regardless of denomination, a healthy church is one that is "on fire."

4. Parentheses indicate a comment from the congregation.

5. Ethnographic discussions of Appalachian religion include Brewer 1962; J. Brown 1951; Dorgan 1987; S. Hill 1972; LaBarre 1976; Peacock 1971; Peacock and Tyson 1989; Photiadis 1978; Sovine 1983; Titon 1988.

Bibliography

Abrahams, R.
  1976 "The Complex Relations of Simple Forms." In *Folklore Genres*, ed. Dan Ben Amos, pp. 193–219. Austin: University of Texas Press.
  1985 "A Note on Neck Riddles in the West Indies as They Comment on Emergent Genre Theory." *Journal of American Folklore* 98:85–94.
Abu-Lughod, Lila
  1991 "Writing against Culture." In *Recapturing Anthropology: Working in the Present*, ed. Richard Fox, pp. 137–62. Santa Fe, N.M.: School of American Research Press.
  1993 *Writing Women's Worlds: Bedouin Stories*. Berkeley and Los Angeles: University of California Press.
Agee, James, and Walker Evans
  1941 *Let Us Now Praise Famous Men*. Boston: Houghton Mifflin.
Althouse, Ronald
  1974 *Work Safety, and Life Style among Southern Appalachian Coal Miners: A Survey of the Men of Standard Mines*. Morgantown: West Virginia University Press.
Anderson, Benedict
  1983 *Imagined Communities: Reflections on the Origin and Spread of Nationalism*. London: Verso.
Anglin, Mary
  1992 "A Question of Loyalty: National and Regional Identity in Narratives of Appalachia." *Anthropological Quarterly* 65(3):105–16.
Appadurai, Arjun
  1988 "Putting Hierarchy in Its Place." *Cultural Anthropology* 3(1):36–49.
  1990 "Disjuncture and Difference in the Global Cultural Economy." *Public Culture* 2(2):1–24.
  1991 "Global Ethnoscapes: Notes and Queries for a Transnational Anthropology." In *Recapturing Anthropology: Working in the Present*, ed. Richard Fox, pp. 191–210. Santa Fe, N.M.: School of American Research Press.
Appalachian Land Ownership Task Force
  1983 *Who Owns Appalachia? Landownership and Its Impact*. Lexington: University Press of Kentucky.
Ardery, Julia, ed.
  1983 *Welcome the Traveler Home: Jim Garland's Story of the Kentucky Mountains*. Lexington: University Press of Kentucky.
Asad, Talal, ed.
  1973 *Anthropology and the Colonial Encounter*. London: Ithaca Press.
Atkinson, Jane
  1990 "How Gender Makes a Difference in Wana Society." In *Power and*

Difference, ed. Jane Atkinson and Shelly Errington, pp. 127–52. Stanford: Stanford University Press.

Atkinson, Paul
  1990   *The Ethnographic Imagination: Textual Constructions of Reality*. New York: Routledge.
Auerbach, Erich
  1953   *Mimesis*. Princeton: Princeton University Press.
Ayers, Edward
  1992   *The Promise of the New South*. Oxford University Press.
Babcock, Barbara
  1977   "The Story in the Story: Metanarration in Folk Narrative." In *Verbal Art as Performance*, ed. Richard Bauman, pp. 61–79. Prospect Heights, Ill.: Waveland Press.
Bachelard, Gaston
  1969   *The Poetics of Space*, trans. Maria Jolas. Boston: Beacon Press.
Bakhtin, Mikhail
  1968   *Rabelais and His World*, trans. Helene Iswolsky. Cambridge: MIT Press.
  1979   *Estetika Slovesnogo Tvorchestva* (The aesthetics of verbal creation). Moscow: S. G. Bocharov.
  1981   *The Dialogic Imagination*, trans. Caryl Emerson and Michael Holquist. Austin: University of Texas Press.
  1984   *Problems in Dostoevsky's Poetics*, ed. and trans. Caryl Emerson. Minneapolis: University of Minnesota Press.
  1986   "The Problem of Speech Genres." In *Speech Genres and Other Late Essays*. Austin: University of Texas Press.
Ball, Richard
  1968   "The Analgesic Subculture of the Southern Appalachians." *American Sociological Review* 38:885–95.
Barthes, Roland
  1957   *Mythologies*. New York: Hill and Wang.
  1974   *S/Z*. New York: Farrar, Straus and Giroux.
  1975   *The Pleasure of the Text*. New York: Farrar, Straus and Giroux.
  1982   *Empire of Signs*, trans. R. Howard. New York: Hill and Wang.
  1986a   "The Death of the Author." In *The Rustle of Language*, trans. R. Howard, pp. 49–55. New York: Farrar, Straus and Giroux.
  1986b   "The Reality Effect." In *The Rustle of Language*, trans. R. Howard, pp. 141–48. New York: Farrar, Straus and Giroux.
Basso, Keith
  1984   "Stalking with Stories: Names, Places, and Moral Narratives among the Western Apache." In *Text, Play and Story: The Construction and Reconstruction of Self and Society*, ed. Edward Bruner. Prospect Heights, Ill.: Waveland Press.
Batteau, Allen
  1980   "Appalachia and the Concept of Culture: A Theory of Shared Misunderstandings." *Appalachian Journal* 7(1):9–31.

1982   "Mosbys and Broomsedge: The Semantics of Class in an Appalachian Kinship System." *American Ethnologist* 9(3):445–66.

1990   *The Invention of Appalachia.* Tucson: University of Arizona Press.

———, ed.

1983   *Appalachia and America: Autonomy and Regional Dependence.* Lexington: University Press of Kentucky.

Bauman, Richard

1977   *Verbal Art as Performance.* Prospect Heights, Ill.: Waveland Press.

1986   *Story, Performance and Event: Contextual Studies in Oral Narrative.* Cambridge: Cambridge University Press.

Bauman, Richard, and Charles Briggs

1990   "Poetics and Performance as Critical Perspectives on Language and Social Life." *Annual Review of Anthropology* 19:59–88.

Bauman, Richard, and Joel Sherzer, eds.

1974   *Explorations in the Ethnography of Speaking.* Cambridge: Cambridge University Press.

Beaver, Patricia

1986   *Rural Community in the Appalachian South.* Lexington: University Press of Kentucky.

Beaver, Patricia, and Burton Purrington, eds.

1984   *Cultural Adaptation to Mountain Environments.* Athens: University of Georgia Press.

Before the Mountain Was Moved

1970   CRM/McGraw-Hill Films.

Behar, Ruth

1993   *Translated Woman: Crossing the Border with Esperanza's Story.* Boston: Beacon Press.

Ben Amos, Dan, and Kenneth Goldstein, eds.

1975   *Folklore: Performance and Communication.* The Hague: Mouton.

Benjamin, Walter

1969a   *Illuminations,* ed. Hannah Arendt, trans. Harry Zohn. New York: Schocken.

1969b   "The Storyteller." In *Illuminations,* ed. Hannah Arendt, trans. Harry Zohn, pp. 83–109. New York: Schocken.

1969c   "Theses on the Philosophy of History." In *Illuminations,* ed. Hannah Arendt, trans. Harry Zohn, pp. 253–64. New York: Schocken.

1972   *Gesammelt Shriften,* ed. Rolf Tiedemann and Hermann Schweppenhäuser. Vol. 5. Frankfurt am Main: Suhrkamp Verlag.

1977   *The Origin of German Tragic Drama,* trans. J. Osborne. London: New Left Books.

Berger, John, and Jean Mohr

1973   *Ways of Seeing.* New York: Viking Press.

1980   *About Looking.* New York: Pantheon.

1982   *Another Way of Telling.* New York: Pantheon.

Berman, Marshall

1982   *All That Is Solid Melts into Air.* New York: Simon and Schuster.

Bhabha, Homi
    1990   *Nation and Narration*. New York: Routledge.
    1994   *The Location of Culture*. New York: Routledge.
Billings, Dwight
    1974   "Culture and Poverty in Appalachia: A Theoretical Discussion." *Social Forces* 53:315–23.
Boon, James
    1982   *Other Tribes, Other Scribes*. New York: Cambridge University Press.
Bourdieu, Pierre
    1984   *Distinction: A Social Critique of the Judgement of Taste*, trans. Richard Nice. Cambridge: Harvard University Press.
Brenneis, Donald
    1984   "Grog and Gossip in Bhatgaon: Style and Substance in Fiji Indian Conversation." *American Ethnologist* 11:487–506.
    1988   "Performing Passions: Aesthetics and Politics in an Occasionally Egalitarian Community." *American Ethnologist* 14:236–50.
Brewer, Earl D.
    1962   "Religion and the Churches." In *The Southern Appalachian Region: A Survey*, ed. Thomas Ford, pp. 201–18. Lexington: University Press of Kentucky.
Briggs, Charles
    1990   *Competence in Performance: The Creativity of Tradition in Mexicano Verbal Art*. Philadelphia: University of Pennsylvania Press.
Briggs, Charles, and Richard Bauman
    1992   "Genre, Intertextuality, and Social Power." *Journal of Linguistic Anthropology* 2(2):131–72.
Brown, James
    1951   "Social Class, Intermarriage, and Church Membership in a Kentucky Community. *American Journal of Sociology* 57(3):232–42.
Brown, Karen
    1991   *Mama Lola: A Vodou Priestess in Brooklyn*. Berkeley and Los Angeles: University of California Press.
Bruner, Edward
    1985   "Ethnography as Narrative." In *The Anthropology of Experience*, ed. Victor Turner and Edward Bruner, pp. 139–55. Urbana: University of Illinois Press.
Bruner, Edward, and Phyllis Gorfain
    1984   "Dialogic Narration and the Paradoxes of Masada." In *Text, Play, and Story*, ed. Edward Bruner, pp. 56–79. Prospect Heights, Ill.: Waveland Press.
Bruner, Jerome
    1986   *Actual Minds, Possible Worlds*. Cambridge: Harvard University Press.
Bryant, Carlene
    1983   "Family Group Organization in a Cumberland Mountain Neighborhood." In *Appalachia and America: Autonomy and Regional Dependence*, ed. Allen Batteau, pp. 28–47. Lexington: University Press of Kentucky.

Buck-Morss, Susan
    1989   *The Dialectics of Seeing: Walter Benjamin and the Arcades Project.*
            Cambridge: MIT Press.
Butler, Judith P.
    1987   *Subjects of Desire: Hegelian Reflections in Twentieth-Century France.*
            New York: Columbia University Press.
    1990   *Gender Trouble.* New York: Routledge.
Cantwell, Robert
    1984   *Bluegrass Breakdown: The Making of the Old Southern Sound.* Ur-
            bana: University of Illinois Press.
    1993   *Ethnomimesis: Folklore and the Representation of Culture.* Chapel
            Hill: University of North Carolina Press.
Carawan, Guy, and Candie Carawan
    1982   *Voices from the Mountains.* Urbana: University of Illinois Press.
Caton, Steven C.
    1990   *"Peaks of Yemen I Summon": Poetry as Cultural Practice in a North
            Yemeni Tribe.* Berkeley and Los Angeles: University of California
            Press.
Chambers, Ross
    1984   *Story and Situation: Narrative Seduction and the Power of Fiction.*
            Minneapolis: University of Minnesota Press.
    1991   *Room for Maneuver: Reading (the) Oppositional (in) Narrative.* Chi-
            cago: University of Chicago Press.
Chock, Phyllis, ed.
    1986   *Discourse and the Social Life of Meaning.* Washington: Smithsonian
            Institution Press.
Clark, Katerina, and Michael Holquist
    1984   *Mikhail Bakhtin.* Cambridge: Harvard University Press.
Clifford, James
    1983a   "On Ethnographic Authority." *Representations* 1(2): 118–46.
    1983b   "Power and Dialogue in Ethnography: Marcel Griaule's Initiation."
            In *Observers Observed: Essays on Ethnographic Fieldwork*, ed. George
            Stocking, pp. 121–56. Madison: University of Wisconsin Press.
    1986a   "Introduction: Partial Truths." In *Writing Culture: The Politics and
            Poetics of Ethnography*, ed. James Clifford and George Marcus, pp.
            1–26. Berkeley and Los Angeles: University of California Press.
    1986b   "On Ethnographic Allegory." In *Writing Culture: The Politics and
            Poetics of Ethnography*, ed. James Clifford and George Marcus, pp.
            98–121. Berkeley and Los Angeles: University of California Press.
    1988   *The Predicament of Culture: Twentieth-Century Ethnography, Litera-
            ture and Art.* Cambridge: Harvard University Press.
Clifford, James, and George Marcus, eds.
    1986   *Writing Culture: The Politics and Poetics of Ethnography.* Berkeley and
            Los Angeles: University of California Press.
Coles, Robert
    1971   *Migrants, Sharecroppers and Mountaineers.* Vol. 2 of *Children of Cri-
            sis.* Boston: Little, Brown/Atlantic Monthly.

Come All You Coal Miners
  1973   Rounder Records.
Cook, Sylvia
  1976   *From Tobacco Road to Route 66.* Chapel Hill: University of North
         Carolina Press.
Corbin, David
  1981   *Life, Work and Rebellion in the Coal Fields: Southern West Virginia
         Miners, 1880–1922.* Urbana: University of Illinois Press.
Cosentino, Donald
  1982   *Defiant Maids and Stubborn Farmers: Tradition and Invention in
         Mende Story Performance.* Cambridge: Cambridge University Press.
Cottom, Daniel
  1989   *Text and Culture: The Politics of Interpretation.* Minneapolis: Univer-
         sity of Minnesota Press.
Couto, Richard
  1975   *Poverty, Politics and Health Care: An Appalachian Experience.* New
         York: Praeger.
  1989   "The Political Economy of Appalachian Health." In *Health in Ap-
         palachia: Proceedings from the 1988 Conference on Appalachia,* ed.
         Appalachian Center, University of Kentucky, pp. 5–16. Lexington: Ap-
         palachian Center.
Crapanzano, Vincent
  1977   "The Writing of Ethnography." *Dialectical Anthropology* 2(1):69–
         73.
  1980   *Tuhami: Portrait of a Moroccan.* Chicago: University of Chicago Press.
  1992   *Hermes' Dilemma and Hamlet's Desire: On the Epistemology of Inter-
         pretation.* Cambridge: Harvard University Press.
Culler, Jonathan
  1975   *Structuralist Poetics.* Ithaca: Cornell University Press.
Cunningham, Rodger
  1987   *Apples on the Flood: The Southern Mountain Experience.* Knoxville:
         University of Tennessee Press.
de Certeau, Michel
  1984   *The Practice of Everyday Life,* trans. Steven Randall. Berkeley and Los
         Angeles: University of California Press.
de Lauretis, Teresa
  1984   *Alice Doesn't: Feminism, Semiotics, Cinema.* Bloomington: Indiana
         University Press.
  1987   *Technologies of Gender: Essays on Theory, Film and Fiction.* Bloom-
         ington: Indiana University Press.
Deleuze, Gilles, and Felix Guattari
  1983   *Anti-Oedipus: Capitalism and Schizophrenia,* trans. Robert Hurley,
         Mark Seem, and Helen R. Lane. New York: Viking.
  1986   *Kafka: Toward a Minor Literature.* Minneapolis: University of Minne-
         sota Press.
  1990   "What Is a Minor Literature?" In *Out There: Marginalization and Con-*

temporary Cultures, ed. R. Ferguson, M. Gever, M. Trinh, and C. West, pp. 59–69. New York and Cambridge, Mass.: The New Museum of Contemporary Art and the MIT Press.

1991   *A Thousand Plateaus.* Minneapolis: University of Minnesota Press.

Derrida, Jacques
1970   "Structure, Sign, and Play in the Discourse of the Human Sciences." In *The Languages of Criticism and the Sciences of Man*, ed. R. Macksey and E. Donato, pp. 246–72. Baltimore: Johns Hopkins University Press.

1974   *Of Grammatology*, trans. Gayatri Spivak. Baltimore: Johns Hopkins University Press.

1978   *Writing and Difference*, trans. Alan Bass. Chicago: University of Chicago Press.

1981   *Positions*, trans. Alan Bass. Chicago: University of Chicago Press.

Dickey, James
1971   *Deliverance.* New York: Dell.

di Leonardo, Micaela
1991   *Gender at the Crossroads of Knowledge: Feminist Anthropology in the Postmodern Era.* Berkeley and Los Angeles: University of California Press.

Dix, Keith
1988   *What's a Coal Miner to Do? The Mechanization of Coal Mining.* Pittsburgh, Pa.: University of Pittsburgh Press.

Dorgan, Howard
1987   *Giving Glory to God in Appalachia: Worship Practices of Six Baptist Subdenominations.* Knoxville: University of Tennessee Press.

Dorst, John
1983   "Neck-Riddle as a Dialogue of Genres: Applying Bakhtin's Genre Theory." *Journal of American Folklore* 96:413–33.

1989   *The Written Suburb.* Philadelphia: University of Pennsylvania Press.

Dumont, Jean Paul
1978   *The Headman and I.* Austin: University of Texas Press.

1986   "Prologue to Ethnography or Prolegomena to Anthropology." *Ethos* 14:344–67.

1988   "The Tasaday: Which and Whose? Toward the Political Economy of an Ethnographic Sign." *Cultural Anthropology* 3(3):261–75.

Dwyer, Kevin
1977   "On the Dialogic of Fieldwork." *Dialectical Anthropology* 2(2):143–51.

1982   *Moroccan Dialogues: Anthropology in Question.* Baltimore: Johns Hopkins University Press.

Eller, Ronald
1982   *Miners, Millhands and Mountaineers: Industrialization of the Appalachian South, 1880–1930.* Knoxville: University of Tennessee Press.

Erikson, Kai
1976   *Everything in Its Path: Destruction of Community in the Buffalo Creek Flood.* New York: Simon and Schuster.

Fabian, Johannes
   1983   *Time and the Other: How Anthropology Makes Its Object.* New York:
          Columbia University Press.
Favret-Saada, Jeanne
   1980   *Deadly Words: Witchcraft in the Bocage,* trans. Catherine Cullen.
          Cambridge: Cambridge University Press.
Feld, Stephen
   1982   *Sound and Sentiment: Birds, Weeping, Poetics and Song in Kaluli Ex-
          pression.* Philadelphia: University of Pennsylvania Press.
   1984   "Communication, Music and Speech about Music." *Yearbook for Tra-
          ditional Music* 16:1–18.
   1987   "Dialogic Editing: Interpreting How Kaluli Read Sound and Senti-
          ment." *Cultural Anthropology* 2(2):190–210.
   1988   "Aesthetics as Iconicity of Style, or, 'Lift-Up-Over-Sounding': Getting
          into the Kaluli Groove." *Yearbook for Traditional Music* 20:74–113.
Feldman, Allen
   1991   *Formations of Violence: The Narrative of the Body and Political Ter-
          rorism in Northern Ireland.* Chicago: University of Chicago Press.
Fetterman, John
   1967   *Stinking Creek.* New York: E. P. Dutton and Company.
Finnegan, Ruth
   1967   *Limba Stories and Storytelling.* Oxford: Clarendon Press.
   1977   *Oral Poetry: Its Nature, Significance, and Social Context.* Cambridge:
          Cambridge University Press.
Fischer, Michael
   1984   "Towards a Third World Poetics: Seeing Through Short Stories and
          Films in the Iranian Culture Area." *Knowledge and Society* 5:171–241.
   1986   "Ethnicity and the Post-Modern Arts of Memory." In *Writing Culture:
          The Politics and Poetics of Ethnography,* ed. James Clifford and George
          Marcus, pp. 194–233. Berkeley and Los Angeles: University of Califor-
          nia Press.
Fisher, Stephen, ed.
   1993   *Fighting Back in Appalachia: Traditions of Resistance and Change.*
          Philadelphia: Temple University Press.
Fisher, Stephen, and Jim Foster
   1979   "Models for Furthering Revolutionary Praxis in Appalachia." *Appala-
          chian Journal* 6:170–94.
Ford, Thomas, ed.
   1962   *The Southern Appalachian Region: A Survey.* Lexington: University
          Press of Kentucky.
Foster, Hal
   1985   *Recodings: Art, Spectacle, Cultural Politics.* Seattle, Wash.: Bay Press.
   ———, ed.
   1983   *The Anti-Aesthetic: Essays on Postmodern Culture.* Port Townsend,
          Wash.: Bay Press.
Foster, Stephen William
   1988   *The Past Is Another Country: Representation, Historical Conscious-*

ness, and Resistance in the Blue Ridge. Berkeley and Los Angeles: University of California Press.

Foucault, Michel
1970 *The Order of Things.* New York: Random House.
1972 *The Archaeology of Knowledge,* trans. A. M. Sheridan Smith. London: Harper Colophon.
1977 "Nietzsche, Genealogy, History." In *Language, Counter-Memory, Practice,* pp. 139–64. Ithaca: Cornell University Press.
1978 *The History of Sexuality.* Vol. 1. New York: Pantheon.
1979a *Discipline and Punish,* trans. Alan Sheridan. New York: Vintage.
1979b "What Is an Author." In *Textual Strategies: Perspectives in Post-Structuralist Criticism,* ed. Josué Harari, pp. 141–60. Ithaca: Cornell University Press.
1980 *Power/Knowledge: Selected Interviews and Other Writings, 1972–1977,* ed. Colin Gordon. New York: Pantheon Books.

Fox, Aaron
1992 "The Jukebox of History: Narratives of Loss and Desire in the Discourse of Country Music." *Popular Music* 11(1):53–72.
1993 "Split Subjectivity in Country Music and Honky-Tonk Discourse." In *All That Glitters: Country Music in America,* ed. George Lewis, pp. 131–39. Bowling Green, Ohio: Bowling Green State University Popular Press.
1994 "The Poetics of Irony and the Ethnography of Class Culture." *Anthropology and Humanism* 19(1):61–66.

Freud, Sigmund
1953 "Mourning and Melancholia." In *The Standard Edition of the Complete Psychological Works of Sigmund Freud,* 14:237–336. London: Hogarth Press.

Frykman, Jonas, and Orvar Löfgren
1987 *Culture Builders: A Historical Anthropology of Middle-Class Life,* trans. Alan Crozier. New Brunswick, N.J.: Rutgers University Press.

Gates, Henry Louis
1988 *The Signifyin(g) Monkey.* Oxford: Oxford University Press.

Gaventa, John
1980 *Power and Powerlessness: Quiescence and Rebellion in an Appalachian Valley.* Urbana: University of Illinois Press.

Gazaway, Rena
1969 *The Longest Mile: A Vivid Chronicle of Life in an Appalachian Hollow.* New York: Penguin Books.

Geertz, Clifford
1988 *Works and Lives: The Anthropologist as Author.* Stanford: Stanford University Press.

Genette, Gerard
1979 "Valéry and the Poetics of Language." In *Textual Strategies: Perspectives in Post-Structuralist Criticism,* ed. Josué Harari, pp. 359–73. Ithaca: Cornell University Press.
1980 *Narrative Discourse.* Ithaca: Cornell University Press.

Ghosh, Amitav
  1992   *In an Antique Land.* Delhi: Ravi Dayal.
Gilroy, Paul
  1990   *"There Ain't No Black in the Union Jack": The Cultural Politics of Race and Nation.* Chicago: University of Chicago Press.
Ginsburg, Faye, and Anna Tsing, eds.
  1990   *Uncertain Terms: Negotiating Gender in American Culture.* Boston: Beacon Press.
Gitlin, Todd, and Nancy Hollander
  1970   *Uptown: Poor Whites in Chicago.* New York: Harper and Row.
Glassie, Henry
  1982   *Passing the Time in Ballymenone: Culture and History of an Ulster Community.* Philadelphia: University of Pennsylvania Press.
Gordon, Deborah
  1988   "Writing Culture, Writing Feminism: The Poetics and Politics of Experimental Ethnography." *Inscriptions* 3/4:7–26.
Green, Jim
  1978   "Holding the Line: Miners' Militancy and the Strike of 1978." *Radical America* 12(3):2–27.
Green, Rayna
  1984   "Magnolias Grow in Dirt: The Bawdy Lore of Southern Women." In *Speaking for Ourselves: Women of the South,* ed. Maxine Alexander, pp. 20–28. New York: Pantheon.
Halliday, M.A.K.
  1978   *Language as Social Semiotic: The Social Interpretation of Language and Meaning.* London: Edward Arnold.
Halperin, Rhoda
  1990   *The Livelihood of Kin: Making Ends Meet "the Kentucky Way."* Austin: University of Texas Press.
Handler, Richard, and Joyce Linnekin
  1984   "Tradition, Genuine or Spurious." *Journal of American Folklore* 97: 273–90.
Hanks, William
  1989   "Text and Textuality." *Annual Review of Anthropology* 18:95–127.
Hanson, A.
  1989   "The Making of the Maori: Culture Invention and Its Logic." *American Anthropologist* 91(4):890–902.
Haraway, Donna
  1985   "A Manifesto for Cyborgs: Science Technology and Socialist Feminism in the 1980s." *Socialist Review* 80:65–107.
  1989   *Primate Visions: Gender, Race and Nature in the World of Modern Science.* New York: Routledge.
Harding, Susan
  1987   "Convicted by the Holy Spirit: The Rhetoric of Fundamental Baptist Conversion." *American Ethnologist* 14(1):167–81.
  1990   "If I Should Die before I Wake: Jerry Falwell's Pro-Life Gospel." In

Uncertain Terms: Negotiating Gender in American Culture, ed. Faye Ginsburg and Anna Tsing, pp. 76–97. Boston: Beacon Press.

Harrington, Michael
1962   *The Other America.* New York: Macmillan.

Hartigan, John
1992   "Reading Trash: *Deliverance* and the Poetics of White Trash." *Visual Anthropology Review* 8(2):8–15.

Health/Pac Bulletin
1977   "Health Care by the Ton." November/December.

Heath, Shirley Brice
1983   *Ways with Words.* Cambridge: Cambridge University Press.

Hebdige, Dick
1988   *Hiding in the Light: On Images and Things.* London and New York: Routledge.

Heidegger, Martin
1971   *Poetry, Language, Thought*, trans. A. Hofstadter. New York: Harper and Row.

Herzfeld, Michael
1981   "Performative Categories and Symbols of Passage in Rural Greece." *Journal of American Folklore* 94:44–57.

1982   *Ours Once More: Folklore, Ideology and the Making of Modern Greece.* Austin: University of Texas Press.

1985   *The Poetics of Manhood: Contest and Identity in a Cretan Mountain Village.* Princeton: Princeton University Press.

1987   *Anthropology through the Looking Glass: Critical Ethnography in the Margins of Europe.* New York: Cambridge University Press.

Hicks, George
1976   *Appalachian Valley.* New York: Holt, Rhinehart and Winston.

Hill, Jane
1985   "The Grammar of Consciousness and the Consciousness of Grammar." *American Ethnologist* 12(4):725–37.

1986   "The Refiguration of the Anthropology of Language." *Cultural Anthropology* 1:69–102.

1990   "Weeping as a Meta-Signal in a Mexicano Women's Narrative." In *Native Latin American Cultures through Their Discourse*, ed. Ellen Basso, pp. 29–49. Bloomington: Folklore Institute, Indiana University.

Hill, Samuel S., ed.
1972   *Religion and the Solid South.* Nashville, Tenn.: Abington Press.

Hobsbaum, Eric, and Terrence Ringer, eds.
1983   *The Invention of Tradition.* Cambridge: Cambridge University Press.

Hooks, Bell
1989   *Talking Back: Thinking Feminist, Thinking Black.* Boston: South End Press.

1994   *Outlaw Culture: Resisting Representations.* New York: Routledge.

Howell, Joseph
1973   *Hard Living on Clay Street.* New York: Doubleday.

Hume, Brit
    1971   *Death and the Mines: Rebellion and Murder in the United Mine Work-*
           ers. New York: Grossman.
Hurston, Zora Neale
    1935   *Mules and Men.* New York: Harper and Row.
Hymes, Dell
    1975   "Folklore's Nature and the Sun's Myth." *Journal of American Folklore*
           88:345–69.
    1981   *"In Vain I Tried to Tell You": Essays in Native American Ethnopoetics.*
           Philadelphia: University of Pennsylvania Press.
    1985   "Language, Memory and Selective Performance: Cultee's 'Salmon's
           Myth' as Twice Told to Boas." *Journal of American Folklore* 98:391–
           434.
Jackson, Michael
    1982   *Allegories of Wilderness: Ethics and Ambiguity in Karanko Narrative.*
           Bloomington: Indiana University Press.
Jakobson, Roman
    1960   "Closing Statement: Linguistics and Poetics." In *Style in Language*, ed.
           T. A. Sebeok, pp. 350–77. Cambridge: MIT Press.
Jameson, Frederic
    1981   *The Political Unconscious: Narrative as a Socially Symbolic Act.* Ithaca:
           Cornell University Press.
Jauss, Hans Robert
    1982   *Toward an Aesthetic of Reception*, trans. Timothy Bahti. Minneapolis:
           University of Minnesota Press.
Johnstone, Barbara
    1990   *Stories, Community, and Place: Narratives from Middle America.*
           Bloomington: Indiana University Press.
Kahn, Kathy
    1973   *Hillbilly Women.* New York: Doubleday.
Kaplan, Berton
    1971   *Blue Ridge: An Appalachian Community in Transition.* Morgantown:
           West Virginia University Press.
Karp, Ivan, and Steven Lavine
    1991   *Exhibiting Cultures: The Poetics and Politics of Museum Display.*
           Washington: Smithsonian Institution Press.
Keeler, Ward
    1987   *Javanese Shadow Plays, Javanese Selves.* Princeton: Princeton Univer-
           sity Press.
Kephart, Horace
    1922   *Our Southern Highlanders: A Narrative of Adventure in the Southern*
           Appalachians and a Study of Life among the Mountaineers. New York:
           Macmillan.
Kingsolver, Ann
    1992   "Contested Livelihoods: 'Placing' One Another in 'Cedar,' Kentucky."
           Anthropological Quarterly. 65(3):128–36.

Kirshenblatt-Gimblett, Barbara
   1975   "A Parable in Context: A Social Interactional Analysis of Storytelling
          Performance." In *Folklore: Performance and Communication*, ed.
          Dan Ben Amos and Kenneth Goldstein, pp. 105–30. The Hague:
          Mouton.
Kondo, Dorinne
   1986   "Dissolution and Reconstitution of Self: Implications for Anthropo-
          logical Epistemology." *Cultural Anthropology* 1:74–88.
   1990   *Crafting Selves: Power, Gender and Discourses of Identity in a Japa-
          nese Workplace*. Chicago: University of Chicago Press.
Kristeva, Julia
   1976   "The System and the Speaking Subject." In *The Tell-Tale Sign*, ed.
          Thomas Sebeok, pp. 47–55. Lisse: de Ridder.
   1980   *Desire in Language: A Semiotic Approach to Literature and Art*. New
          York: Columbia University Press.
   1982   *Powers of Horror*. New York: Columbia University Press.
LaBarre, Weston
   1976   *They Shall Take Up Serpents*. New York: Schocken.
Lacan, Jacques
   1977   "The Subversion of the Subject and the Dialectic of Desire in Freud's
          Unconscious." In *Ecrits*, trans. A. Sheridan, pp. 292–375. New York:
          Norton.
Lane, Winthrop D.
   1921   *Civil War in West Virginia*. New York: Oriole Chapbooks.
Langer, Susanne
   1953   *An Introduction to Symbolic Logic*. New York: Dover.
Lavie, Smadar
   1990   *The Poetics of Military Occupation*. Berkeley and Los Angeles: Univer-
          sity of California Press.
Least Heat Moon, William
   1982   *Blue Highways: A Journey into America*. Boston: Little, Brown and Co.
LeGuin, Ursula
   1981   "It Was a Dark and Stormy Night: or, Why Are We Huddling around
          the Campfire?" In *On Narrative*, ed. W.J.T. Mitchell, pp. 187–96. Chi-
          cago: University of Chicago Press.
Lesy, Michael
   1973   *Wisconsin Death Trip*. New York: Pantheon.
Levinas, Emmanuel
   1981   *Otherwise Than Being or Beyond Essence*, trans. A. Lingis. Boston:
          Martinus Nijhoff.
Lewis, Helen Mathews, Linda Johnson, and Donald Askins, eds.
   1978   *Colonialism in Modern America: The Appalachian Case*. Boone, N.C.:
          Appalachian Consortium Press.
Lewis, Ronald L.
   1987   *Black Coal Miners in America: Race, Class, and Community Conflict,
          1780–1980*. Lexington: University Press of Kentucky.

Limon, José
    1991 "Representation, Ethnicity, and the Precursory Ethnography: Notes of
          a Native Anthropologist." In *Recapturing Anthropology: Working in
          the Present*, ed. Richard Fox, pp. 115–36. Santa Fe, N.M.: School of
          American Research Press.
    1994 *Dancing with the Devil*. Minneapolis: University of Minnesota Press.
Looff, David
    1971 *Appalachia's Children*. Lexington: University Press of Kentucky.
Lord, Albert
    1960 *The Singer of Tales*. Cambridge: Harvard University Press.
Lowe, Donald M.
    1982 *History of Bourgeois Perception*. Chicago: University of Chicago
          Press.
Lukács, Georg
    1968 *History and Class Consciousness*. Cambridge: MIT Press.
Lyotard, Jean-François
    1984 *The Postmodern Condition: A Report on Knowledge*. Minneapolis:
          University of Minnesota Press.
MacCormack, Ann, and Marilyn Strathern, eds.
    1980 *Nature, Culture and Gender*. Cambridge: Cambridge University
          Press.
Maclean, Marie
    1988 *Narrative as Performance: The Baudelairean Experiment*. London and
          New York: Routledge.
Mannheim, Bruce
    1991 *The Language of the Inca since the European Invasion*. Austin: Univer-
          sity of Texas Press.
Marcus, George, and Michael Fischer, eds.
    1986 *Anthropology as Cultural Critique*. Chicago: University of Chicago
          Press.
Martin, Emily
    1987 *The Woman in the Body: A Cultural Analysis of Reproduction*. Boston:
          Beacon Press.
Mason, James Murray
    1884 *West Virginia Tax Commission, Second Report, State Development*.
          Wheeling, W.V.
Mathews, Elmora M.
    1965 *Neighbor and Kin: Life in a Tennessee Ridge Community*. Nashville,
          Tenn.: Vanderbilt University Press.
McGrane, Bernard
    1989 *Beyond Anthropology*. New York: Columbia University Press.
McNeil, W. K., ed.
    1988 *Appalachian Images in Folk and Popular Culture*. Ann Arbor: UMI
          Research Press.
Mercer, Colin
    1991 "Neverending Stories: The Problem of Reading in Cultural Studies."
          New Formations 13:63–74.

Moore, Marat
  1990   "Hard Labor: Voices of Women from the Appalachian Coalfields."
         Yale Journal of Law and Feminism 2:199–239.
Nägele, Rainer, ed.
  1988   *Benjamin's Ground: New Readings of Walter Benjamin.* Detroit:
         Wayne State University Press.
Narayan, Kirin
  1989   *Storytellers, Saints and Scoundrels: Folk Narrative in Hindu Religious
         Teaching.* Philadelphia: University of Pennsylvania Press.
Newcomb, Horace
  1979–1980   "Appalachia on Television: Region as Symbol in American Popu-
         lar Culture." *Appalachian Journal* 7(1–2):155–64.
Obermiller, Phillip J., and William W. Philliber, eds.
  1987   *Too Few Tomorrows: Urban Appalachians in the 1980s.* Boone, N.C.:
         Appalachian Consortium Press.
Ortner, Sherry, and Harriet Whitehead, eds.
  1981   *Sexual Meanings: The Cultural Construction of Gender and Sexuality.*
         Cambridge: Cambridge University Press.
Peacock, James
  1968   *Rites of Modernization: Symbolic and Social Aspects of Indonesian
         Proletarian Drama.* Chicago: University of Chicago Press.
  1971   "The Southern Protestant Ethic Disease." In *The Not So Solid South*,
         ed. Kenneth Morland, pp. 108–13. Athens: University of Georgia Press.
Peacock, James, and Ruel Tyson
  1989   *Pilgrims of Paradox: Calvinism and Experience among the Primitive
         Baptists of the Blue Ridge.* Washington: Smithsonian Institution Press.
Pearsall, Marion
  1959   *Little Smoky Ridge.* Birmingham: University of Alabama Press.
Peirce, C. S.
  1974   *Collected Papers.* Vols. 1 and 2, ed. C. Hartshorne and P. Weiss. Cam-
         bridge: Harvard University Press.
Philliber, William W., and Clyde B. McCoy, eds.
  1981   *The Invisible Minority: Urban Appalachians.* Lexington: University
         Press of Kentucky.
Photiadis, John, ed.
  1978   *Religion in Appalachia.* Morgantown: West Virginia University Press.
Pratt, Mary Louise
  1977   *Toward a Speech Act Theory of Literary Discourse.* Bloomington: Indi-
         ana University Press.
  1986   "Fieldwork in Common Places." In *Writing Culture: The Politics and
         Poetics of Ethnography*, ed. James Clifford and George Marcus, pp.
         27–50. Berkeley and Los Angeles: University of California Press.
  1992   *Imperial Eyes: Travel Writing and Transculturation.* London and New
         York: Routledge.
Preston, Dennis
  1982   "Ritin' Fowklower Daun' Rong: Folklorists' Failures in Phonology."
         Journal of American Folklore 95:304–26.

Propp, Vladamir
   1968   *Morphology of the Folktale*, trans. Laurence Scott. Austin: University of Texas Press.
Puckett, Anita
   1992   "'Let the Girls Do the Spelling and Dan Will Do the Shooting': Literacy, the Division of Labor, and Identity in a Rural Appalachian Community." *Anthropological Quarterly* 65(3):137–47.
Puckett, John
   1989   *Foxfire Reconsidered: A Twenty-Year Experiment in Progressive Education.* Urbana: University of Illinois Press.
Rabinow, Paul
   1977   *Reflections on Fieldwork in Morocco.* Berkeley and Los Angeles: University of California Press.
   1985   "Discourse and Power: On the Limits of Ethnographic Texts." *Dialectical Anthropology* 10:1–14.
   1986   "Representations Are Social Facts: Modernity and Post-Modernity in Anthropology." In *Writing Culture: The Poetics and Politics of Ethnography*, ed. James Clifford and George Marcus, pp. 234–61. Berkeley and Los Angeles: University of California Press.
Rabinow, Paul, and William Sullivan, eds.
   1979   *Interpretive Social Science: A Reader.* Berkeley and Los Angeles: University of California Press.
Ramanujan, A. K.
   1989   "Telling Tales." *Daedalus* 118(4):239–61.
Rapp, Rayna
   1979   "Anthropology: Review Essay." *Signs* 4(3):497–513.
Reed, T. V.
   1988   "Unimagined Existence and the Fiction of the Real: Postmodernist Realism in *Let Us Now Praise Famous Men.*" *Representations* 24:156–75.
Reiter, Rayna Rapp, ed.
   1975   *Toward an Anthropology of Women.* New York: Monthly Review Press.
Ricoeur, Paul
   1981   "Narrative Time." In *On Narrative*, ed. W.J.T. Mitchell, pp. 165–86. Chicago: University of Chicago Press.
   1984   *Time and Narrative.* Vol. 1. Chicago: University of Chicago Press.
Roberts, John
   1989   *From Trickster to Badman.* Philadelphia: University of Pennsylvania Press.
Rosaldo, Michelle Zimbalist
   1974   "Women, Culture and Society: A Theoretical Overview." In *Women, Culture and Society*, ed. Michelle Zimbalist Rosaldo and Louise Lamphere, pp. 67–88. Stanford: Stanford University Press.
   1980   "The Use and Abuse of Anthropology: Reflections on Cross-Cultural Understanding." *Signs* 5(3):389–417.
Rosaldo, Michelle Zimbalist, and Louise Lamphere, eds.
   1974   *Women, Culture and Society.* Stanford: Stanford University Press.

Rosaldo, Renato
    1984   "Grief and a Headhunter's Rage: On the Cultural Force of Emotions."
            In *Text, Play, and Story*, ed. Edward Bruner, pp. 178–98. Seattle: Amer-
            ican Ethnological Society.
    1989   *Culture and Truth: The Remaking of Social Analysis*. Boston: Beacon
            Press.
Said, Edward
    1978   *Orientalism*. New York: Random House.
    1983   "Opponents, Audiences, Constituencies and Community." In *The Anti-
            Aesthetic: Essays on Postmodern Culture*, ed. Hal Foster, pp. 135–59.
            Port Townsend, Wash.: Bay Press.
    1984   "The Mind of Winter: Reflections on Life in Exile." *Harpers*
            269(1612):49–55.
    1986   *After the Last Sky: Palestinian Lives*. New York: Pantheon.
Salvati, Raymond E.
    1957   *Island Creek: Saga in Bituminous*. New York: Newcomen Society in
            North America.
Savage, Lon
    1990   *Thunder in the Mountains: The West Virginia Mine War, 1920–21*.
            Pittsburgh, Pa.: University of Pittsburgh Press.
Scheper-Hughes, Nancy
    1993   *Death without Weeping: The Violence of Everyday Life in Brazil*.
            Berkeley and Los Angeles: University of California Press.
Schieffelin, Edward
    1985   "Performance and the Cultural Construction of Reality." *American
            Ethnologist* 12(4):707–24.
Scholte, Bob
    1973   "Toward a Reflexive and Critical Anthropology." In *Reinventing An-
            thropology*, ed. Dell Hymes, pp. 430–57. New York: Pantheon.
Schwartweller, Harry K., James Brown, and J. J. Mangalam, eds.
    1971   *Mountain Families in Transition*. University Park: Pennsylania State
            University Press.
Scott, Joan W.
    1988   *Gender and the Politics of History*. New York: Columbia University
            Press.
    1991   "The Evidence of Experience." *Critical Inquiry* 17:773–97.
Shapiro, Henry
    1978   *Appalachia on Our Mind: The Southern Mountains and Mountaineers
            in the American Consciousness, 1890–1920*. Chapel Hill: University of
            North Carolina Press.
Sherzer, Joel
    1983   *Kuna Ways of Speaking: An Ethnographic Perspective*. Austin: Univer-
            sity of Texas Press.
    1987   "A Discourse-Centered Approach to Culture." *American Anthropolo-
            gist* 89(2):295–309.
Sherzer, Joel, and Anthony Woodbury, eds.
    1987   *Native American Discourse: Poetics and Rhetoric*. Cambridge: Cam-
            bridge University Press.

Shifflett, Crandall A.
  1991   *Coal Towns: Life, Work, and Culture in Company Towns of Southern
          Appalachia, 1880–1960*. Knoxville: University of Tennessee Press.
Smith, Barbara Herrnstein
  1981   "Narrative Versions, Narrative Theories." In *On Narrative*, ed. W.J.T.
          Mitchell, pp. 209–32. Chicago: University of Chicago Press.
Sovine, Melanie
  1983   "Studying Religious Belief Systems in their Social Historical Context."
          In *Appalachia and America: Autonomy and Regional Dependence*, ed.
          Allen Batteau., pp. 48–67. Lexington: University Press of Kentucky.
Sperber, Daniel
  1975   *Rethinking Symbolism*, trans. Alice Morton. Cambridge: Cambridge
          University Press.
Spivak, Gayatri Chakravorty
  1988   "Can the Subaltern Speak?" In *Marxism and the Interpretation of Cul-
          ture*, ed. Cary Nelson and Lawrence Grossberg, pp. 271–315. Urbana:
          University of Illinois Press.
  1990   "Explanation and Culture: Marginalia." In *Out There: Marginaliza-
          tion and Contemporary Cultures*, ed. R. Ferguson, M. Gever, M. Trinh,
          and C. West, pp. 377–93. New York and Cambridge, Mass.: The New
          Museum of Contemporary Art and the MIT Press.
Stallybrass, Peter, and Allon White
  1986   *The Politics and Poetics of Transgression*. Ithaca: Cornell University
          Press.
Steedly, Mary
  1993   *Hanging without a Rope: Narrative Experience in Colonial and Post-
          colonial Karoland*. Princeton: Princeton University Press.
Stephenson, John B.
  1968   *Shiloh: A Mountain Community*. Lexington: University Press of
          Kentucky.
  1984   "Escape to the Periphery: Commodifying Place in Rural Appalachia."
          Appalachian Journal 11:187–200.
Stewart, John O.
  1989   *Drinkers, Drummers and Decent Folk: Ethnographic Narratives of Vil-
          lage Trinidad*. Albany: State University of New York Press.
Stewart, Kathleen
  1988   "Nostalgia: A Polemic." In *Cultural Anthropology* 3(3):227–41.
  1990   "Back-talking the Wilderness: 'Appalachian' En-genderings." In *Un-
          certain Terms: Negotiating Gender in American Culture*, ed. Faye
          Ginsburg and Anna Tsing, pp. 43–56. Boston: Beacon Press.
  1991   "On the Politics of Cultural Theory: A Case for 'Contaminated' Cri-
          tique." *Social Research* 58(2):395–412.
  1993   "Engendering Narratives of Lament in Country Music." In *All That
          Glitters: Country Music in America*, ed. George Lewis, pp. 221–
          25. Bowling Green, Ohio: Bowling Green State University Popular
          Press.
  1995   "An Occupied Place." In *Senses of Place*, ed. Keith Basso and Steve
          Feld. Santa Fe, N.M.: School of American Research Press.

Stewart, Susan
   1983   "Shouts on the Street: Bakhtin's Anti-Linguistics." *Critical Inquiry*
          10:265–81.
   1984   *On Longing: Narratives of the Miniature, the Gigantic, the Souvenir,
          the Collection.* Baltimore: Johns Hopkins University Press.
   1991   *Crimes of Writing: Problems in the Containment of Representation.*
          New York and Oxford: Oxford University Press.
Stocking, George, ed.
   1983   *Observers Observed: Essays on Ethnographic Field-Work.* Madison:
          University of Wisconsin Press.
   1989   *Romantic Motives: Essays on Anthropological Sensibilities.* Madison:
          University of Wisconsin Press.
Stoler, Ann
   1989a "Making Empire Respectable: The Politics of Race and Sexual Moral-
          ity in Twentieth-Century Colonial Cultures." *American Ethnologist*
          16(4):634–60.
   1989b "Rethinking Colonial Cultures: European Communities and the
          Boundaries of Rule." *Comparative Studies in Society and History*
          31:134–61.
   1992   " 'In Cold Blood': Hierarchies of Credibility and the Politics of Colonial
          Narratives." *Representations* 37:151–89.
Strathern, Marilyn
   1987a "An Awkward Relationship: The Case of Feminism and Anthropol-
          ogy." *Signs* 12(2):276–92.
   1987b "Out of Context: The Persuasive Fictions of Anthropology." *Current
          Anthropology* 28(3):251–81.
   1991   *Partial Connections.* Savage, Md.: Rowman and Littlefield.
   1992   *After Nature: English Kinship in the Late Twentieth Century.* Cam-
          bridge: Cambridge University Press.
Taussig, Michael
   1987   *Shamanism, Colonialism, and the Wildman.* Chicago: University of
          Chicago Press.
   1989   "Terror as Usual: Walter Benjamin's Theory of History as a State of
          Siege." *Social Text* 23:3–20.
   1991   "Tactility and Distraction." *Cultural Anthropology* 6(2):147–53.
   1992   *The Nervous System.* New York: Routledge.
   1993   *Mimesis and Alterity: A Particular History of the Senses.* New York:
          Routledge.
Taylor, Elizabeth
   1992a "Drinking from the Rock: Self and Story in Appalachian Coal-Mining
          Communities." Ph.D. diss., University of Michigan.
   1992b "The Taxidermy of Bioluminescence: Tracking Neighborly Practices
          in Appalachian Coal-Mining Communities." *Anthropological Quar-
          terly* 65(3):117–27.
Taylor, Mark C.
   1990   *Altarity.* Chicago: University of Chicago Press.
Tedlock, Barbara
   1992   *The Beautiful and the Dangerous.* New York: Penguin Books.

Tedlock, Dennis
  1972   "On the Translation of Style in Oral Narrative." In *Toward New Per-
         spectives in Folklore*, ed. Americo Paredes and Richard Bauman, pp.
         114–33. Austin: University of Texas Press.
  1983   *The Spoken Word and the Work of Interpretation.* Philadelphia: Uni-
         versity of Pennsylvania Press.
Terdiman, Richard
  1985   *Discourse/Counter-Discourse.* Ithaca: Cornell University Press.
Thibault, Paul
  1991   *Social Semiotics as Praxis.* Minneapolis: University of Minnesota Press.
Thornton, Robert
  1988   "The Rhetoric of Ethnographic Holism." *Cultural Anthropology* 3(3):
         285–303.
Titon, Jeff Todd
  1988   *Powerhouse for God: Speech, Chant and Song in an Appalachian Bap-
         tist Church.* Austin: University of Texas Press.
Todorov, Tzvetan
  1981   *Introduction to Poetics.* Minneapolis: University of Minnesota
         Press.
  1984   *Mikhail Bakhtin: The Dialogic Principle*, trans. Wlad Godzich. Minne-
         apolis: University of Minnesota Press.
Tompkins, Jane P., ed.
  1980   *Reader-Response Criticism.* Baltimore: Johns Hopkins University
         Press.
Trinh, Min-Ha T.
  1991   *When the Moon Waxes Red: Representation, Gender, and Cultural
         Politics.* New York: Routledge.
Trotter, Joe W., Jr.
  1990   *Coal, Class and Color: Blacks in Southern West Virginia, 1915–32.*
         Urbana: University of Illinois Press.
Tsing, Anna
  1994   *In the Realm of the Diamond Queen.* Princeton: Princeton University
         Press.
Turner, Victor
  1979   *Process, Performance, and Pilgrimage: A Study in Comparative Sym-
         bology.* New Delhi: Concept.
  1981   "Social Dramas and Stories about Them." In *On Narrative*, ed. W.J.T.
         Mitchell, pp. 137–64. Chicago: University of Chicago Press.
Turner, William H., and Edward J. Cabell, eds.
  1985   *Blacks in Appalachia.* Lexington: University Press of Kentucky.
Tyler, Stephen
  1984   "The Vision Quest in the West, or What the Mind's Eye Sees." *Journal
         of Anthropological Research* 40(1):23–40.
  1986   "Post-Modern Ethnography: From Document of the Occult to Occult
         Document." In *Writing Culture: The Politics and Poetics of Ethnogra-
         phy*, ed. James Clifford and George Marcus, pp. 122–40. Berkeley and
         Los Angeles: University of California Press.

Ulmer, Gregory
    1983   "The Object of Post-Criticism." In *The Anti-Aesthetic: Essays on Postmodern Culture*, ed. Hal Foster, pp. 83–110. Port Townsend, Wash.: Bay Press.
    1985   *Applied Grammatology: Post(e)-Pedagogy from Jacques Derrida to Joseph Beuys.* Baltimore: Johns Hopkins University Press.

Urban, Greg
    1985   "The Semiotics of Two Speech Styles in Shokleng." In *Semiotic Mediation: Sociocultural and Psychological Perspectives*, ed. E. Mertz and R. Parmentier, pp. 311–29. Orlando, Fla.: Academic Press.
    1988   "Ritual Wailing in Amerindian Brazil." *American Anthropologist* 90: 385–400.
    1991   *A Discourse-Centered Approach to Culture.* Austin: University of Texas Press.

Van Mannen, John
    1988   *Tales of the Field: On Writing Ethnography.* Chicago: University of Chicago Press.

Visweswaren, Kamala
    1988   "Defining Feminist Ethnography." *Inscriptions* 3/4:27–46.
    1994   *Fictions of Feminist Ethnography.* Madison: University of Wisconsin Press.

Volosinov, V. N.
    1976   "Discourse in Life and Discourse in Art." In *Freudianism: A Marxist Critique*, trans. I. R. Titunik. New York: Academic Press.
    1986   *Marxism and the Philosophy of Language*, trans. Ladislav Matejka and I. R. Titunik. Cambridge: Harvard University Press.

Wagner, Roy
    1981   *The Invention of Culture.* Chicago: University of Chicago Press.

Wallace, Michael
    1987   "Dying for Coal: The Struggle for Health and Safety Conditions in American Coal Mining, 1930–82." *Social Forces* 66(2):336–64.

Waller, Altina L.
    1988   *Feud: Hatfields, McCoys, and Social Change in Appalachia, 1860–1900.* Chapel Hill: University of North Carolina Press.

Walls, David, and John B. Stephenson
    1972   *Appalachia in the Sixties.* Lexington: University Press of Kentucky.

Webster, Steven
    1982   "Dialogue and Fiction in Ethnography." *Dialectical Anthropology* 7(2):91–114.
    1983   "Ethnography as Storytelling." *Dialectical Anthropology* 8(3):185–206.
    1986   "Realism and Reification in the Ethnographic Genre." *Critique of Anthropology* 6(1):39–62.

Weiner, Annette
    1976   *Women of Value, Men of Renown.* Austin: University of Texas Press.

Weller, Jack
    1965   *Yesterday's People.* Lexington: University Press of Kentucky.

West Virginia Land Task Force
  1980   *Appalachian Land Ownership Study*. Vol. 7. Appalachian Regional
          Commission.
Whisnant, David
  1973   "The Folk Hero in Appalachian Struggle History." *New South* 28:30–
          47.
  1980   *Modernizing the Mountaineer: People, Power and Planning in Ap-
          palachia*. New York: Burt Franklin & Co.
  1983   *All That Is Native and Fine: The Politics of Culture in an American
          Region*. Chapel Hill: University of North Carolina Press.
White, Hayden
  1973   *Metahistory*. Baltimore: Johns Hopkins University Press.
  1981   "The Value of Narrativity in the Representation of Reality." *Critical
          Inquiry* 7:5.
Wigginton, Eliot
  1972–1980   *The Foxfire Book*. Vols. 1–8. Garden City, N.Y.: Doubleday.
Williams, Raymond
  1973   *The Country and the City*. New York: Oxford University Press.
  1977   *Marxism and Literature*. Oxford: Oxford University Press.
Willis, Paul
  1981   *Learning to Labour: How Working Class Kids Get Working Class
          Jobs*. New York: Columbia University Press.
Wilson, W.
  1973   "Herder, Folklore, and Romantic Nationalism." *Journal of Popular
          Culture* 6:819–35.
Yanagisako, Sylvia, and Jane Collier, eds.
  1987   *Gender and Kinship: Essays toward a Unified Analysis*. Stanford: Stan-
          ford University Press.
Yarrow, Mike
  1991   "The Gender-Specific Class Consciousness of Appalachian Coal
          Miners: Structure and Change." In *Bringing Class Back In: Historical
          and Contemporary Perspectives*, ed. Scott G. McNall, Rhonda Levine,
          and Rick Fantasia, 285–310. Boulder, Co.: Westview.
  1978   "Second Time Around." *Seven Days*, April 7.
Žižek, Slavoj
  1991   *For They Know Not What They Do: Enjoyment as a Political Factor*.
          New York: New Left Books.